YOUR TIME IS NOW

THE SAMMY PETRILLO STORY

DAVE ABRAMSON

Your Time Is Now
The Sammy Petrillo Story

By Dave Abramson

ISBN: 9781627311861

Designed by Bill Smith, designSimple

Feral House
PO Box 100099
Cudahy, WI 53110

www.feralhouse.com
info@feralhouse.com

FOR NANCY

“I DON’T WANT TO BE SOMETHING THAT I’M NOT. I DIDN’T LIKE BEING SOMEONE ELSE. AT THE SAME TIME, I’M VERY GLAD I WAS. ’CAUSE I FOUND OUT SOMETHING THAT I NEVER KNEW. YOU MIGHT AS WELL LIKE YOURSELF. JUST THINK ABOUT ALL THE TIME YOU’RE GOING TO HAVE TO SPEND WITH YOU.”

—Jerry Lewis as Prof. Julius Kelp
in *The Nutty Professor*

FOREWORD

BY SCOTT ALEXANDER

What did it mean to be Sammy Petrillo? What did it mean to have the core of his existence predicated upon the life of another person?

Was he alive when he wasn't pretending to be Jerry? Did he have other dreams, other aspirations, other joys? He lived a life, but his wives and children were discarded along the way. His friends were scarce. His day jobs were a foggy mystery. What he left us is *Brooklyn Gorilla* and that stunning performance. We can assume he wanted more out of life, but . . . what would that be? What did he think when he looked in the mirror? "Hey, there's the guy who's not Jerry Lewis"?

Did Sammy realize the existential hellscape he had created? He liked to play coy and say, "I wasn't even trying to copy Jerry! But once I got that haircut . . . things just sorta snowballed." But that argument is dubious. Sammy chased the idea of becoming Jerry in a way that takes your breath away. Yes, he was incredibly young and naïve when all this started (sixteen!), but was he really oblivious to his own insane hubris? "I am going to commit myself to pretend to be another person." This is crazy. It's a bizarre goal. Sammy isn't allowed to shrug off the very awkward situation he created.

Also, unfortunately, he was trying to borrow the act of one of the most self-absorbed personalities who ever lived. Jerry Lewis was an egomaniac with a capital E. How many performers have their own trademarked caricatures? Sammy was willfully appropriating one of the most *specific* personalities of all time. Jerry's "kid" persona is so overpowering, it's hard to think of other performers to even compare him to. The classic Hollywood icons—Bogie, Marilyn, Cagney, James Dean—they pale in comparison. They resemble real human beings we may have met in our lifetimes. "The Kid" is something else.

And Sammy was something else, squared and cubed.

I have always been fascinated by showbiz knockoffs and look-alikes. I love the tribute acts, the impressionists, even the wax dummies. (Yes, I own the Smothers Brothers in wax.) I'll admit that sometimes I even prefer impersonators to the real thing. Is it perverse to admit I'd rather watch Johnny Carson interview Rich Little than watch him interview Jimmy Cagney? Is *Beatlemania* possibly more fun than *Magical Mystery Tour*?

In classic Hollywood, movie stars shone brightly, and studios shamelessly tried to rip them off, producing smudged copies. "You got Errol Flynn? We got Tyrone Power!" "You got Deanna Durbin? We got Gloria Jean!" "You got Clark Gable? We got James Craig!" "You like Betty Grable? You'll love June Haver!" "Forget Marilyn Monroe! We got Jayne Mansfield, Sheree North, *and* Mamie Van Doren!" Rock Hudson begat Tab Hunter who begat Troy Donahue. It was simply commerce. Studios produced an "answer" to a competitor's star.

But the Sammy situation is stranger in that he was competing head-to-head with Jerry. It was ballsy. The producers of *Bela Lugosi Meets a Brooklyn Gorilla* were clearly attempting to confuse the innocent movie-going public. One ad actually read, "Have you seen Jerry Lewis in his first hit?" Well, I think I did, but . . . maybe I didn't? Now I'm confused! Of course, Jerry had every right to be indignant, though we can't blame Sammy for this chaos. He didn't make the ads. He just hit his marks and did his schtick. When George Lazenby became James Bond, the early posters for *On Her Majesty's Secret Service* actually obscured his face. He posed with the gun, Connery style, but his face is in silhouette! The ad cleverly screams, "Bond is back!" Did Sean Connery get annoyed? Did audiences on opening night howl that they had been played? You pay your money, you take your chances.

For me, only one other guy in history was in Sammy's class: the Man with Bogart's Face, the amazing Robert Sacchi. Like Sammy, Sacchi was born with a bone structure eerily matching that of the Hollywood screen legend. One day he looked in the mirror and said, "Holy shit, I look like someone else! And that could be my job!" Like Sammy, he also nailed the voice, the mannerisms, the posture. Sacchi worked hard to deliver the goods. He had a fine twenty-year run, when his facial resemblance was so uncanny that he could pull off the act. Like Sammy, he was showcased in a starring part in exactly one feature film, which seemed to exist just for him.

Unlike Sammy, from all accounts Sacchi was a mellow guy who was easy to work with. He parlayed his talent into a long career. He booked hundreds of commercials as Bogie, and anytime he needed to pay the bills, he could join a production of *Play It Again, Sam.*

Two observations comparing and contrasting Sammy and Sacchi:

They each seemed to be emulating their guy, on screen and off. Humphrey Bogart was a pro who everybody liked to work with. Jerry was a pain in the ass.

Sacchi had a home-field advantage: he wasn't competing with Bogie, because Bogie was dead. Nobody in the audience could pretend they got ripped off. But Sammy had the temerity to steal his act in real time. He and Jerry were contemporaries. And Jerry was probably the most popular entertainer on the planet. Jerry and Dean ruled film, TV, and nightclubs. When Sammy and his faux Dean, the passable Duke Mitchell, started showing up in movies and clubs, they had inadvertently declared war.

If Jerry had been a nicer guy, he would have laughed it off and let Sammy eat his scraps in the corner. But Jerry wasn't that kind of mensch, and so Sammy was doomed to get crushed. And once Sammy's rickety little enterprise collapsed, he didn't have a Plan B. Decades of futility and oblivion lay ahead.

There is one other fellow who played this game: back in the silent days, Billy West was another real-time knockoff. Billy West cleverly ripped off Charlie Chaplin. Yes, Billy did a spot-on simulation of the most popular entertainer on the planet. (Sound familiar?) Billy had it easier, in that he could hide his face under the Little Tramp's costume, mustache, and hat. Suited up, he looked just like the guy. Plus, he had the delicate gestures and impressive comic chops. When Charlie found himself unable to quench the public demand he had created, Billy leapt in. Billy started pumping out competing look-alike two-reelers at a frantic pace. He even had supporting players from Charlie's repertory company. The audience was perfectly satisfied with these knockoffs, and Billy had years of success. Crazily, when Billy switched studios, his former studio hired a fake Billy West. Yes, they hired an impersonator to impersonate Billy impersonating Charlie.

This is a level of meta-success Sammy could only dream of.

Surprisingly, the real Chaplin seemed unbothered by the fake Chaplin. He didn't try to shut Billy down. He probably felt (reasonably) that his fame was so monumental that a cheeky doppelgänger couldn't hurt business. As the kids say, it's just a rounding error. So he let Billy keep it up. If only Jerry Lewis had been as big-hearted as Charlie. Then Sammy's life might have gone in a less dismal direction. Maybe we could have had a series of Duke and Sammy movies. Jack Broder presents: *Duke and Sammy on the Moon*! But now I'm just dreaming.

And what of other simulacra? All the many replicas and human counterfeits? If done well, these artists tickle us and even elicit emotions. At the top of this showbiz pyramid, it goes without saying, are Fake Elvises. We have been overrun by them since Real Elvis first appeared. They will never quench the demand. Even Elvis wasn't Elvis enough to satisfy everyone.

In their wake are musical tribute acts. Dozens of Zeppelins, Metallicas, and Grateful Deads travel the circuit, playing civic theaters and small rock venues. Vegas has endless Rat Packs. These entertainers are trying to put a smile on your face, sing the hits, and bring back memories from high school. They are essentially magicians. If you're seated farther back than row ten, the effect is swell, and you can convince yourself that you're seeing the real deal. But if you meet them at the merch table afterwards, the illusion will collapse, and you're just talking to a guy in a funny wig.

Now that we live in the future, our favorites are even simulated by technology. There is an audio-animatronic robot Johnny Depp at Disneyland. Tupac Shakur showed up unannounced at Coachella. Holograms of the deceased singers Whitney Houston and Roy Orbison tour the country. Digital avatars of ABBA sing nightly in London. AI produces instant movies of Elvis boxing Stephen Hawking. But we are gathered here today to salute human beings. Flesh-and-blood workers like Sammy. So let us praise a few of the greats. Some of these imposters are as beguiling as the real thing.

• In the world of tribute impressionists, I am particularly fond of two titans. Frank Ferrante has been delivering a wonderful Groucho Marx for forty years and counting. He's so good, Groucho's son Arthur Marx co-wrote a biographical play that Frank starred in. And Jim Bailey spent his life delivering a staggeringly accurate Judy Garland. He was so amazing, the real Judy actually came onstage and performed with him! Later, he performed concerts with Liza Minnelli, as mother and daughter! How crazy is that?

• There is the face of *Beatlemania*, Mitch Weissman. Mitch looked shockingly like Paul McCartney, plus he could sing and play the bass. In my opinion, he was single-handedly responsible for the massive success of this show on Broadway. In the TV commercials, it truly looked as though Paul were starring in the musical! For $15 a ticket, how could you say no?

• There are the astonishing Chuck McCann and Dick Van Dyke, specifically on a 1958 episode of *The Garry Moore Show*, performing "The Vacuum Cleaner Salesman." In this double-switch sketch, the guys play the two parts as Laurel and Hardy, and then, seconds later, they perform the same two parts as Jackie Gleason and Art Carney. Seventy years later, this switch-up remains mind-blowing. They are so good, you forget, twice, that you are not watching the real people.

• There is the disastrous *All New Adventures of Laurel & Hardy in For Love or Mummy* (yes, that is the title). This is an actual feature motion picture, produced by Larry Harmon, who somehow ended up controlling the likeness rights to Stan and Ollie. He made a "brand new" Laurel and Hardy film, cast with look-alikes, shot in South Africa. It's worse than it sounds. Duke and Sammy could beat these guys in a wrestling match, any day of the week.

• There is the extraordinarily weird *Angels with Angles* (2005), which is a fake George Burns comedy, with George played by Frank Gorshin in heavy rubber makeup. I have no idea what the George Burns estate made of this film.

• There is the legendary Vaughn Meader, who became a superstar performing his comedic version of John F. Kennedy. Like Sammy, like Billy West, Vaughn hitched his wagon to the most beloved guy around, and everything was hunky-dory. That is, until JFK went to Dallas. Vaughn is probably the case history for "don't bet your career on just one impression."

• There is the Sammy-like Charles Bronson look-alike Robert Bronzi, who is king of this domain, starring in a dozen low-budget *Death Wish* knockoffs. Poor Sammy only got one movie, and this guy got a dozen. How unfair is the world? Bronzi is pretty good at punching bad guys and shooting a gun, though his heavy Hungarian accent is problematic, to be kind.

• There is *Back to the Future Part II*. After a salary dispute, Crispin Glover didn't return for the sequel. But his character was still needed, so the filmmakers got creative and pulled his makeup face casts out of storage from the first movie. As a result, *Part II* has a different actor brazenly pretending to be Crispin Glover, hidden under rubber facial prosthetics. The real Crispin was unamused, and his lawyers allegedly settled for a lot of money.

• There are the publicity stills to the Marx Brothers' *Go West*. Some movie stars are so famous, they don't even pose for their own photos. Groucho Marx didn't feel like leaving his house, so the screenwriter Irving Brecher slathered on the greasepaint and eagerly stood in for him. The photos are rather astonishing. You've got a twenty-five-year-old Groucho, posed with fifty-year-old Harpo and Chico. It's like Saddam Hussein look-alikes, waving at parades and showing up at mall openings in Iraq.

• There are the notorious Fake Shemps. This refers to four infamous Three Stooges shorts filmed *after* Shemp Howard died. The thrill is in figuring out: how'd they do that? This is more like a corporate takeover: there is no single performer behind this ruse. There is stock footage, old audio, misleading editing, and quick shots of the bit player Joe Palma, his hair cut like Shemp and his face stubbornly turned away from camera. These films are a tribute to the tightfisted ethos of Columbia Pictures, which wouldn't let the death of a star get in the way of violent entertainment.

• There are the misadventures of Gallagher and Gallagher 2. The watermelon-hating "comedian" Gallagher decided he could franchise himself, so he licensed his rights to his look-alike brother. The brother was restricted to smaller markets, where he would perform in the identical costume. Audiences rightfully couldn't tell the difference. It's a sledgehammer, fruit, and a guy in a striped shirt. And hell, his name is Gallagher. You'd have to be really suspicious to suspect foul play! Eventually Gallagher 1 regretted his decision and felt threatened by Gallagher 2, so he sued his brother in federal court. After much confusing finger-pointing and family warfare, the real Gallagher successfully won back the exclusive rights to play himself.

• And then there is the master of this look-alike universe, Bruce Lee. Somehow, after he died, Bruce managed to star in more movies than when he was alive. His magnum opus is *Game of Death*—or . . . sort of. Eleven minutes of unseen Bruce fight footage was interpolated into this ghastly production. The rest of the movie is tricked out with an army of doubles wearing funny beards, stock shots, film from Bruce's actual funeral, and a cardboard photo of Bruce glued onto a bathroom mirror. It has to be seen to be believed.

• Which is not to be confused with Bruceploitation. After Lee's unexpected death in 1973, every producer in Hong Kong frantically tried to fill the void. Theaters were suddenly flooded with films starring Bruce Li and Bruce Le and Bruce Liang. These flicks were promoted by hucksters, not unlike how Jack Broder had promoted Sammy. These wiseguys were winking, sort-of promising that you *might* get the real thing. It was a pact between the film, the audience, and the actors. Let's all pretend. Unlike Sammy, who at least had the glory of full billing and could invite his cousins to see it, poor "Bruce Li" didn't even get his real name onscreen! And what of the fans? Did they really think that Li was Lee? As a fellow entered the drive-in, a six-pack of beer ready, excited for his triple bill of kung fu . . . was he full of misplaced hope? But after five minutes, as the fake Bruce revealed a face that didn't look quite right, and as he performed moves that weren't as beautiful and perfect as Bruce's . . . perhaps then it hit our sucker, and he turned to his buddies and said, "Hey! We've been ripped off!" To which they probably replied, "Carl, Bruce Lee died three years ago. Just watch the shitty movie."

In 1975, *Esquire* devoted an issue to celebrity look-alikes. I was enthralled. The cover, with two Telly Savalases, is still an all-timer. Inside, the magazine has pages of doppelgängers, all struggling to get some attention from an uncaring world. This was their moment in the sun. The one who makes me dizzy is essentially a poor man's Sammy Petrillo, if such a thing is possible. This guy named Steven L. Shoup complains that he can't get work as a comedian, because he looks just like Woody Allen! Well, this is a paradox inside of a riddle! What a hellish fate! What's a guy to do? I guess he should have started telling rabbi jokes.

Which takes us back to Sammy. What makes Sammy more special? Why is he greater than the rest? Why does he fascinate us in a way that all the others don't? Well . . . Sammy wore his heart on his sleeve. He desperately, almost uncomfortably desired that blaze of glory. He had big feelings. We know he wanted to be up on that Mount Rushmore of showbiz. He's different from all these other guys. Robert Sacchi and Billy West and Jim Bailey weren't screaming, "Love me!" Sammy was. Constantly. He wanted to be adored, which makes the source of his beliefs ("I'm gonna do a really good impression") all the stranger. Sammy is the performer some of us may wish to avert our eyes from. But we have to stare.

When the trailer for *Brooklyn Gorilla* showed up in theaters, I like to believe that it created widespread pandemonium and national confusion. It's an astonishing piece of flim-flammery. It's two minutes of a Martin and Lewis film from another dimension. It seems to be the guys . . . kind of. Well, there's something wrong with Dean, but damn, that's Jerry, right? I think?

Whoops. Am I supposed to discuss Duke? Well, what of Duke? Let's just say, he didn't really do much of a Dean. He was just an attractive Italian guy with a pleasant singing voice. But, ladies and gentlemen, he provided *value*. Standing next to Sammy, he magically made Sammy look more like Jerry. It's a trick of the eye. Duke made the fake monkey look more like the real monkey. For that, we thank him.

Today, we celebrate Sammy, because he pulled off the impossible. He thought Jerry was the greatest, and he wanted to be the greatest too. So he gifted us Jerry's face, voice, and rubbery limbs. He gave us the big-eyed reactions and the double takes. Sammy is endlessly endearing, in his own terrible way. As a boy he loved showbiz, with the ratty sawdust dream coursing through his blood. He kicked his way in the door, in a strange, wacky manner that nobody else has done, before or since. He didn't just have a job to do—he was *driven*. By the time he was eighteen, he had peaked. By the time he was twenty, the dream was on life support. What a burden for a kid! This is why I feel such warmth towards him. And I hope that, after reading this book, you will too.

Dave Abramson has committed an insane amount of his life to this project. His devotion to this single idea (Sammy!) is beyond belief. He and I started corresponding about it in 2009. We first met about the book more than a dozen years ago. I'm not sure how he kept his sanity. At times, it seemed that he was going to surrender, that Sammy Petrillo was just too big a burden for one man to wrap his arms around. But I'm glad, for all of us, that he stuck with Sammy and made it to the finish line.

Enjoy.

PREFACE

On Sunday night, November 12, 1950, a sixteen-year-old kid popped his head out of a baby's crib on national TV and a six-decade career was born. He was onscreen for all of five seconds—the five seconds that would define the rest of his life.

His name was Sammy Petrillo, and he was the greatest Jerry Lewis impersonator that ever lived. Others mimicked Lewis, yet none else came close: no one inhabited and bounced around inside that rubbery skin like Petrillo. The mugging and guffawing, those faces . . . *that voice!*

It was as if someone had fed Jerry Lewis into a sputtering mimeograph machine and Sammy Petrillo rolled out the other end. At first glance, in a 1950 black-and-white world, they were so nearly identical that even decades later telling them apart can pose a challenge. In 1982, *The Today Show* mistakenly ran a clip of Sammy as an example of Jerry Lewis's genius to a bewildered and darkly amused Jerry Lewis. The resemblance was unbelievable.

Sammy's most notable pairing was with the Dean-Martin-ish (heavy on the "-ish") Duke Mitchell. Together they triumphed in the cult movie favorite *Bela Lugosi Meets a Brooklyn Gorilla* (1952)—a Martin and Lewis knockoff movie that was as funny as or funnier than any Martin and Lewis movie. Realart Pictures, a Poverty Row (meaning very-low-budget) studio that had had success with *Bride of the Gorilla,* produced *Bela Lugosi Meets a Brooklyn Gorilla* with half an eye on a kill fee from the Martin and Lewis people before the cameras even turned over. Fortunately, for the sake of humanity, shooting commenced as lawsuits were threatened and then forgotten.

It's sacrilege in some film circles to utter *Brooklyn Gorilla* in the same breath as Martin and Lewis's *Artists and Models,* the latter, directed by Frank Tashlin, considered to be a gem, the former a Poverty Row quickie starring a strung-out Bela Lugosi. Far from his 1930s matinee-idol status as the suave and sexy Count Dracula, the now methadone-addicted Lugosi's acting jobs consisted of getting chased by guys in gorilla suits and the East Side Kids. Whether *Brooklyn Gorilla* is described in hushed tones or with derisive laughter, the power of this movie can't be denied.

The ridiculousness of pairing an aging horror icon with a pair of Martin and Lewis wannabes is monumental enough to earn it the crown jewel of lowbrow cinema. At the New York City premiere at the once-majestic Rialto Theatre, jungle-themed cardboard cutouts of Sammy and Duke and Bela lined the marquee at the corner of Broadway and 42nd Street. Sammy's family and high-school pals were duly impressed and strangers recognized him in the street. Sammy was famous now, and the showbiz gods had invited him into their elite club.

After *Brooklyn Gorilla,* at age eighteen, it all came crashing down for Sammy Petrillo. Canceled bookings, unpaid IOUs, and an entertainment-wide blacklisting that may or may not have come from Jerry Lewis, whom Sammy may or may not have signed an exclusive contract with, contributed to his failure. It was a heartbreaking mess. Sammy would later say that he "held the record for the world's youngest has-been."

Working in a Martin and Lewis impersonation act became less tenable, and, especially with the breakup of Martin and Lewis in 1956, Sammy and Duke had no choice but to split up the act. They each continued with their respective showbiz careers, both forever tethered to the ineffable magic that was *Brooklyn Gorilla*.

Bela Lugosi Meets a Brooklyn Gorilla was one of the last highlights in Sammy's long career. His journey was of the pie-in-the-puss variety, one strewn with minor victories scattered among large and numerous failures. However, Sammy was the eternal optimist. After each crushing professional defeat, he'd find some other way to infiltrate the business that he loved best, the business that rewarded his true talent—not just the take at the end of the night, but the primal need to hit that stage, stare into the lights, read a room like a pro, and get them on your side and keep them there using only your sheer talent. It was selfish and selfless at the same time.

Sammy would eventually grow to resent Jerry Lewis's fame and accomplishments. He'd ask himself why Jerry was so successful when he was doing a similar schtick. Decades later, Sammy's pal Stephen Kroninger recalled a candid moment that might serve as a punchline to the longest shaggy-dog story ever told. "I was with Sammy. He was eating a grilled cheese sandwich and Sammy had false teeth and he didn't have his teeth in and he's eating without any teeth and he turns to his brother and he goes, 'I never thought Jerry Lewis was funny.'"

Millions thought that Jerry Lewis was funny. For decades, Jerry Lewis was one of the most famous entertainers on the planet. Cherished and despised in equal portions, Lewis spoke to the multitudes through the universal language of acting like an idiot. A humanitarian, an inventor, a franchise, Lewis was an uncompromising genius whose charitable nature was matched only by his massive ego. As a performer, there was no one else like him, except possibly his father, the Catskills comic and impersonator Danny Lewis. When Jerry's razor-sharp comic timing clicked into place, he was swinging at an expert level, riffing infinitely on all of the varieties of stupid. It was a monster act, and Jerry could be funny as hell. When he struggled, there wasn't a worse person to be around. Lewis famously directed, starred in, and then shelved his Holocaust magnum opus *The Day the Clown Cried*. Self-styled as a serious auteur as well as a pandering clown, Lewis morphed through the years from a skinny kid into a curmudgeonly lump, all while retaining his place as the ambassador of comedy with a conscience. Brilliant, difficult, and insanely popular in his heyday, Jerry scorched a path of hilarity and tears that the world had never seen.

Jerry's rise to fame began as half of one of the most successful acts in the history of show business. Dean Martin (born Dino Paul Crocetti) was the other half. Together from 1946 to 1956, Dean Martin and Jerry Lewis were a phenomenon, the fast and funny kick in the pants that post-war entertainment in America had been aching for. Martin and Lewis bounced through the nightclubs, blasted over the radio waves, tore a hole in the silver screen, broke through walls and windows, and virtually jumped into the laps of an ever-emerging TV audience. They were fresh and hot, and nobody could touch them. With their juvenile wisecracking, leaping about, and ad-libbing, they were idolized by men, women, and children nationwide and then worldwide. At their height, a single appearance leaning out a window in Times Square drew crowds that shut down several blocks. Dean Martin and Jerry Lewis dragged entertainment into the second half of the twentieth century by the short hairs.

After the initial success of *Bela Lugosi Meets a Brooklyn Gorilla,* Sammy doubled down on the life of the peripatetic nightclub comic. As his parents once had, he followed the work, settling in towns where the seltzer sprayed and carny talk echoed in the dressing rooms. Sammy's Jerry Lewis imitation was his calling card into the business, a backstage pass into the rarefied world where fellow entertainment legends strode with impunity. It was an impersonation that would take on a life of its own, and the act of getting inside another idiot's skin transformed itself into something that elevated the schtick way beyond the edge of the stage. There were moments when that comic up there was neither Sammy nor Jerry but an absurd combination of two imperfect morons that passed in the night. It was perfection, and it was the fire that Sammy spent his entire life running into and away from at the same time.

Few remember Sammy these days, and for those that do, for most of them, he's nothing more than a footnote, a cipher, an odd blip in the pulse of showbiz. Sammy traversed pop culture from the last gasps of burlesque and skin flicks to the world of stand-up comedy and cable TV, yet he never broke through. Some see Petrillo as a rip-off of Jerry Lewis's act—an untalented hack who leeched off Lewis's fame with all of the fury and none of the artistry. There are others who consider Sammy Petrillo as brilliant as, if not more brilliant than, the muse he sought to emulate. Originality does not necessarily make the man. No one remembers who Jackie Gleason stole his "How sweet it is!" schtick from. In his heyday, even Charlie Chaplin came in twenty-seventh when he entered a Charlie Chaplin look-alike contest. Sammy was a natural-born kosher ham, a fearless, have-schtick-will-travel kind of a kid, who was happy to be in the spotlight, even if it was someone else's.

Sammy worked with many other partners over the years besides Duke Mitchell, including a few strippers, a gorilla, a robot, and the first Black comedian to make a million dollars. Some of his sidekicks found fame in funny places after leaving the act. Sammy's early partner Ric Marlow, a.k.a. Mr. Mood, racked up a fortune co-composing the 1960 adult-contemporary pop hit "A Taste of Honey." The intriguingly named Petrillo and Petrillo featured the comedian and singer Carme Pitrello who ended up replacing Sammy with Paul Salos, a lesser Jerry Lewis impersonator. Salos hailed from Dallas, was pals with Jack Ruby, and earned a mention as a person of interest in the Warren Commission Report. In 2008, he advanced three rounds on *America's Got Talent* with his fedora-hatted Sinatra impersonation. One of Sammy's most enduring partners was his ex-girlfriend Suzie Perkovic, an on-again-off-again roommate, muse, and confidante. Billed as Suzie and Sammy, they were familiar faces in the Pittsburgh comedy boom of the early 1980s.

Sammy was a private man who was many things to many people. Depending on whom you spoke with, Sammy was always there for you or gone without a trace. Some of the Sammy Petrillo people refuse to talk to each other. The only thing that they can agree on is how smart and funny he was. They all imitate him in the exact same raspy voice.

In my early stages of research, I had no idea how many conflicting opinions of Sammy's life and legacy would be conjured up. To use a crude image that anyone familiar with Jerry Lewis would get, it was like a Jerry Lewis *Rashomon* parody complete with bucked teeth and oversized glasses.

Some dissension was more critical than others. That night in the diner, when Sammy jumped into a lady's lap and asked for a shave, was it whipped cream or sour cream that he slathered on his face? Is it true that Jerry Lewis actually signed Sammy to a contract to keep him from working? What incredible offers did Mitchell and Petrillo pass on, and was Dean Martin behind some of those offers? How did Sammy end up getting co-writing credit on the first Isley Brothers single? Did Sammy really come up with the idea for *The Munsters*? Did Sammy discover and mentor Richard Pryor in a Pittsburgh comedy club when they weren't selling off-brand perfume door-to-door? Did Sammy invent a fart-propelled superhero ten years before Howard Stern? Why did the future wife-murderer Spade Cooley want to kill Duke and Sammy? How did that bullet get in Sammy's leg? Did Sammy really step out one night for a pack of smokes, leaving a wife and four kids, never to return? Was Sammy working on a remake of or sequel to *Brooklyn Gorilla* starring himself and his once-estranged son? What happened at that 2008 Jerry Lewis event with Peter Bogdanovich, when security attempted to remove Sammy from a front-row seat?

Questions led to more questions, and soon Sammy's story unspooled into a sprawling narrative that only years of research and dozens of interviews could piece back together. His other non-specifically-Jerry-Lewis ventures deserved further investigation as well. Sammy was involved in several unreleased movies, but two that escaped into the public were the nudie cutie *Shangri-La* (1961) and his nudie roughie for Doris Wishman, *Keyholes Are for Peeping* (1972). His comedy LPs *All about Cleopatra* and the genuinely hilarious *My Son, the Phone Caller* have intriguing backstories that involve the Ed Sullivan impersonator Will Jordan and the independent filmmaker Barbara Loden. As a radio host, Sammy produced *Protect Yourself,* the world's first and last martial-arts instructional radio show. Sammy's pals resembled an outtake reel from *Broadway Danny Rose*: Tiny Tim, Al "Grandpa Munster" Lewis, the *Car 54* legend Joe E. Ross, the kid-show host Chuck McCann, the "Nature Boy" composer and kook eden ahbez (lowercase intentional), the *Reservoir Dogs* star and real-life tough guy Lawrence Tierney, and Joey

Bishop's partner, the unrelated Rummy Bishop. Ever the journeyman, Sammy was as comfortable twisting balloons at a five-year-old's birthday party as he was working blue with Linda Lovelace at a Passaic, New Jersey, burlesque house.

His substantial under-the-radar showbiz journey will hopefully entertain most of you and serve as a cautionary tale for the rest. Sammy's life is a conundrum inside a fortune cookie inside a whoopee cushion inside a gorilla cage. Consider it a handbook for what to do and what not to do in show business.

CHAPTER 1

A STAR IS HATCHED

There were two Kid Skellys.

The first Kid Skelly got walloped in an illegal boxing match in Lakewood Park, Indiana, in 1911. It was a three-round bout that was supposed to go ten. The fight ended just before the cops arrived. A couple weeks later, Kid Skelly popped up at another match in Brazil, Indiana. After his introduction to the crowd, Skelly offered to take on anyone 150 pounds or less. The outcome of this fight was not recorded for posterity.

Two years later the second man to be known as Kid Skelly was born. Classified as a lightweight, he also would take up boxing, among other vocations. Abraham Patrello and his family were Greek Jews whose ancestors had spent enough time in Italy to be able to blend in unnoticed. Some Italian blood seeped into the family tree, which might account for the Patrello name. As a first-generation American, young Abraham honored his family's nomadic tendencies. By bus and rail, he would criss-cross the new land as much as he could, once he was able to. Stationed in San Diego during a naval stint, Patrello rebranded himself "Kid Skelly" and had the name proudly tattooed on his arm. After his boxing career ended, this Skelly continued as a dancer, a comedian, an agent, a jeweler, a cab driver, and eventually an owner of a novelty joke shop in Florida.

Skelly had pizzazz and was a master of schtick. One of Skelly's routines was a pantomime bit in which he would dry himself off with a towel. First, he'd mimic drying his face, then his neck and under his arms. Then, with the towel threaded between his legs, he'd cast a knowing glance at his audience and floss back and forth with a frenzy that never failed to elicit howls of laughter. Family, friends, strangers—all were slain by this solid bit of business. Skelly loved the attention, and he knew how to get it.

Anna (sometimes known as Annie) Jackowitz (sometimes Jalovitz) was a comely Romanian Jew who was also drawn to showbiz. An amateur dancer herself, Anna was so enraptured by Skelly's charms that on January 7, 1934, she married the aspiring entertainer. It was the heyday of burlesque, and, together, Skelly and Anna were booked into the circuit, or "the wheel," of the variety acts that traveled to theaters across the country by rail. Burlesque flourished because both vaudeville and the movies, even in the "pre-code" days, held themselves to a semi-decent code of conduct. The implied sex appeal and salacious gags might get pushed to the limit, yet would never be taken beyond the realm of wholesome fun. Burlesque was vaudeville's raunchier cousin and was unafraid to add some skin to the game. Adding "exotic" dancers and tassel-twirling striptease acts added to burlesque's already growing popularity. Working-class men in towns large and small found solace in this new form of entertainment that would one day evolve into the modern strip club.

Cross-country travel could be rough, even though the burlesque theaters paid for the performers' train tickets. Arriving in a new town, a performer's trunk would go to the hotel and another trunk would be delivered backstage at the theater. With a typical assortment of unsavory types on and off the stage, many of the chorus girls and strippers would marry the comics on the bill, if only for safety reasons. Sometimes a dancer would get paid a little extra to act as a foil or a "straight man" for a comic—an arrangement that worked out well for Skelly and Anna.

Taking a break from burlesque on a stopover in Hollywood, Anna doubled for the movie star Alice Faye, standing under the hot lights while cameramen set up shots and took exposure readings off her face. Shuttling between the Bronx, New York, and Phoenix, Arizona, Skelly and Anna were back to hitting the burlesque circuit hard when a new talent popped his head into the world.

Hatched nine months and seventeen days after Skelly and Anna's wedding night, Sam Albert Patrello made his first appearance on October 24, 1934. Even though Sammy always claimed to have been born in the Bronx, his birth certificate cites Arizona as his place of origin. A newspaper article in 1952 reported that Sammy was "literally born backstage when his dancer-parents were touring the country with variety shows." For the sake of the story, let's go with the Bronx. It makes for better copy anyway.

By 1940, Skelly, Anna, and Sammy centered their lives in the Bronx—a reasonable commute to the Catskill Mountains, where Skelly hoofed and joked for the summer vacationers. Nineteen-forty was also the year that six-year-old Sammy first ran out onstage to compete with his father for the crowd's attention.

"I used to watch my dad perform, then I'd go onstage and do some bits too," Sammy recalled. "My mother taught me comedy and how to ad-lib." Anna would draw pictures, put them on the wall, and ask Sammy how he'd reply to a heckler: "'Here's a man who says you stink! What's your retort?' Some parents discourage their kids from pursuing a show business career. With me, it was just the opposite."

With a performing son as an asset, the Patrellos hit the road again, stopping off long enough in Arizona for the arrival of Sammy's younger brother, Marvin. In 1944, during World War II, Skelly enlisted in the Navy, stayed stateside, got that tattoo, and was in civvy clothes again by 1946.

The Patrellos hunkered down in the Bronx for a spell, but that wasn't a good fit for burlesque performers trying to eke out a living. A few years earlier, Mayor Fiorello La Guardia had squeezed the industry out of New York City, and burlesque now lived on in working-class neighborhoods scattered across the country. In the right towns, the work was plentiful, since there was always a need for seltzer-spraying comics and passable singers to prop up the striptease acts. For the next few years, Skelly and family lived out of suitcases as they helped provide much needed ribald entertainment to working stiffs everywhere.

Baby Marvin didn't take to the spotlight like Sammy but unwittingly went along for the ride. "We lived like gypsies," Marvin recalled. "I was brought up in Florida, California, Arizona. I don't know why. They would just get a bug and would want to move out of the state. My dad used to blame my mother and my mother used to blame my dad."

At one point, the Patrellos called Phoenix home for a few years as they took a stab at living a normal life. They found a place in a government-housing community at 16th and East Roosevelt Street. Sammy honed his class-clown skills a block away at Thomas A. Edison Elementary School. An 8mm home movie is the first glimpse of a thirteen-year-old Sammy Patrello hamming it up for the camera. Shot in Arizona in 1948, about a minute of existing footage opens with a buck-toothed, smiling Sammy pointing a cap gun at the camera. Wearing a striped shirt and baggy trousers, topped off by a ten-gallon cowboy hat that's too low on his head, Sammy gets off a quick round before catching a bullet himself. Clutching his shoulder, Sammy falls backwards to the ground, gunned down by an imaginary assailant. Four years later, Sammy would reenact this bit in his debut motion picture.

Sammy's first write-up was courtesy of a local newspaper, the *Arizona Republic*. On what was allegedly the hottest day of 1948, "newspaper salesboy Sam Patrello" is pictured with his pal Charles Edward Lawrence as they mug for the cameras. Both clutch ice-cream cones in the 112-degree heat, yet Sammy is seen wiping his brow with his ice-cream cone hand, precariously close to smashing it into his head.

Almost a year later the *Republic* covered Sammy again: "One of the latest moppets to try his hand at the entertainment angle is 14 year old Sam Patrello, eighth grader at Edison School, who'll be on deck this week as a comedian. Young Sam appeared on KOOL [radio] at 10:30 am Saturday in his newly publicized role."

Exactly what Sammy did on KOOL and how long he did it for is lost to time. We do know that a KRUX sportscaster, Ed de Forest, handled the emcee chores along with "his famous Jub Jub Bird" sidekick. We also can be fairly certain that Sammy hadn't discovered Jerry Lewis yet. Martin and Lewis had debuted their nationally syndicated radio show just one month earlier, and their first motion picture, *My Friend Irma,* wouldn't be released until later that year.

By 1950, the wandering Patrellos were back in the Bronx, this time in the 149th Street projects. Three blocks away, the main shopping district known as the Hub provided the bustle of department stores, luncheonettes, decrepit movie palaces, and other lowbrow thrills. The Patrellos took up residence in a five-room ground-floor apartment at 209 East 196th Street, one block east of the Grand Concourse. Once referred to as the "Park Avenue of the middle class," the Grand Concourse connected the North Bronx to Manhattan via three expansive roadways divvied up by two strips of trees. It was originally conceived by the French topographical engineer Louis Aloys Risse in 1909 to be a knockoff of Paris's Champs-Élysées. By the late 1940s, its continental mystique grew a little rough, thanks in no part to the side streets that provided the seedy pleasures that could be found in the Hub. Sammy shared a bed with younger brother Marvin, whose tossing and turning kept Sammy awake throughout most of those Grand Concourse nights.

Occasionally, Skelly and Anna would skip town with Marvin and drop Sammy off with their wealthier relatives a few stops north on the subway line in Morris Heights. The Jackowes (formerly Jackowitz and Jalovitz) lived right off University Avenue and Featherbed Lane, above a steep hill from Jerome Avenue.

Sammy's favorite movie theater, the Zenith, was nearby on 170th Street. Its typical fare was second- and third-run features along with serials. It would set Sammy back 25 cents, but it's likely that he took advantage of the 11-cent admission before 10 a.m. on the weekends. The first 500 kids to show up received free comic books. Sammy would sit in the theater and dream about appearing on the big screen.

Sammy's cousin Martin Jackowe recalled their cramped living situation: "It was a one-bedroom apartment, and I shared a bed in the living room with Sammy. It was a Hollywood bed. I had a sister and me and my mother and father. Sammy's my first cousin and his mother was my father's sister and for whatever reason his mother and father always moved around. [The actor] Vince Edwards slept in my living room. This was before the *Ben Casey* thing. I remember that he was big and hairy."

On September 1, 1950, Sammy placed an ad in the *New York Post*: "If you are a teen ager with musical aspirations and desire to join a band, Sammy Patrello 328 E. 145th St., would like to hear from you . . . Sam's not a musician himself; comedy and MC work are his forte. He wants recruits to join him and pianist Alan Kalsky . . ." It's possible that 328 E. 145th Street was Kalsky's address. The majority of Sammy's acquaintances, especially his partners, are notable either for some outside achievement or for reappearing later in Sammy's life. The pianist Alan Kalsky fits neither of these descriptions, and his involvement with Sammy, for our purposes, ends right here.

Sammy was floundering. He was sixteen and knew that he was destined for a life in showbiz without having any idea how he was going to make that happen. Nearly two months later, on a whim, Sammy's life was irrevocably changed by a single seemingly mundane event. It was a life-changing incident that shoved him into the fast lane of fame; it propelled Sammy to heights beyond imagination. It was the impetus, the seismic kick in the pants, the unseen hand that guided our hero to legendary status. On a weekday afternoon in early November 1950, Sammy Patrello got a haircut.

CHAPTER 2

THE HAIRCUT

"It was a freebie," Sammy recalled when interviewed on the author's radio show on WFMU in 1992. "A freebie haircut. What happened was, I was going to Performing Arts High School, or High School of Performing Arts as it were. I went down to their annex, which was called Metropolitan High School, and the annex was like a trade school and they were learning how to cut hair. And so I got a freebie haircut and the guy cut my hair and he started to laugh, and I said, 'What are you laughing at?' and he said, 'You look just like that guy Jerry Lewis,' and I said, 'Get out of here,' and he said, 'Yes, you do,' and I said, 'Wow, that's interesting.' You know?

"In the meantime, everywhere I walked, people laughed, people asked me if I was Jerry Lewis. It was unbelievable. And Jerry Lewis, at the time, I guess he had made his first or second motion picture, *My Friend Irma Goes West*. I really didn't know that much about him, and I kinda caught some glimpses of the movie and I saw he went, "Ah ah ah," and he talked kinda high like *this, you know?* And I said, 'Gee, you know, maybe I do resemble that guy, and I could do that kind of a laugh. I could do that kind of a voice.' I was an impersonator and comic, as you know, as well as an actor and so forth. And I thought, 'Gee, that's really cute, you know? I decided I was gonna give up school, so I went down to get some working papers, and I said to myself, 'Do you really want to get a job or do you want to be in show business? That's where your heart is. That's you—you've been brought up with that.' My dad was a comic and my mother was a dancer and Alice Faye's double, and so I was kind of born and bred in show business. And I said to myself, 'Gee, you gotta do something with show business.'"

Sammy ran down to a local candy store, rang up *Variety,* and asked where Milton Berle held rehearsals for his hit TV show. *Texaco Star Theater* was a comedy-variety weekly hour that had originated as a radio show in 1938. Initially hosted by Adolph Menjou, then John Barrymore, and finally the comedian Ken Murray, *Texaco Star Theater* transitioned to television in 1948 with a rotation of hosts before settling on Milton Berle after a few months.

Milton Berle (born Mendel Berlinger) got his start at age six by winning a Charlie Chaplin look-alike contest. A few years later, Berle's mother landed him a gig posing as a child model for Buster Brown shoes. Determined for her son to break into showbiz, she dragged him into Eddie Cantor's dressing room so he could show off his Eddie Cantor impersonation. She crashed Al Jolson's sold-out Winter Garden show and pushed young Milton onstage to show Joley how to do Joley. Fueled by a stage mother and his own brash hamminess, Berle made his vaudeville debut in 1920 in Atlantic City before eventually taking his act to Broadway. At age sixteen, his quick wit secured the vaunted role as master of ceremonies on the vaudeville circuit. Berle found success in radio, movies, and even songwriting; however, nothing had the profound, industry-changing impact as his *Texaco Star Theater* gig. After almost forty years in the biz, Berle, the master ad-libber, brought his seasoned jackassery to the small screen.

In more ways than one, nobody was bigger than the man so beloved by the public that he was often referred to as Uncle Miltie. As much as 90% of the country shut down on Tuesday nights from eight to nine Eastern to gasp at this Borscht Belt titan. Berle's over-the-top ad-libbing and physical antics sold a nation on this new medium by repurposing hoary old vaudeville gags for the stay-at-home crowd. TV set sales skyrocketed as a nation quickly adapted to the schticky, life-changing technology. It was the Golden Age of Television, and Berle quickly became the reigning king, an entertainer so closely entwined with the medium that he was nicknamed "Mr. Television."

Oh, and Milton Berle, by all accounts, had a monster-sized schlong. The story goes that another similarly-structured personality, possibly Forrest Tucker or maybe Huntz Hall, held a competition at the Friars Club to see who was more well-endowed. Henny Youngman, or possibly Jack Carter, advised Miltie to "only take out enough to win." Miltie won. You didn't think that you were getting out of here without the Milton Berle schlong contest story? Now let's get our minds out of the gutter and rejoin our hero down at the candy-store phone booth.

Variety gave Sammy the address and phone number for Nova Studios, where Berle drilled and aggravated his writers for countless hours a week before bringing the act into the TV studio. Sammy called up Nova and quickly got clearance to the set by claiming to be Milton Berle's cousin. Just as Berle and television met each other at exactly the right time in history, Sammy, sporting the world's greatest haircut, crashed the only party in town that knew what to do with him.

"I walked right into Milton Berle's rehearsal," Sammy recalled years later. "Berle was there with a whistle and a towel around his neck—that's how he rehearsed—and he had a bunch of people, great writers, and they were fabulous comedy writers, and what I did was I ran over to Milton Berle and jumped right in his arms and I started throwing lines at him, and every line I threw at Berle, his comedy writers—of course I didn't know they were comedy writers, but they broke up. They screamed. And every time he threw a line back at me, they clammed up. They did it to put Berle on, and it was really cute—they were cute guys, really nice fellas—and Berle says, 'Gee, you know you look a lot like Jerry Lewis.' I said, 'I know, I know. Maybe that could help me get into show business here or something?' He said, 'Well, you know, Jerry is doing a show where they need someone to look like him, to play his baby.' He said, 'And I'm gonna send you over to MCA.'"

In 1950, MCA was one of the largest talent agencies in the world. Their activities included booking acts, publishing music, running a record label, and representing film, television, and radio stars. Miltie instructed Sammy to go up to MCA headquarters and meet up with Freddie Fields, an agent. Five months earlier Freddie had scored the coup of his career by convincing Dean Martin and Jerry Lewis to sign with MCA.

When the elevator doors opened, high atop the lush MCA offices on West 57th Street, Sammy came flying out, bouncing off the walls and falling over the leather chairs. "I started shouting at them," Sammy recalled years later, "'Hey, come on, everybody!' You know, I started doing, like, a Jerry Lewis type voice. I was really a crazy kid, very brash. And people just freaked out—they were laughing all over the place." Sammy made a beeline for Freddie Fields's office: "I walked past his secretary and she said, 'Jerry, what did you do? Shrink?'—because he's much taller than I am—you know, he's six foot one and a half—and I just kept making faces and clowning around and saying, 'I wanna see Freddie, I wanna see Freddie,' and she said, 'Okay.' So she said, 'Freddie, here's Jerry,' she said, 'but he shrunk.' And I walked into his office and he said, 'My goodness, I can't believe this.'"

With trembling hands, Freddie Fields picked up the phone and dialed up Milton Berle's agent, Herb Jaffe.

"Herb Jaffe came in and Freddie Fields said, 'Your hair is a little long.'" Freddie grabbed a pair of scissors from his secretary's desk. "He said, 'Basically, just cut it a little bit right here in the front,' and he cut my hair, and he and Herb Jaffe said, 'Come on, we got to go over to Sherry Netherland's [the Sherry-Netherland hotel] to see Jerry.'"

In 1950, after headlining their own radio show for NBC, Martin and Lewis were given the opportunity to host NBC's new Sunday night TV variety show, *The Colgate Comedy Hour*. Alternating weeks with other hosts (Abbott and Costello, Eddie Cantor) they slayed the nation with their breaking-the-fourth-wall antics. No act was hotter, and Jerry Lewis in particular was starting to be hailed as a comedy genius, an intriguing notion that would stick with him throughout the years.

According to Sammy's cousin, Martin Jackowe, Sammy knocked on Jerry's hotel-room door and Dean Martin was there: "Dean saw Sammy and went to Sammy like this—[finger on lips]—'Shhh!' [He] opened the door and let him in."

Up until that moment, Jerry Lewis was secure in the knowledge that he was the only Jerry Lewis in the world. Sammy continues, "And they ushered me in there and Jerry Lewis was in the bathroom in his shorts shaving, and, so help me, he almost cut his throat when he saw me. I came in and sat on the toilet seat and he did a double take and the razor almost went through his neck and he couldn't believe it and he said, 'My goodness, where did they get this guy?' He wasn't being funny—he was being kinda serious." (In another version of this story that Sammy told his cousin Martin, Jerry put his hands around Sammy's neck and choked him.) "Jerry said a couple of derogatory things to me which I don't even want to go into now. But he was a little paranoid, you know. He said something to the effect of, 'Don't sign any checks.' He said, 'Don't be me . . . Jerry Lewis.'"

CHAPTER 3

JERRY LEWIS

Jerry Lewis's father wasn't just an Al Jolson impersonator. Besides appearing as an accomplished mimic, Daniel "Danny" Levitch could reel off a string of gags with the best of the clowns. Shuffling onstage in his ill-fitting suit, he was a real "a little song, a little dance, a little seltzer down the pants" kind of entertainer. That said, even Danny would tell you that nothing touched his Jolson impression. Decades after Al Jolson walked the boards with his blackface routines, it's now difficult to imagine how popular he was. Conquering stage, screen, radio, and the recording industry, Jolson entertained the pants off America and was billed on phonograph records as "the World's Greatest Entertainer." When Danny Levitch got down on one knee with arms outstretched to the heavens to belt out a maudlin tearjerker, he could deliver Joley for a fraction of the price—and a fraction of the paycheck, too, but Danny knew that would change in time. He had a solid act that worked, and one that might be able to pay all of the bills someday. It was the 1920s, and the future was looking bright.

Danny found work wherever he could. He entertained at birthday parties, at weddings, for kids waiting in line for smallpox vaccines—anywhere he could bank five or ten bucks at a time. For a more reliable paycheck, he sold sheet music for the music publisher Fred Fischer, Inc. In the spring of 1923, he noticed a beautiful, slightly zaftig Rachel ("Rae") Brodsky selling sheet music at an S. S. Kresge store in Newark, New Jersey.

Rae was an accomplished pianist who could accommodate any customer's request. She also performed regularly on the radio station WOR, played cocktail lounges, and dated Jimmy Ritz of the famed Ritz Brothers. Danny made a play for Rae by handing her the sheet music from Fischer's 1917 hit "They Go Wild, Simply Wild over Me" and singing along with it, complete with a Jolson-esque bird-whistle break.

Rae was smitten with her singing Romeo, and they hitched up after a two-year Newark–Brooklyn courtship. They lived in a series of small apartments and even out of a hotel room in Times Square for a spell while they chased down the dream. The sporadic Borscht Belt gigs paid the bills, and Rae provided piano arrangements for the both of them.

On March 16, 1926, they ushered into the world their only child, Jerome, who was named for Rae's father. Jerry later claimed that he was born Joseph and changed his name to Jerry, but his birth certificate and the 1930 and 1940 censuses have him down as Jerome. Jerry would casually play with many facts concerning his early years, sculpting dates and events into an approved past that he was more comfortable with. The controversy over his birth name is just another in the burnishing of the Lewis rags-to-riches story.

Danny and Rae changed their surnames to the more marquee-friendly Lewis and followed the action wherever they could get work, moving frequently, often dropping young Jerry off with relatives for months at a time. The Lewises schlepped all over the Catskills and New Jersey, pursuing their Borscht Belt dreams as much as two could without ever breaking into the big time.

Jerry was a lonely kid. He never got over the abandonment by his parents, and existential self-doubt nagged at him for the rest of his life. Luckily for Jerry and the rest of mankind, he learned to cope with his debilitating depression by acting like an idiot whenever and wherever he could. Jerry recalled, "I used to climb the pipes in the kitchen and dangle like a monkey." He was a pencils-up-the-nose, drooling class clown who had learned enough from his attention-grabbing father to know how to get some of that for himself.

Sometimes, to Jerry's delight, Danny and Rae would drag him along on tour when they ran out of relatives to drop him off with. Jerry slept in dressing rooms, was baby-sat by hotel maids, and quickly acquired a taste for the nomadic biz of show. In 1932 the Lewises were booked into a ten-week engagement at the President Hotel in Swan Lake, New York. The highlight of the act was when Danny would lean into the wildly popular dirge "Brother,

Can You Spare a Dime?" Jerry watched and made mental notes every night from the wings. He started bugging the old man to let him perform it onstage. Danny shut that down right away. He didn't want his nutty kid going into show business. Aware of his son's emotional ups and downs, Danny was concerned about what that kind of attention might do to him, and he didn't want to spend the rest of his life trying to get that toothpaste back in the tube. Rae took her little *bubbeleh* monkey's side and pressured Danny into letting the six-year-old sing just one song. Danny relented.

While the big songs of 1932 were upbeat anthems like "Life Is Just a Bowl of Cherries" and "Happy Days Are Here Again," "Brother, Can You Spare a Dime?" was a compelling indictment of American values gone wrong. Sung from the point of view of Joe Everyman, soldier, worker, father, son, and brother, who gave everything for his country and got nothing in return, the haunting verses and resigned refrain of "Brother, can you spare a dime?" scored with a Depression-weary public. The feel-bad lyrics were courtesy of Yip Harburg, who, along with the composer, Jay Gorney, retrofitted the melody from a Jewish lullaby that Jay had heard back in his native Russia. It was introduced in the short-lived Broadway revue *Americana* and sung by the now forgotten Rex Weber, who was known in the trade for his "standard routine of ventriloquistic singing." "Brother" became one of the most popular songs of 1932, thanks to emotionally charged versions by Rudy Vallée and Bing Crosby. Naturally, when Jolson got hold of it, he crushed it, and most people, including the Lewises, probably heard it for the first time on his weekly NBC radio show. Decades later at the MGM Grand in Las Vegas, Dean Martin, who at that point in his career couldn't be bothered to make it through an entire number without cracking up or forgetting the lyrics, would occasionally roll out a somber and stunning rendition of "Brother, Can You Spare a Dime?" It was a hell of a song and a gift from the showbiz gods for those who successfully tackled it.

Jerry always cited September 17, 1931, as the date that he first suited up in a pint-sized tuxedo and performed "Brother, Can You Spare a Dime?" The song would not be written for another full year. However, whenever this occurred, it was still a life-changing event for the young entertainer. In one of Jerry's accounts, the orchestra didn't have time to change the key, and squeaky-voiced Jerry's out-of-tune screeching elicited unexpected peals of laughter from the audience. Another version of the story has Jerry solely accompanied by his mother on piano without so much of the off-key screeching. In 2012, at an eighty-sixth-birthday celebration at the 92nd

Street Y in New York City, Jerry recalled that when he took his bow he stepped into a footlight which exploded, spewing smoke all over the stage. Cue uproarious laughter. In any case, his debut was intoxicating, and it was the sweet poison that young Jerry could now not live without. "From that moment on," Jerry recalled, "showbiz was in my blood. So was loneliness."

Jerry asked Danny if he could perform "Brother" the following night and Danny refused. He genuinely wanted his son to have a more secure livelihood than showbiz. Also, the pest got bigger laughs with that one bit than Danny got all night. The kid pleaded, he cajoled, he screamed, all in that moronic, idiot voice that fans and connoisseurs of Lewis's oeuvre know so well. When that failed, Jerry ran through the audience begging the hotel guests to scream for him and request that he sing a song. The scheme worked and Jerry started opening the show every night and getting laughs that Danny didn't even know existed.

The Hotel Arthur in Lakewood, New Jersey, was a prime vacation spot for Newark and Philly Jews, and for the 1938 holiday season Danny was their genial emcee. Jerry got a job serving tea and cookies twice a day to hotel guests in the lobby. After seeing a Ken Maynard western in a downtown movie theater, Jerry and a couple of his work buddies began acting out parodies of the latest westerns, complete with flying stunts and goofy gunplay. The act was a hit with the tea-and-cookies crowd. Jerry was getting more confident in the spotlight: "I was tall, skinny, gawky—cute, but funny-looking. With the voice God had given me, I certainly wasn't going to be a singer like my dad, with his Al Jolson baritone. I always saw the humor in things, the joke possibilities." One of those joke possibilities was miming along to popular records of the day, a catapult and eventually a crutch for the young comic.

Reginald Gardiner was an English comedian whose hit Broadway act in the 1930s included a routine in which he would comically lip-synch to a record. Dozens of comedians performed this bit; however, it was Gardiner who inspired Jerry to fool around with his own version of it. Just for their own amusement, Jerry and his childhood crush, Lonnie Brown, worked up an act where they would duet to Jeanette MacDonald and Nelson Eddy's "Indian Love Call." One night at the Arthur in February 1939, the headliner, Red Buttons, didn't show up on time. Jerry and Lonnie were quickly recruited to entertain the crowd. Even though the loud applause at the end of their act was for a just-arriving Red Buttons, it still encouraged Jerry enough to double down on this showbiz thing. Miming to records was a solid act, and Jerry ate off it for the next five years.

Initially billing himself as "Joey Levitch and His Hollywood Friends," Jerry recalled in his memoir, *Dean & Me (A Love Story),* "I would put on a fright wig with a frock coat and lip-sync to the great baritone Igor Gorin's 'Largo al factotum' from *The Barber of Seville*. I'd come out in a Carmen Miranda dress, with fruit on my head, and do Miranda. Then a pin-striped jacket, suck in my cheeks and I'd do Sinatra singing 'All or Nothing at All.'" Soon he'd perform as "Jerry Lewis—Satirical Impressions in Pantomimicry" and as "the Gay Imposter." Like many comedy legends before him, Jerry also worked for no pay as a *tummler* at the Borscht Belt resorts. A *tummler* was the greeter who did a little bit of everything—guiding and amusing the guests through their stay in several capacities. From check-in to check-out, there was Jerry, fumbling around with luggage, leading the exercise class, and screaming out bingo numbers. It was an invaluable education for any aspiring entertainer.

School never meant a hell of a lot to Jerry. His freshman nicknames were Ug, for ugly, and Id, for idiot, so at sixteen he dropped out of school and devoted himself to showbiz full time. By seventeen, he was making a better living than Danny. Realizing that his son's career had eclipsed his, Danny came to terms with it and was now talking up Jerry to his showbiz pals. After Broadway shows let out for the night, Danny and Rae would drag Jerry over to Lindy's, at Broadway and 49th Street. The famed eatery was Schmooze Central—a Damon Runyon–esque hub where gangsters and their henchmen, song-pluggers and bookies, runners and flunkies, working and non-working actors all sat side by side joking and nailing down high-powered deals over coffee and the best cheesecake in the world. The Lewises couldn't afford to go in, so they would stand outside and catch celebrities on their way out. Rae would nudge Jerry: "There's Milton Berle—make like an idiot and talk funny."

One night, Jerry talked funny to the right talent agent, Abner "Abby" Greshler, who took an interest in the kid. Greshler was a pioneer in the art of package deals ("the super deal") and would eventually represent A-list names like Al Jolson, Danny Kaye, Benny Goodman, Eddie Cantor, Milton Berle, Vince Edwards, the Monkees, Jack Klugman, and Tony Randall. (In tribute to their beloved agent, Randall and Klugman saw to it that Murray the Cop's last name on the *Odd Couple* TV series was Greshler.) Sixteen-year-old Jerry, accompanied by his dad, signed a management contract with Greshler in his midtown office. Greshler immediately booked Jerry into the deceptively named Palace Theatre, a run-down burlesque house in Buffalo, New York. Jerry eventually worked his way up from a string of sketchy venues to the occasional nightclub and theater. August 1944 was a momentous month for Jerry. He met his future wife. And then he met his soulmate.

Patti Palmer (née Esther Grace Calonico) was singing with the bandleader Fio Rito at the Downtown Theater in Detroit when she met Jerry. Patti initially broke into the biz by learning Dinah Shore's repertoire on accordion and acing her way into singing on a kiddie radio show. Raised as a devout Catholic in Wyoming, Patti spent her childhood in a succession of foster homes. She was a lonely kid and felt a connection with the brash and insecure comic. Jerry, in turn, charmed and courted her in true Jerry Lewis fashion. One time at a diner he dumped a bowl of hot cereal over his head because Patti wasn't paying enough attention to him. When the waitress asked Jerry why he had oatmeal on his head, he replied in his moron voice, "Because I didn't have Cream of Wheat . . .?" Patti was twenty-two, and Jerry was eighteen. In October they were married by a justice of the peace in a quick trip up to Connecticut. Six knocked-up months later, Patti converted to Judaism to appease Jerry's family and they were remarried by a rabbi under a *chuppah*. Patti intended to name her first-born son after her favorite matinee idol, Cary Grant, but a clerical error rendered the future rock 'n' roll pop star as Gary.

On August 31, 1944, Jerry was cooling his heels in the lobby of the Belmont Plaza Hotel when a singer known as "the Boy with the Tall, Dark, and Handsome Voice" walked out of the elevator, passing the ground-floor Glass Hat Club where he was performing nightly. Sporting a camel-hair suit, red patent-leather shoes, and noticeable scars from a recent $500 nose job (paid for by his manager, Lou Costello), Dean Martin sauntered past Jerry into the night. Their paths crossed again, this time at the corner of Broadway and 49th Street when a mutual friend, the ex-boxer Sonny King, introduced them to each other. A few nights later Jerry visited Dean in the basement of the Havana-Madrid Club at Broadway and 51st, where he was appearing. Dean took a liking to the kid and was unusually chatty, pouring drinks and spinning some of the latest records. Coming across as much older than his twenty-seven years, Dean recounted his upbringing in Steubenville, Ohio, as a steelworker, bootlegger, card shark, and unsuccessful welterweight boxer known as Kid Crochet. Out of his twelve bouts, he casually remarked that he "won all but eleven." He was cavalier about his convoluted business arrangements, selling percentages of himself to numerous agents that he could never make good on. Dean was stoic, laid-back and world-weary—everything that Jerry wasn't—and it made

Jerry Lewis before the Haircut. Courtesy of BearManor Media.

an impression on the young comic. Dean also imparted some tips on how to work the room and helpful one-liners to use in a pinch. Jerry listened carefully to the man that he was coming to think of as the older brother that he never had.

While never sharing the bill together, in the next year and a half Dean and Jerry passed through the same clubs and towns, always missing each other by a day or two. They would leave each other notes in the dressing rooms concerning food, lodging, broads, and other random observations.

In March 1946, Dean and Jerry were both booked at the Havana-Madrid, where they had first hung out in the basement. Dean was getting fair reviews but was in hock to his eyeballs, with oversold percentages of himself. Jerry was bombing with his now-creaky record act, and he wasn't winning any fans with his over-the-top impression of the Andrews Sisters singing "Beer Barrel Polka."

A few nights into the engagement Jerry asked if he could "fool around" with Dean's act after he was done singing a full set, and Dean figured sure, why not? Jerry dressed up as a busboy and dropped a full load of dishes during a ballad. Dean yelled at Jerry and Jerry heckled back. It was funny, and the sparse 3 a.m. crowd ate it up. When the gig was over the following week, Dean and Jerry went their separate ways, both impressed by their thrown-together act but with neither one of them, especially Dean, interested in becoming a team.

In the summer of 1946, Jerry was booked into the 500 Club on the Atlantic City boardwalk. The 500 Club, also known as the 500 Cafe or the Fives, was owned by the gangster Skinny D'Amato, who ran a lucrative gambling operation in the back room while his legit partner Irving Wolf booked talent in the front. Even with Jerry's newly-added Louis Prima routine, "Please No Squeeza da Banana," he was tanking and was either fired or about to be fired, depending on who you talked to. In any case, Jerry had to plead for his job. Knowing that D'Amato and Wolf also hated the other singer on the bill, Jack Randall, he engineered a plan to get Dean to replace Randall so that he and Dean could unleash their magic. After some tense negotiations, Dean's agent, Lou Perry, took a pay cut and sent Dean down to the Jersey Shore to save Jerry's ass.

When Dean arrived backstage, he was mystified as to how they could turn some scattered ad-libs and insults from a few months before into a solid comedy routine. Jerry tore apart the brown paper bag from a pastrami sandwich, grabbed a makeup pencil and wrote down notes between the grease stains. Jerry remembered what his dad had gotten laughs with

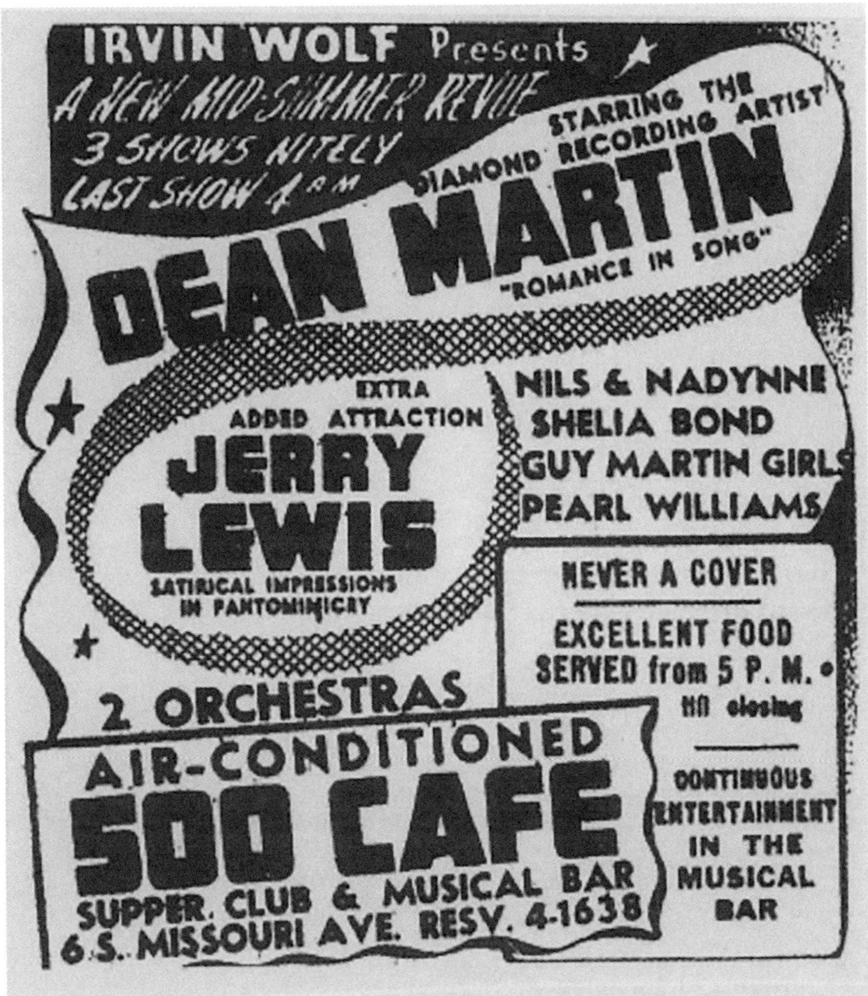

The birth of an act. *The Press of Atlantic City,* August 29, 1946.

everywhere he went and jotted down an outline: "Filler," "Busboy," "That Old Gang of Mine," "Italian Lumberjack," and "April Showers."

"'Filler' is how we get from your intro into the Busboy bit," Jerry told Dean. "Whatever we do, I'm the kid and you're the big brother. I'm the busboy, you're the captain. You're the organ grinder, I'm the monkey. You're the playboy, I'm the putz. Follow?" Dean followed.

The show started with Jerry doing seventeen minutes of his record act to polite applause. When Dean began his set, Jerry sat ringside and let him finish a couple of songs before screwing with him. A few notes into "Where or When," Jerry put his pastrami-bag plans into action. "Waiter!" Jerry yelled in his loudest moron voice. "Where's my Chateaubriand for two, for chrissakes?" Dean appeared perturbed and stopped the band: "Hey, I'm trying to make a living up here."

"Doing that?! Hah-hah-huh-huh!"

Dean invited Jerry up onstage to see if he could do a better job singing. Jerry squinted into the lights and Dean handed him some sheet music. Jerry babbled out some Yiddish double-talk which got yuks. Dean sprayed seltzer into Jerry's mouth, nearly drowning him. Jerry ran out in the crowd, grabbed a large celery, came back onstage, and hit Dean over the head with it. They ran between the tables pelting each other with bread rolls. Jerry took a steak someone was working on and flung it across the room. Dean grabbed a cocktail from a passing waiter, drank some of it, choked on it like it was poison, and threw the rest of it at the diners. Jerry ran into the crowd, smashing dishes along the way and cutting neckties with scissors before jumping behind the drum set with a pair of wind-up novelty teeth in his mouth. When Jerry grabbed the orchestra leader's baton and tried to conduct, he shut off all the light in the room, causing waiters to drop trays of dishes. Together, they bullied the customers into singing campfire songs on the stage floor and then forming a conga line. The crowd went nuts.

The comic singer Sophie Tucker, known as "the Last of the Red Hot Mamas," was in the audience and later raved to the local press that Martin and Lewis were "a combination of the Keystone Kops, the Marx Brothers and Abbott and Costello." After a few nights, customers were lined up around the block and New York papers were sending columnists down the shore to report back on the hottest new act in town. Dean and Jerry had unwittingly hit upon the secret formula for their newfound success: ignore the audience and play to each other. When you have two comics at the top of their respective games, hitting on all cylinders in a way that was spontaneous, ridiculous and real, all at the same time, magic happens and fortunes follow.

Martin and Lewis had taken off.

APTER 4

FIVE SECONDS

May 1947: asleep in a barber's chair, Jerry Lewis was catching a much-needed fifteen-minute snooze between acts. Martin and Lewis were knockin' 'em dead for four sold-out weeks at the Rio Cabana in Chicago. Dean had bribed a barber a couple bucks to cut Jerry's prized, high pompadour down into a little kid's buzzcut. At least that's how one version of the story goes. Jerry's recollection was that he had been awake for the trimming. He recalled that Dean, being a barber's son, had sat him down in the chair and personally scissored off the curly locks. Regardless of how it happened, the result was extraordinary. Unlike Samson, this bolstered Jerry's strength (comically speaking). Gone was the proto-Elvis pompadour that worked against Jerry's nerd schtick. This juvenile crewcut summed up everything that Jerry was going for as an adult-sized five-year-old. Jerry kept it short like that for nearly a decade before regrowing the thick, greased down coiffure, the one that he would sport well into his *King of Comedy* years.

Even before the haircut, things were going pretty well for the duo. After their success at the Fives, they returned to the Havana-Madrid for more sold-out shows and accolades. Jerry's manager, Abby Greshler, cleaned up Dean's complicated finances and ended up managing Dean as well. Greshler booked them into the palatial Loew's State Theatre in Manhattan—the first time that they were billed as "Martin and Lewis." They rolled through their fifteen-minute routine five or six times a day, on a bill with the featured movie, *The Jolson Story*, starring Larry Parks as Al

Jolson. Dean and Jerry were already satirizing Jolson's hit "Sonny Boy" as part of the act so it was a good fit.

"Sonny Boy" was written in 1928 by Ray Henderson, Buddy De Sylva, and Lew Brown as a middle finger to Al Jolson for constantly bugging them for material. On a lark, they came up with the most maudlin slop they could conceive, a tear-soaked rag of a song about a father praising his soon-to-be-dead three-year-old. Jolson flipped the bird right back and took the clunker to the number-one spot on the charts for twelve weeks and sold a million copies.

Martin and Lewis satirizing "Sonny Boy" no doubt drove the Al Jolson sycophant Danny Lewis nuts with envy. To smooth things over, Greshler booked Danny a nightly fifteen-minute slot at the Latin Casino in Philadelphia so he could perform his Jolson act. He also hired the publicist-to-the-stars George Evans to make sure that everyone knew that Martin and Lewis were the hottest act in town. Evans was the marketing genius who had amped up Sinatra's image by hiring bobby-soxers to scream and faint on cue at his shows back in 1943.

Hollywood arrived in the form of Hal B. Wallis, a high-powered independent producer who enjoyed a long-term distribution deal with Paramount Pictures. Wallis had started as a publicist at Warner Bros., where one of his early projects was promoting the first talkie feature in 1927, *The Jazz Singer,* starring Al Jolson. Moving up to the head of productions at Warner, Wallis produced hundreds of movies, including *Casablanca, The Adventures of Robin Hood, Dark Victory,* and other classics. He was an invaluable asset to Paramount Pictures as a headhunter, where he discovered Burt Lancaster, Kirk Douglas, and his soon-to-be mistress, the film-noir hellcat Lizabeth Scott. Wallis didn't have a knack for comedy and wasn't even a fan of nightclubs, so it was with low expectations that he flew out to New York to catch Dean and Jerry's act at the Copa. He was knocked out. Having never seen an audience scream with laughter like that, he declared the team to be an "outright sensation." Greshler engineered a two-picture-a-year contract, plus the freedom to make one independent movie for each two they made for Wallis. That same week, a generous recording contract was inked with Capitol Records that guaranteed them eight releases a year.

The bookings now included theaters and auditoriums in addition to swank nightclubs. They played the Rio Cabana in Chicago, the Stanley Theatre in Camden, New Jersey, the Earle Theatre and Latin Casino in Philadelphia, and the Loew's Capitol in Manhattan, where Jerry had once worked as an usher. In the fall of 1947, they performed at the sprawling Riviera, a nightclub in the Palisades section of Fort Lee, New Jersey, that sported floor-to-ceiling windows with a majestic view of Manhattan. After the shows, Jerry could typically be found in the parking lot, where he clowned around as an inept valet.

Jerry was starting to get referred to in the trades as a "one man *Hellzapoppin',*" a reference to the anything-goes, fourth-wall-breaking Broadway comedy. Being a discerning gag thief, Jerry ramped up his manic stage act by studying other comics and swiping their best mannerisms and comic tics for himself. According to the future Ed Sullivan impressionist Will Jordan, "Jerry stole everybody's act. He admitted it. He got a lot from Joey Adams. '*What's that up the street . . . a head*?' That's all from Joey Adams."

Jerry tended to steal schtick only from the best, and one of the best was Harry Ritz. Harry was the youngest and funniest of the four Joachim brothers from Newark, New Jersey. Rebranding themselves "Ritz" after seeing the name on the side of a laundry truck, three of the brothers formed a singing and dancing comedy act that rivaled the popularity of the Marx Brothers in the 1930s. Forgotten today, Harry Ritz was once the king of the rubber-faced, mush-mouthed idiots. His inspired, anything-for-a-laugh lunacy caused a generation of fellow funny men to swoon at his slapstick feet. Milton Berle called him "the funniest man that I ever met," and Mel Brooks referred to Harry as "the funniest man ever." Jerry would later somberly recount that "Harry was the teacher. He had the extraordinary ability to deny himself dignity onstage. Harry taught us that the only thing that mattered was getting a laugh—whether you did it with a camel or with two rabbis humping a road map. Harry spawned us all. We all begged, borrowed, and stole from him, every one of us. Without him, we wouldn't be here."

As obscure as Harry Ritz is today, the highly influential Gene Baylos was forgotten even in his own time. Thought of as the comedian's comedian, in the early 1940s Catskills scene Gene Baylos befriended a teenaged Jerry Lewis and shared comedy wisdom with him. Baylos ended up regretting his generosity when he realized how much Jerry had lifted from his act: "He stole my body," Baylos later said. "I asked Dean to tell him to stop, and he didn't. I didn't talk to Dean for five years." Jerry took Baylos's manic, rapid-fire delivery and infused it into the soul of his own stage personality. By grabbing funny bits from here and there, Jerry Frankensteined his way into the fully formed jackass that his fans now know and love. He had officially outgrown his record-miming days. Jerry cracked the code for getting large, sustained laughs, and he used this new formula to his advantage. The paying public were merely stand-ins for doting parents, applauding and encouraging Jerry's bad behavior. As Jerry himself explained in the late 1960s, "An audience is nothing more than eight or nine hundred mamas and papas, clapping their hands and saying, 'Good boy, baby.' You'll find that people who have had enough 'good boy, baby' from their actual parents rarely turn to comedy."

Dean was upping his game as well. As a singer, he modestly thought of himself as "100% Crosby"; however, any significant percentage of Bing Crosby's magic was more than enough. By the late '40s, Crosby was a titan in the industry, conquering stage, screen, and radio and ultimately becoming one of the most popular and successful entertainers of the twentieth century. Bing got his first taste of showbiz in 1917 by catching Al Jolson's act while working as a stagehand in Spokane, Washington. He was impressed not so much by Jolson's hamminess but by his ad-libbing and easy rapport with the audience. Deeply affected by what he witnessed, Bing would later describe Jolson's act as being "electric." Ironically, it was literal electricity that would short-circuit Jolson's career about a dozen years later. Innovations in microphones and amplification in the early '30s would render Jolson's belting-it-to-the-rafters style obsolete. The microphone allowed a more nuanced and intimate performance, and, with his mellow baritone, Der Bingle was perfect for the new medium. He created a softer, yet more dynamic performance by treating the microphone as another instrument rather than a megaphone. Bing Crosby modernized the great American songbook and today his singing could pass for something that's almost contemporary, while Al Jolson's histrionics seem to emanate from another planet. At the time, "crooners" like Bing were expected to be a short-lived craze. The *New York Times* predicted that "crooners would soon go the way of tandem bicycles, mah jongg and midget golf." Frank Sinatra, Russ Columbo, Perry Como, Tony Bennett, Dean Martin, and all of their disciples and imitators owe Bing credit for legitimizing this new style of singing.

Dean Martin took Bing Crosby's savoir faire and updated it with a post-war indifference. Patti Lewis, who considered Dean to be "Jerry's other wife," described him in her autobiography as "a study in slow motion, . . . suave, a good communicator, unsure, a ladies' man, charming, talented, a ladies' man, laid-back, slow-paced, introverted, a ladies' man, creative, a crooner with great looks, a golfer, party boy, and a ladies' man." Dean's nonchalant attitude effortlessly carried over to the stage. A *Variety* review of a Latin Casino show nailed it: "Martin of the swoon-croon school, doesn't take himself too seriously." His easygoing personality served him well in the comedy department as well. Pegged by lazy columnists as merely a straight man to Jerry's clown, his impeccable timing and improv chops kept a modicum of control over the stage-hogging Lewis. Like others before him, Bud Abbott notably, Dean was a natural comic who only *played* a straight man. He augmented his style by also borrowing mannerisms from an old nightclub pal, the comedian Buddy Lester. A frequent Vegas opening act for Frank Sinatra, Lester later specialized in portraying funny, gruff mobsters on television. In his first movie role, Lester played himself as a nightclub entertainer in *The Gene Krupa Story,* starring Sal Mineo as Krupa. Lester eventually teamed up with the tap dancer Steve Condos in an act that was compared to Martin and Lewis.

Dean and Jerry's stage personas took shape quickly. Jerry was informally known as "the kid" or "the monkey" or "the idiot," and Dean neatly filled the the role of "older brother" or "organ-grinder." Being showbiz pros by this point, Dean and Jerry's purloined material only served as starting points for their own original routines. By the end of the night, you could still find a buck-toothed Jerry jumping into the crowd and knocking over trays of food while Dean attempted to sing a chorus of "All of Me."

Jerry's ease and overfamiliarity with the audience almost ended his career—and his life, on at least two occasions. The first was at the Chez Paree in Chicago when he jumped off the stage and whacked some guy on the back who wasn't paying attention to the show. It was Al Capone's cousin and bodyguard, Charles "Trigger-Happy" Fischetti.

"Hey pal, the show is up here!" Jerry yelled in his high-pitched moron voice.

Fischetti looked up at him and said, "If you don't move away right now, I'll blow your fuckin' head off."

Dean interceded and amends were quickly made. Two years later at the Copa in New York, Jerry pulled an almost identical stunt, this time by pissing off the Lord High Executioner of Murder, Inc., the Butcher of Brooklyn himself, Albert Anastasia. Jerry was heckling the crowd when the much-feared head of the Gambino family told him to shut the fuck up. Jerry, in idiot mode, suggested loudly that Anastasia's parents might've been cousins that married. Dean jumped between them and saved the monkey's life once again.

Filming started in February 1949 for Martin and Lewis's first feature, *My Friend Irma,* on the Paramount lot. The misadventures of Marie Wilson as the ditzy Irma had been a radio show as well as a comic strip drawn by the future *Archie* artist Dan DeCarlo and a pre-Marvel Stan Lee. Dean and Jerry had supporting roles and successfully reprised their organ-grinder-and-monkey nightclub act.

The gigs kept coming. They were guests on the inaugural broadcast of *Toast of the Town,* the Sunday-night television variety program that would one day be known as *The Ed Sullivan Show*. Almost half of the entire show's $475 budget went to Martin and Lewis for a six-minute bit.

There were a couple of appearances on the wildly popular *Texaco Star Theater* on NBC, hosted by Milton Berle. Before the second show, Berle made them swear up and down that they wouldn't go over their eight-minute time limit. Dean and Jerry promised. That was Sunday morning at rehearsal. Tuesday night Berle couldn't get them off the stage. Jerry stuck his face into the camera: "Milton Berle night! Big deal!" The ratings were off the charts. It was the birth of live, unscripted comedy on television, and an outraged Uncle Miltie was loving every moment of it.

In April, they signed up for a weekly radio show on NBC, but it never really took off, ratings-wise or otherwise. Despite Dean's crooning and Jerry's nutty dialects and pidgin talk, they still were too much of a visual act to translate to radio. Also, the material was all used up after a handful of episodes, so something had to change. George Burns, after a long vaudeville career with his wife Gracie Allen as half of the team of Burns and Allen, faced the same problem. "In vaudeville," George said, "seventeen minutes of good material lasts for years, while on radio, seventeen minutes of good material would last seventeen minutes." George's solution was to hire a crack comedy-writing team that included the future *Beverly Hillbillies*, *Petticoat Junction,* and *Green Acres* creator Paul Henning. With the help of a talented staff, Burns and Allen conquered the radio and television airwaves for the next ten years.

Taking note, Dean and Jerry wisely allocated a substantial portion of their paycheck to the hot, young comedy-writing team of the former door-to-door upholstery and baby-photo salesmen Norman Lear and Ed Simmons. Twenty years later, Lear's production company would change the television industry. His "adult" comedies *All in the Family*, *Maude,* and *Good Times* would replace Henning's hillbilly sitcoms overnight in what was referred to at CBS as the "rural purge." Lear and Simmons were smart and funny, and, working under Martin and Lewis, they became the highest paid writers in radio and television.

Dean and Jerry were now commuting between Hollywood and New York, taking nightclub gigs in Chicago, St. Louis, and Miami and playing for twenty thousand people at a clip in auditoriums in Dallas, San Antonio, and Fort Worth. With their packed schedules, they found time in Hollywood to indulge in classic bad-boy bi-coastal shenanigans. Jerry quickly went into debt by acquiring Dean's gambling habit, and both men openly cheated on their wives: Dean with the actress June Allyson and Jerry with June's showbiz pal Gloria DeHaven.

My Friend Irma was an unremarkable movie, yet Martin and Lewis shone in their supporting roles, and they were signed up for a sequel. First, they needed to film *At War with the Army,* which was one of the independent movies for their own company, York Productions, the deal which Greshler had baked into the Paramount contract. Dean and Jerry worked for next to nothing in exchange for 90% of the film's profits. Its release got pushed back two years and led to an extended legal battle. *At War with the Army* is a cheap-looking, unfunny dog of a movie that turned out to be a lucrative hit with the Martin-and-Lewis-loving public. In 1977 its copyright wasn't renewed, and by the 1980s you could pave a highway to the moon out of public-domain VHS copies of *At War with the Army.*

My Friend Irma Goes West lacked the sexy star power of their initial outing (Hans Conreid, Don DeFore, Percy Helton); however, it delivered a satisfying performance from Tamba the Chimp as Pierre. Tamba was variously billed as Tamba the Chimp, Tampa the Chimp, and Tamba the Ape in a series of *Jungle Jim* movies that starred a post-Tarzan and thankfully clothed Johnny Weissmuller. As punishment for not sleeping with producer Hal Wallis, the twenty-five-year-old Corinne Calvet was cast against her will as the Hollywood vixen Yvonne Yvonne, who travels cross-country with her dressed-alike chimp. This was a big step down after recently co-starring with Burt Lancaster in the gritty blockbuster *Rope of Sand.* Her discomfort with the role was worsened by the sexual advances of Tamba, who made her life a living hell whenever he was within humping distance. Jerry made a bad situation worse by imitating the randy chimp on the set and, by Calvet's account, "turning into a human monkey, harassing me without restraint."

Production wrapped on the chimp movie and Martin and Lewis hit the road again. However, they were outgrowing nightclubs and were getting booked more and more into auditoriums and state fairs. Anything

Jerry exploring his inner chimp. *My Friend Irma Goes West,* 1950.
Courtesy of BearManor Media.

resembling subtlety in the act was being lost in the din of screaming fans. The radio show wasn't gelling, and the movies were dreary, low-budget affairs; so far, nothing captured the anarchic energy of their live act, including, most importantly, Dean and Jerry's brilliant ad-libbing. Live television would be the inevitable step in transforming the team into comedy superstars.

Sylvester "Pat" Weaver, older brother to the zany comedian Doodles and father to the actress Sigourney, was head of programming at NBC. Weaver offered a sweet deal for a weekly television variety show. Colgate-Palmolive-Peet would pony up $60,000 per episode, which was a record-setting amount in the nascent world of television budgets. Knowing the potential for burnout, Dean and Jerry smartly passed on the weekly offer and opted for monthly appearances to be shared in rotation with Eddie Cantor and Fred Allen as hosts. *The Colgate Comedy Hour* would air the first three Sundays of the month, with the last Sunday sponsored by Frigidaire and hosted by the now-forgotten comedian Bobby Clark if Bob Hope wasn't available. It was a bold move to go toe-to-toe with Ed Sullivan's *Toast of the Town,* which was on CBS in the same slot. In addition to A-list radio personalities, *Toast of the Town* and *The Colgate Comedy Hour* would both draw from the same talent pool of former burlesque and vaudeville variety acts. It was an unexpected second act for the magicians and mimics, the hoofers and ventriloquists, and all of the dog acts and dish-balancers that had seen their business dwindle in the post-war years. Colgate's faith in lowbrow entertainment in general, and Martin and Lewis in particular, was not misplaced.

The Colgate Comedy Hour aired on Sunday nights at 8 p.m. in the Eastern time zone. The other half of the country would have to wait a week for a kinescope to be flown out to the coast. In the days before videotape and coaxial cross-country cables, television shows were filmed off a TV screen in 35mm to produce kinescopes, or "kinneys," for rebroadcast.

NBC had bought the 1,400-seat International Theatre in 1949 and wired it up as a television studio. Centrally located on West 59th Street, the hit weekly variety show *Your Show of Shows* was broadcast from its massive stage. It was a no-brainer securing the venerable Eddie Cantor to launch the first episode. Treading the boards since 1907, Cantor was a natural for live television. Born in New York City as Isidore Itzkowitz and nicknamed "the Apostle of Pep" and "Banjo Eyes" (for his gigantic peepers), Cantor was a multi-hyphenate tap-dancing entertainer, author, and composer. Among his compositions was "Merrily We Roll Along," used as the theme song for Warner Bros.' *Merrie Melodies* cartoons. In 1912 he created his blackface alter ego, Jefferson, playing the smart-aleck son of the legendary Black performer Bert Williams. Cantor and George Jessel both turned down the lead in *The Jazz Singer* over salary issues. Al Jolson's portrayal of the conflicted entertainer Jack Robin (née Jakie Rabinowitz), torn between his family's Orthodox Judaism and his showbiz aspirations, would be career-defining.

Beloved by millions for his scene-stealing antics, Cantor was reviled by his peers, who saw him an as an unfunny, stage-hogging lout with a track record of sexual harassment. He worked diligently, though, campaigning for donations to the National Foundation for Infantile Paralysis to wipe out polio, even coining the phrase "March of Dimes" (a riff on the *March of Time* newsreels). When criticized by the network and sponsors for embracing Sammy Davis, Jr., after a *Colgate Comedy Hour* performance, Cantor doubled down and demanded that Davis appear on the next two episodes.

Performing well-worn hits from his long career, including "This Is My Broadway" and the sentimental "We're Having a Baby," Cantor earned rave reviews all while putting a serious dent into Ed Sullivan's audience. The anticipation was high for the following week, which would be the debut Martin and Lewis episode.

Dean and Jerry brought along their top writers from radio, Norman Lear and Ed Simmons, along with the joke-writer Austin "Rocky" Kalish. Raised in the Bronx, Rocky had entered showbiz as a boxer, performed briefly in burlesque, and ended up writing jokes for Abbott and Costello and other comedians. Rocky met his future wife and writing partner, Irma, when they were kids, and together they would be responsible for hundreds of scripts, including episodes of *Johnny Staccato, My Three Sons, I Dream of Jeannie, All in the Family,* and *Maude* and the oddball hippie comedy film *Keep off My Grass!,* directed by Shelley Berman and starring Micky Dolenz.

Who Dean and Jerry didn't bring along to the TV show was their manager, Abby Greshler. Abby was fired on the cusp of the team's rocketship-like success. Turns out Greshler was simultaneously underselling the act while overcharging them at the same time. Tax problems multiplied because Greshler apparently couldn't tell the difference between *net* and *gross* and possibly didn't care. Lew Wasserman, the recently appointed president of MCA, Inc., swooped in, initiated years' worth of Greshler-related lawsuits, and signed up Martin and Lewis for as long as they would continue to be Martin and Lewis.

Kingman T. Moore, veteran of the suspenseful anthology TV series *Lights Out,* was signed on to direct, and Bud Yorkin, fresh out of college, was hired as stage manager. Yorkin would famously go on to work with Norman Lear and produce *All in the Family, Maude, Good Times,* and other hit sitcoms. But right now he was young and hungry and ready to be a cog in the Martin and Lewis machine. Yorkin is also significant in the Jerry Lewis story, if only for bringing the horrible disorder muscular dystrophy to Jerry's attention. After hearing about Yorkin's nephew who was stricken with it, Jerry embarked on a rocky, longtime relationship as spokesperson and fundraiser for the Muscular Dystrophy Association.

Perhaps the most significant of the new hires, as producer and co-director, was Ernest D. Glucksman. Born in Vienna, Glucksman had cut his teeth as a comic in the Borscht Belt under the name Ernie Gilbert. He worked his way up to social director and producing shows in summer stock theater. In an odd coincidence, he had once auditioned Jerry's parents, Danny and Rae, for a Catskills gig that never panned out. The soft-spoken Glucksman appeared ill-prepared for the craziness that he was signing up for. Leaving his burlesque career behind, he looked like just another middle-management advertising executive. With glasses, suspenders, and an expensive homburg hat and attaché case, he was the perfect foil for Jerry Lewis. Glucksman was Margaret Dumont in a Brooks Brothers suit.

The abuse that Ernie Glucksman endured from Dean and Jerry, especially Jerry, was the stuff of legend. Jerry would only refer to him, even in important meetings, as "Mr. Gluckstern," a nickname that Glucksman despised. On an almost daily basis, he was humiliated by slaps, punches, and glasses of water emptied on his head. His expensive ties were getting scissored in half and his homburg would get yanked down over his eyes and ears when he least expected it. It got to the point that, when Glucksman saw Jerry coming down the hall, he would pull his hat down over his eyes and cut off his own tie. One time Jerry cut off one side of his suspenders, Dean cut off the other side, and when that poor schmuck bent down to pull up his pants Jerry cut off his tie. Will Jordan knew Ernie at the time and recalled that "he was a very good-natured guy, and [Dean and Jerry] both considered themselves boxers—well, Dean used to be, and he had gigantic fists. He could kill you with those big hands of his. They used to punch this guy's shoulder until it was horribly black and blue and then they'd give him a twenty-dollar bill for letting them use his shoulder as a punching bag."

When Ernie first took the job, he realized that talking business with the boys was nearly impossible. The format of the show needed to be discussed, but he could never get their attention. Ernie asked to see Jerry alone, and that's when he realized what a different person Jerry was when you got him away from everyone else. In the presence of others, he was a bouncing-off-the-walls maniac with the attention span of a monkey. Alone, Jerry showed Ernie a more measured side of himself, listening to ideas, but mostly sharing press clippings, photographs, scripts, records, tapes—basically anything that he and Dean had done since the beginning. They were all carefully catalogued in file cabinets along with who had been on the bill with them, how much they had gotten paid, and how they had gone over that night. Glucksman said, "He was better organized than IBM." Jerry had specific ideas for the hour: "Two sketches and two songs for Dean and a wrap-up." Dean had specific ideas as well, and they involved teeing off at the nearest golf course. He was fine with Jerry handling the particulars.

September was a busy month. Dean and Jerry toured the northeast with their longtime orchestra leader Dick Stabile, Marilyn Maxwell (the poor man's Marilyn Monroe, who would later star in a TV version of Monroe's hit *Bus Stop*), and Dean's uncle, the eccentric dancer Leonard Barr. Known in the 1930s as "Bananas," Barr performed a "crazy legs" specialty act, and, because he had been good to Dean as a boy, Dean made sure that there was always work for Uncle Leonard. After helping to judge a ballroom dance contest at Madison Square Garden, Dean and Jerry had four days to knock together a live television show.

The first episode was relatively easy— they took the whole troupe, including Uncle Leonard, and squeezed it into the confines of an hour-long program with commercials. It was a triumph. They were able to recreate the intimacy of their nightclub act, only this time in front of millions instead of hundreds. Blasting their lunacy into living rooms across half the nation was a genius stroke and a turning point in the team's success.

The reviews were effusive. *Variety* described the show as "maximum yocks" and Jack Gould in the *New York Times* extolled it as "swell nonsense," referring to the team as "a pair of mad zanies of the first rank." After praising Jerry to the skies, Gould ominously referred to Dean as "a competent straight man" with "a baritone voice that should not offend either the Crosby or Como fans."

In October of 1950, there were six million TV sets in the country, and half of them were now tuning into *The Colgate Comedy Hour* on Sunday nights. Television sets were still a luxury item, so many watched in bars or on sidewalks outside of appliance stores or simply heard tall tales the next day around the water cooler. Martin and Lewis were now on everyone's entertainment radar. Their anarchy translated to the small screen because they had cracked the code on how to astound both the studio audience and the home audience at the same time. Jerry explained, "I was so nuts and I was out of the rules and I never hit the marks and I was into the cameras and I was the first one to bring the camera with me . . . I knew the importance of physicality and [Dean and I] were good together on it. We knew when to pull back and when to feed one another and when to get up close."

Just as Bing Crosby used the microphone as an instrument, Dean and Jerry treated the camera as a third partner: giving it the side eye, breaking the fourth wall by speaking directly to it, and sometimes running up and actually grabbing it. When props didn't work or lines were forgotten, Dean and Jerry were at their best, cracking themselves up and sharing the joy of the moment with the studio audience.

For the next five years, Dean and Jerry spent two weeks out of every month in full rehearsal mode for one hour's worth of programming. When in town, Jerry lived at either the Sherry-Netherland or the Essex House, and Dean rented a ten-room apartment on the Upper West Side. Week one would start with read-throughs in hotel rooms, rented apartments, and offices. As space was required for the more physical bits, they would move over to Paramount Caterers in the West 40s or the Mayflower Hotel on 61st Street and Central Park West, just around the corner from the studio. Rehearsal was Monday through Saturday, "all day and half the night," Jerry recalled, "with hardly enough time to take a leak in the john, much less run out for a quick nosh at the Stage Delicatessen on Seventh Avenue." Towards the end of week two, there would be a full dress rehearsal at the International Theatre. The time set aside for blocking was usually interrupted by Dean and Jerry chasing after the cameras and sticking pornographic photos in front of the lenses. On Saturday nights, the day before showtime, according to Jerry, they'd be back at the Essex House:

> All the writers, directors, and producers bunched around, sweating over sketches, bits and jokes, production numbers; everybody anxiously discussing what to keep in, what to toss out; the whole thing appearing sensational and hopeless at the same time. Meanwhile, every nerve is frazzled and the awful smell of stale cigarettes smoldering in greasy plates make this final meeting before the actual air date of *The Colgate Comedy Hour* a pleasure to be done with. Satisfied or not, tomorrow night we'll know what the rest of America thinks.

By 9 p.m. the following evening, it was all over. At 9:30, Jerry, Ernie, and the writers would meet to start planning the following month's program. Less than two weeks later, the rehearsals would start all over again. As expected in such a close-knit situation, bonds and alliances were formed.

For the following month's show, Ed Simmons and Norman Lear flew out to Chicago to accommodate the team's engagement at the ritzy Chez Paree. Within a week of their arrival, the historic Ambassador East looked like a frat house. Food fights spilled out into the hallways, and fire hoses were used as large comic props. Dean joined in on the fun, but, being a street-fighting ex-boxer, his horseplay bordered on the sadistic. Amid the pranks and pillow fights, a never-ending exchange of engraved gold lighters and gold pens were given to the writers with the expectation of extravagant gifts in return. When Lear and Simmons would follow Jerry to Los Angeles, he would invite them along to watch him shop at the swank tailor to the stars Sy Devore, down on Sunset and Vine. Jerry would casually pick out a couple dozen handmade custom suits along with socks, shirts, ties, and whatever else was on display. Lear and Simmons tried to emulate the team's swinging lifestyle down to the shoes. "We never knew what loafers were until we saw them wearing loafers," Simmons said, "so we got loafers." Cologne was next. Simmons was friendlier with Dean, so he applied Dean's scent, Woodhue. Jerry preferred Aphrodisia, and, coincidentally, so did Lear. Not wanting to miss a moment of the madness, both writers embarked on a steady diet of Seconal for sleeping and Dexedrine for staying awake. They also found time to write funny scripts for the show.

The ever-suffering punching bag in a business suit, Ernie Glucksman, who had endured the team's maltreatment, now had to contend with the two head writers dressing and smelling like Dean and Jerry. Cast and crew of *The Colgate Comedy Hour* were beginning to notice that Jerry was treating Ernie as a stand-in for his father. Ernie was the fantasy father figure whom, unlike Danny Levitch, Jerry could physically abuse.

Meanwhile, Danny and Rae were thrilled, enjoying the reflected fame and kibitzing with Uncle Miltie at Lindy's best booth. Rae showed off her fur capes and Danny spoke glowingly about his own son to everyone, except to his own son. The success that had bypassed Danny but landed in his son's lap gnawed at him and added to the general chilliness. Jerry gave his parents a check for $25,000 for their anniversary, and even this grand gesture fell flat. Adding to his woes, Jerry was turning into a nitpicking workaholic. It couldn't have helped his peace of mind that Martin and Lewis breakup rumors were already hitting the gossip columns. He was afraid that all of this newfound fame could evaporate overnight. Earlier that year, Jerry and Patti adopted a son, Ronald, as a brother for Gary, but that did little to ease Jerry's neurosis. Dean, the big brother that Jerry never had, was increasingly distant, so he got close to Lear and Simmons. When Jerry needed to be cuddled, he'd curl up in Patti's arms and call her "Momma." He created a new and improved family, one that was non-judgmental, available 100% of the time, and dedicated only to Jerry. As he grew in popularity and throve as an artist, those closest to him were made to suffer.

Meanwhile, preparing for his first television appearance, for which he would receive sixty dollars, Sammy had changed his surname to Petrillo. It cannot be confirmed, but one theory is that Sammy was inspired by the

Appointment television. *Indianapolis Star,* November 12, 1950.

president of the American Federation of Musicians, James Caesar Petrillo. Powerful and controversial, James Petrillo had railed against the trend of radio stations replacing musicians on the radio with what he called "the menace of mechanical music," the phonograph record. He predicted a day when recordings would entirely replace live music on the radio and take work away from card-carrying musicians. Congress tried to rein in his powers, but his "Petrillo bans," two separate strikes in 1942 and 1948, had shut down the recording industry for years at a time.

James Petrillo had a powerful nationwide presence, and his headline-grabbing actions served as comic fodder for everyone from Spike Jones to Jack Benny to Bugs Bunny. It was a punchline of a name and everybody had a joke about the authoritative labor czar. Sammy denied that he changed his name because of James Petrillo. He said that it was a "popular" name at the time; however, when asked on occasion if he was related to the famous union leader, he'd shrug his shoulders and say, "Yeah."

On Monday morning, November 6, 1950, Sammy took the subway down to Columbus Circle for his first rehearsal with Jerry Lewis. The *Colgate* gang was holed up for a few days in a catering hall on the first floor of the Mayflower Hotel. Not a lot of props—just a couch and a giant, waist-high baby's crib against a curtain.

Here's how the sketch was supposed to work:

Jerry and his wife are about to leave for the evening and are giving the babysitter last-minute instructions. They split, and Dean climbs in a window to canoodle with the sitter. Backstage, Jerry has taken off his hat and overcoat and now he's in full baby drag. He crawls under the curtain and into the crib and then climbs out. Near the end of the sketch, Baby Jerry jumps back in the crib, crawls back under the curtain, and after a few moments emerges fully dressed with his wife, stage right. The quick change was a hoary old theatrical gag that went back to Elizabethan times and possibly the Stone Age. The audience is in on the joke and they love it, because what's not to love about Jerry Lewis running around changing costumes like a maniac? Not many entertainers at that point were willing to knock themselves out at that pace just for a gag. Even Berle had his limits.

Here comes the twist: someone else who looks *exactly like Jerry Lewis* would stick his head out of the crib with the real Jerry Lewis standing right next to him. If this were to work out, it would be a hell of a sight gag for live TV, worthy of the great Ernie Kovacs.

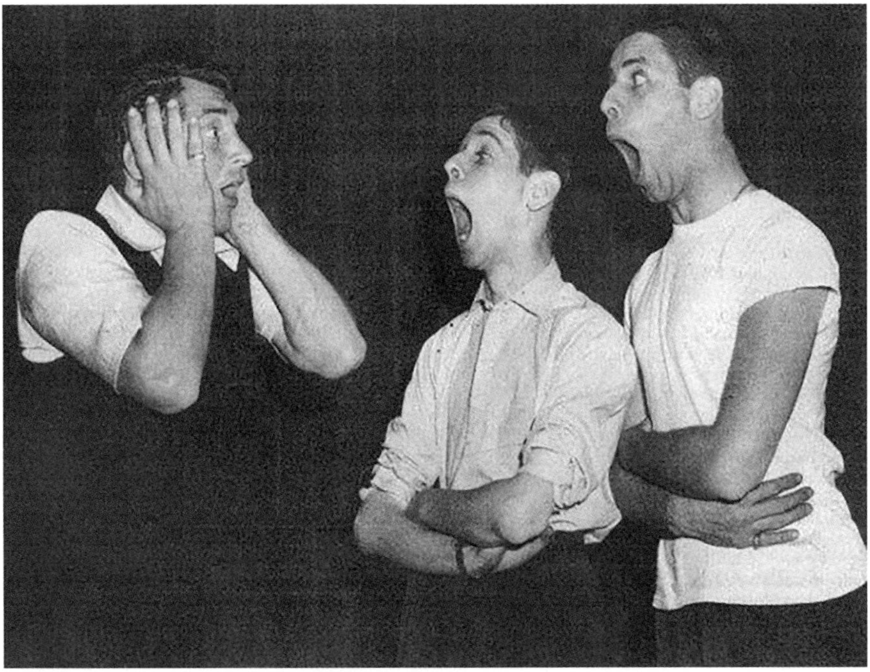

Dean sees double. *The Colgate Comedy Hour,* November, 1950.

Sammy Petrillo's job was to imitate Jerry Lewis as if Jerry Lewis were a full-grown baby. His time on camera would be brief, but it would have to be perfect. Hours were spent rehearsing the tics and grimaces required for the punchline to land. "There also was a prop baby rattle, and Jerry used to hit Sammy over the head with it and he would hurt him," Sammy's cousin Martin recalls Sammy telling him. "You accept it. You're sixteen years old and it's Jerry Lewis, and he's hitting you over the head."

Baby Jerry Lewis had dialogue when he was out of sight and inside the crib. He would scream and yell and have a tantrum; however, it wouldn't be Sammy's voice. For more control over the situation, Jerry pre-recorded the infant's barrage of inanities on a reel-to-reel tape recorder. Tape recorders were a fairly new technology, but by 1950 they had already upended the radio and recording industries. An early cheerleader for audio tape was Bing Crosby, who, for years, had grown weary of broadcasting the same radio show twice—once for the East Coast and once for the West. With reel-to-reel tape, he could record a month's worth of radio shows in a couple of days. He could even ad-lib and then edit out the duds. Bing, like his fellow crooner, Dino, preferred swinging a nine iron on a sunny day rather than being cooped up in a studio.

November 12, 1950, 8 p.m. Eastern time: *The Colgate Comedy Hour* hit the air. An impossibly young-sounding Don Pardo reads off the show's credits while two candy-striped showgirls pull down several window shades bearing large cartoon likenesses of Dean and Jerry. The opening skit finds the boys entertaining at a morticians' convention. After a few strained jokes ("Did you take a bath?" "Why? Is one missing?"), they segue into their old nightclub schtick in front of the curtain. In their element, they're clearly having fun, seamlessly rolling through their live act for the television cameras. Dean tries to sing "The Glory of Love" and Jerry keeps interrupting. Jerry finger-mimes a surgeon cutting off Dean's nose and pasting on a new one. Dean sneaks up behind Jerry and Jerry screams and the audience screams along.

Next up is a dance-lesson sketch that features Uncle Leonard doing his crazy-legs routine. Itching powder is poured down Jerry's back so he can do the rhumba as well as Uncle Leonard. While Jerry holds a life-sized female dummy, they ad-lib a couple of mildly risqué lines and the audience loves it. This is followed by the actor Jack Cassidy reciting the tale of "Millie the Fillie," backed up by the singing group the Skylarks. Next up is the big-band singer Kitty Kallen, an Ajax commercial that goes on too long, and then finally what we all came here for: the babysitter sketch.

The scene opens on Jerry and his wife (a pre-*Honeymooners* Joyce Randolph) leaving the babysitter with Baby Jerry asleep in his crib. When Baby Jerry climbs out of the crib in baby drag, as expected, the audience goes nuts. He's wearing a baggy onesie, a floppy bonnet with a bow that goes down to his crotch, and, inexplicably, a wedding ring that was never off his left hand no matter what role he was playing. The audience finally gets to see this big man-baby as literally a man-baby, and they're loving it. He looks at Dean and says in a deep voice, "Hey! You're not my mother!" Jerry crosses his eyes and purses his lips and screams some more and jumps around on the couch. Jerry finally agrees to go back to sleep if he gets a goodnight kiss. The babysitter gives Jerry a chaste kiss on top of his head. Jerry takes the babysitter into a deep smooch.

"How much does my mommy pay you?"

"Sixty-five cents an hour."

Jerry does a Bogart impression. "From now on, you're gettin' seventy-five!" Another smooch.

The sketch is almost over. In a genuinely inspired bit, Jerry attempts to drink a glass of milk while he's crying hysterically. Every time he takes a big sip, Dean yells something at him, like, "Milk is good for you!" Jerry screams and the milk falls out of his mouth. He tries again. "It's better than spinach!" Dean yells. The milk dribbles all over his onesie and onto the stage floor. The audience is dying. A third time: "You'll get big bones!" More milk. Dean is at his Bud Abbott best. Jerry takes a fourth swig of milk. The studio audience is going bananas. So far everything is playing out as it had in rehearsal, only better.

Near the end of the seven-minute sketch, something happened that simultaneously sent 1,335 jaws to the theater floor and, more significantly, millions more jaws to the carpets of living rooms nationwide. Dean half-tosses and Jerry half-jumps back into the waist-high crib. Dean is back on the couch with the babysitter. And with Jerry changing clothes backstage, a hidden Sammy starts tossing stuffed animals out of the crib. A slightly sped-up tape of Jerry plays, "Yeah, that's what you think, you dirty rotten grown-ups! You no-good, miserable adults!" The tape of Jerry babbles on while Sammy's leg kicks up and he points an outstretched arm at Dean. Jerry and Joyce walk in. Dean and Jerry and the baby start arguing.

DADDY JERRY: You gotta know how to handle these children. You mustn't yell like that.
DEAN: Ah, he's no child.
DADDY JERRY: He is my child. I'll have none of that talk.
DEAN: Whaddaya mean you'll have none of that talk?
BABY JERRY: Daddy! Daddy! Hey, there!
DADDY JERRY: Whaddaya want now?!
BABY JERRY: Since when are you such a great man?
DEAN: You shouldn't talk to your daddy like that!
BABY JERRY: Yeah, well I can talk any way that I want, it's a free country.

All three start yelling over each other, until:

DADDY JERRY: Shut up! This is my child and you can't talk to him the way you do!

On cue, Sammy pops his head out wearing a baby's bonnet. Dean puts his hands to the sides of his head and wails in surprised agony as if he had just seen two Jerry Lewises right next to each other. The camera dollies in tight on the bizarre tableau. Jerry and Sammy move in close to each

The moment that shook the world. *The Colgate Comedy Hour,* November 12, 1950.

other and their idiotic expressions are as one. For five seconds the stunned audience erupts in gasps and screams and then more screams. Jerry Lewis and Sammy Petrillo are now side by side in profile, puckering up their faces and pursing their lips into identical ape-like grins. The camera holds on that shot arrogantly, as if to say, "Don't say that we don't deliver the goods here on *The Colgate Comedy Hour*!" The screams continue for a few seconds more, and the shot goes to black.

It's an event that could have only occurred in the blossoming days of early television. The payoff of the gag relies on the intimacy of those two gangly heads, side by side, a reveal that would be lost on a standard burlesque audience or in a semi-respectable theater. As a movie gag, the gravity of the joke would be undercut by obvious trick photography. The punchline lands because the thousand-plus audience members are freaking out at the exact same time that the millions at home are.

This was a moon-landing moment in the world of drop-your-pants comedy on television and for five seconds Sammy was the most famous man in half the country (the other half the following week when the episode would be broadcast to the Mountain and Pacific time zones). Those five seconds did not feel like five seconds to Sammy. It felt like the rest of his life.

Thirty minutes after the program ended, Jerry, Ernie, and the writers found an empty room backstage and began planning the following month's show. Sammy stood outside the theater and had a smoke. He hopped on the subway back up to 170th Street in the Bronx. Sammy mixed inconspicuously with the Sunday-night subway riders—stenographers and short-order cooks getting home from a swing shift, less fortunate ones on their way to a second job. These fellow travelers, some nodding off, others with their heads in newspapers, were not television-watchers. Sammy was invisible.

Sammy's six-year-old brother Marvin later remembered that night: "When I watched Sammy on *The Colgate Comedy Hour*," Marvin said, "it was like, 'Wow—look at that!' and I had to ask my dad if he knew which one was Sammy. I remember the write-up the next day—it was either the *Post* or the *News*—and it was asking the question, 'Which one was the real Jerry Lewis?' Those are my first memories of Sammy having talent."

Sammy's cousin Martin continues the story:

> That night we were lying in bed and Sammy turned to me and told me that he rode up on the subway from NBC. We lived in the southwest part of the Bronx—the Heights. You had to walk up a hill from Jerome Avenue. It's all hills. He says, "I rode up on the subway. Everything was still. People just sat there." Then, "Martin!" he says (he always had a little rasp in his voice), "As I'm coming up the hill and as I'm approaching the candy store, somebody saw me and they started to cheer me!" Now he was like a conquering hero and he's walking up the street and they're all cheering. They knew Sammy before, but now Sammy is a genuine television star. He was on with Jerry Lewis, and he has to walk into the building and the courtyard. He has to walk up a few steps. People are leaning out of the building. It's almost like "Sammy's Coming! Sammy! Sammy's coming!" And I remember the crowd in my living room. We were one of the few people who had a TV. No food, but we had a TV and people were still milling around and they were just cheering him. He was sixteen. It was 1950.

So he's up in the apartment and my cousin is a TV star. I became a big shot because of that and I go to sleep with him that night and I'm saying to myself, "He was on TV!" and I'm just staring at him. He became totally different to me because of that. That's the first time that I remember Sammy in my life.

CHAPTER 5

GET ME A JERRY LEWIS

'Dean Martin & Jerry Lewis in their third show gave further proof that low comedy pays off with high laugh results. Zanies continue to prove that their antic style is as potent on video as it's been in the theatres, cafes and films. For this show they drew upon the services of one Sammy Petrillo (no relation to JP) who is an amazing double for Lewis, both visually and vocally. Petrillo was used to excellent advantage in a babysitter scene with Petrillo enacting the infant. Bit also involved some clever staging since it originally might have represented a quick change by Lewis. Confusion had greater humorous impact when both Lewis and Petrillo were seen simultaneously."

Variety, November 15, 1950

The joke landed.

In a career populated with scores of outlandish visual gags, this was one of Jerry's first, and it was a grand slam. That line about Sammy being an amazing double, "both visually *and vocally,*" no doubt needled Jerry since that was really his voice, not Sammy's. He let his own ingenuity bite him on the *tuchis* that time. And four mentions of Sammy Petrillo for a five-second bit seemed excessive. Jerry was not happy. A few days after the show, one of his secretaries rang up Sammy to tell him how pissed off he was. Not planning to let something like that happen again, Jerry cooked up a plan.

Dean and Jerry took the following month off of *The Colgate Comedy Hour*, but it was a whirlwind for the team nonetheless. There were nightclub bookings in Cleveland and Chicago, and they filmed their fourth motion picture, and third for Paramount, *That's My Boy*. By the time they returned to the show, they were on fire, working on a telepathic level of comic timing previously reserved for the masters of funny. Martin and Lewis had taken the leap into the beloved pantheon of legendary comedy teams, alongside Laurel and Hardy, Abbott and Costello, and the Marx Brothers. And they were walking through the fire once a month on live TV for an audience of millions, tweaking and honing their act as the laughs only got louder. Dean and Jerry were young, talented, successful, and getting more popular every day. They were also starting to hate each other.

Initially, they were thick as thieves, with showgirls, gambling, and the abasement of Ernie Glucksman as their common interests. They were promoted as paisans onscreen and off, down to their matching shirts—Dean's with "boy singer" stitched on his front pocket and Jerry with "child star" embroidered on his. It was a sore point for both of them when critics dismissed Dean as a replaceable straight man. Jerry stuck up for his partner, often reminding Ernie to tell the writers to "write for Dean like he's a comedian."

In some ways, Jerry was Dean's greatest cheerleader, but it killed him that Dean was more naturally funny than he was. An aside from Dean, muttered under his breath, or a raised eyebrow at the right moment, could be five times as funny as Jerry hanging upside down from a ladder with a plunger stuck to his head, and Jerry knew it.

Sometimes Dean would invent hilarious lines in rehearsal only to have Jerry steal the ad-lib just before Dean had a chance to use it on live TV. "Jerry would get screams from the audience and applause," their stage manager, Bud Yorkin, remembered. "Dean would just stand there dumbfounded and look at Jerry as if he couldn't believe his ears. That happened on a number of occasions. It was unbelievable how he could pull that on his own partner."

Jerry would also literally double over in pain if Dean got any laughs during rehearsal. According to Norman Lear, "Jerry would wind up in a corner on the floor someplace with a bellyache. And a doctor would have to come. This was always true. Whenever Dean was very funny, strange physical things happened to Jerry. Sometimes he would go to the extreme of calling Marvin Levy, who was his doctor at the time, to fly in from California to treat him."

No one was safe from Jerry's manic jealous fits. The comedy writer Rocky Kalish recalled the moment when Jerry turned on him:

> I opened my mouth when we were working on a skit. Everybody was struggling for a line for a climax to a scene and Jerry opened his mouth and I said something quietly to Dean and Dean said to me, "Hey, why don't you tell him? Tell him what you just told me." And I did. Everybody laughed, except Jerry, 'cause I overrode a thought of Jerry's and it was a good ending for the scene. From that moment on, Jerry had a hard-on for me. Immediately, it got me in trouble with Martin and Lewis and Glucksman too, I guess. I was under contract at the time. The contract was not renewed.

It's no secret that Jerry suffered with lifelong issues of abandonment and rejection. His early triumphs were hobbled by crippling self-doubt. "I was afraid," Jerry said, "that I would wake up some morning, and everything would be gone—my house, my swimming pool, my job at the studio." It's not unlikely that Jerry worked himself into a frenzy thinking about that kid that *Variety* loved, this "Sammy Petrillo," that could usurp all that he had worked towards. Lewis knew that he had cornered the market in the world of abrasive man-child comedy. He also knew that, through his genius, he probably opened a path for scores of fumbling schlemiels to follow, carefully aping his act and stealing what was rightfully his. This Pandora's box of stupid needed to be riveted shut.

By Sammy's account, he was summoned to the palatial MCA offices on West 57th Street to sign an exclusive contract courtesy of Jerry Lewis. Various projects were discussed and Sammy was instructed to turn down any TV offers that didn't come from MCA or Jerry.

Weeks went by. Sammy and his family began to notice that neither Jerry nor MCA were tossing him any offers or even answering the phone. The entertainment columnist Jack O'Brien at the *New York Journal-American* noticed also. He wrote in his column about Sammy not getting any work and wondered if Jerry Lewis might have something to do with it.

According to Will Jordan, "Jerry also put his father under contract. It's similar to the situation that also happened with Al Jolson's brother and Charlie Chaplin's brother. They were put under contract so that they wouldn't work."

Ernie Glucksman's nephew Rick Saphire, an agent who would one day represent both Sammy *and* Jerry, surmised that what Sammy signed was what's referred to in the trade as a "Little Rascals contract":

During the *Our Gang* comedies, Alfalfa had a dream that he wanted to be an opera singer and he walked into an opera house and signed a contract with the opera. It was a "wink-wink" contract, where the guy winked at the secretary and told her to draw up a contract that looked like a real contract just to make the guy feel good. The contract that Sammy signed might not have been a legitimate contract. But Jerry was known to have invited several people, who I personally know, to California because he was gonna give them their big break, and these people ended up sitting in their hotel rooms and Jerry didn't follow through. So it's not unique what might have happened with Sammy, but I know that Jerry never liked any type of competition and there was some competition there.

Rocky Kalish never believed that there was a contract in the first place.

"He was sixteen years old! To sign the contract, his parents would have had to sign it also and they didn't. I'm sure that Sammy wanted to tell the story that he was under contract, but there was no such thing. It couldn't have existed. Possibly, Jerry might've said something about helping represent him or something along those lines."

In 2011, Jerry was asked outright if he had signed Sammy to a contract. "I don't know anything about him," Jerry replied. "I saw the kid in the street and put him on the show that week. That's it."

"Did you sign him to a contract?"

"No. Your information is wrong."

Whether the contract existed or not is immaterial. If Sammy thought that it was real, or at least told people that it was, then that's all that mattered. Jerry Lewis would be in charge of Sammy Petrillo's career.

The phone wasn't ringing, and by January Sammy suspected that Jerry was blackballing him. The contract, whether it existed or not, was worthless. Fortunately, Sammy knew someone who knew how to place items with the columnist Bert Gumpert at the *New York Post*. Sammy landed in the good graces of Gumpert and his column, "The Bronx Bandwagon," at least twice in January 1951. First Gumpert reported that "Sam Patrello, 328 E. 145th St., guest-stars for John Carroll University over Cleveland TV station tonight." Then the encouraging, "Sammy Patrello doin' fine on smaller nightclub circuit, and getting closer to the big time." According to *Variety* that same month, Sammy was "currently lining up his own teenage variety program."

During the day, Sammy cooled his heels down at Hanson's Drugstore with every other type of showbiz act that haunted midtown in search of a gig. From the unwashed to the elite, Hanson's was the main hangout to see and be seen. With payphones ringing off the hook, handshake deals were brokered over grilled cheese sandwiches and egg creams. Located at the corner of 51st Street and Seventh Avenue, Hanson's occupied a relatively tiny corner in a massive structure that stretched all the way over a block west to Broadway. The building housed every agent in town, so the drugstore was typically the entry or egress from an important huddle upstairs.

The comedian and TV host Chuck McCann first met Sammy at Hanson's along with the usual gang of funnymen: Buddy Hackett, Jack Carter, Uncle Miltie, Huntz Hall, and Jack E. Leonard. Even Jerry Lewis would frequent the lowbrow soda shop. "Sammy loved Jerry," Chuck recalled. "You can't do an impression of Jerry without loving him, and Sammy was highly influenced by him. What most comedians do is absorb little traits of everybody so you get an amalgamation of influences in the mix. It's like an honor or a tribute to them. For me it was Gleason and Laurel and Hardy, and whatever. But you just don't take just one central guy to imitate."

By the end of the month, *Variety* was announcing that Sammy was "starting dates as single" for a show at the Boulevard Tavern in Forest Hills, New York, with the caveat, "Petrillo will use some of Lewis's material, but will depend largely on his own script. He's letting his hair grow so that the resemblance to Lewis won't be too marked."

In March, the *New York Post* reported that Sammy would appear with perhaps the first of his many partners, George DeWitt. They were booked "on a 46-day Mediterranean tour as shipboard entertainers." It isn't confirmed if this ship actually left port with Sammy and George aboard; however, they did appear together at the Paramount in Times Square, a prestigious gig to be certain. George DeWitt was a suave and easygoing comic who would later go on to replace Bill Cullen as the host of *Name That Tune* from 1955 to 1959. DeWitt cozied up to the Rat Pack by sabotaging Sammy Davis, Jr.'s Jack Benny impersonation one night with his own ad-libbed impersonation of Jack Benny's sidekick, Eddie "Rochester" Anderson. He was also one of the first comedians to open for Frank Sinatra, until he was replaced by Joey Bishop.

In an April solo appearance, Sammy entertained at a Damon Runyon Carnival Dance in Brooklyn to raise funds to fight cancer. Also featured on the bill were Red Buttons, the magician Jackie Flosso, and the Skylarks, who regularly toured as backup singers for Dinah Shore and

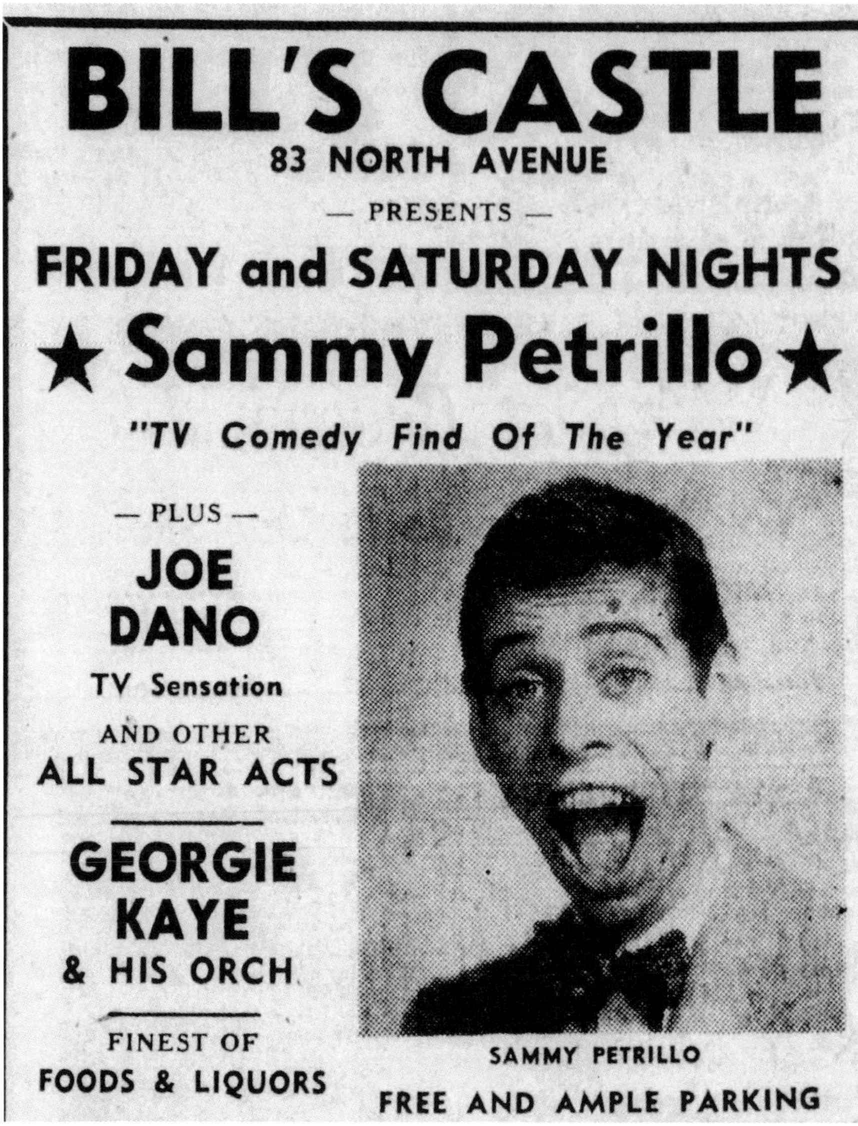

Bridgeport Telegram, October 27, 1951.

Martin and Lewis. A few weeks later, Sammy played another fundraiser in Brooklyn, this one a "Dark Dance" benefit for the National Council to Combat Blindness.

In an interview years later, Sammy mentioned that one of his first partners was Eddie Schaeffer. Not much is known about the pairing except that it presumably included some Martin and Lewis impersonations. Eddie Schaeffer left the Sammy Petrillo universe around this time as quietly as he had arrived in it.

Next up was Danny Wald. The "comic team of Sammy Petrillo and Danny Wald" appeared on a local WPIX baseball-related TV quiz show that preceded a New York Giants game. Intriguingly, the panel also featured the "hipsemantic"-spouting proto-beatnik Lord Buckley, whom *Billboard* described as "the vaudevillian, who supplies some humor altho he does little in the way of nailing down the answers." In the early '60s, Danny Wald formed a Martin and Lewis tribute act with Buddy Boylan that played the 500 Club in Atlantic City, the Playboy in Miami Beach, and numerous nightspots up and down the eastern seaboard. The multi-talented Danny switched from imitating Dean Martin to becoming Jerry Lewis, which turned out to be a better fit. Danny and Buddy both appeared uncredited on TV in *Car 54, Where Are You?,* and Danny had an unbilled role in Bob Fosse's *Lenny*. In the 1980s, Danny teamed up with Chuck Morro, who impersonated Dean Martin for years.

Fresh on the heels of receiving an honorary Doctor of Humane Letters degree at Temple University in Philadelphia, and a day before signing another lucrative contract with NBC, Eddie Cantor appeared on *The Colgate Comedy Hour* for his final show of the season. The roster of guests was stacked. Ads for the show promised "merry, madcap Milton Berle as [Eddie Cantor's] entirely unpredictable guest! You've seen them separately on TV before, now for the first time see them together. Things will bust out all over with laughter tonight FOR SURE." The rest of the cast, according to Virginia's *Portsmouth Star,* included "fast-rising young comedian, Phil Foster, June Keegan, Paul Whiteman's 13-year-old singing protege, and Sammy Petrillo, youthful impersonator who is a ringer for Jerry Lewis (of Dean Martin &)." The *Dallas Morning News* clarified that "Sammy Petrillo [was] no relation to the musician's czar," with the *Chicago Tribune* adding that "There also will be impersonations of Groucho Marx and Dean Martin and Jerry Lewis."

Sammy appeared as Jerry, for over thirty seconds this time, in a hospital-based skit that was designed to make light of Eddie Cantor's recent health issues. (Cantor was plagued with a bad ticker and would have a heart attack after performing on an episode of *The Colgate Comedy Hour* the following year.)

In the sketch, Cantor is sitting upright in a hospital bed with a thermometer in his mouth. Sammy enters from a door, stage left, wearing an oversized suit and bow tie. He's surprised to see Cantor in bed and does a "take" for the audience. Sammy grabs the thermometer out of Cantor's mouth, breaks it in half, puts one half back into Cantor's mouth, the other half into his mouth, and proceeds to eat it. Cantor breaks character and turns his head to the side, laughing for a moment. Sammy looks at the camera and exclaims, "I like it! I like it!!" while baring his teeth. Cantor yells at Sammy to get out of the room. Medium shot on Sammy again, looking at the camera, gesturing his thumb at Cantor, and in his best Jerry voice, says "He's *craaay—zee!*" Sammy exits whence he came, not in a straight line but walking in an arc toward the camera and then out the door for maximum effect.

Less than a month earlier on *The Colgate Comedy Hour,* Jerry had also eaten a thermometer and had also exclaimed, "I like it! I like it!" Sammy was now recycling specific Jerry gags. To be clear, Jerry didn't invent the eating of the modern glass thermometer for comic effect. Fatty Arbuckle gobbled one down in *Good Night, Nurse!* in 1918, and Harpo Marx gleefully revived the gag in 1937's *A Day at the Races.*

If this freshly stolen joke rankled Jerry Lewis, he might have been too busy to do anything about it. (He did steal back the thermometer-eating bit in the Navy induction scene in the team's fifth movie, *Sailor Beware.*) During a stint at the Paramount a few weeks later, the boys were busy being kings of the entertainment world. Promoting their next movie, *That's My Boy,* they shut down a section of Times Square by merely sticking their heads out the window a few floors above the rear of the theater. It was a scene of bedlam that would not be matched until a decade later, at the height of Beatlemania. Dean and Jerry dumped photos on the thousands waiting below with Dean drolly doling out the glossies one at a time. "I tell ya what, you wanna come up for coffee?" Jerry screamed down to the multitudes, followed by, "We ain't got any!" Before being comically pulled back inside the window by a policeman, Dean said to the crowd, "We just want you guys to know that we're the happiest guys in the whole, whole world. It's the greatest thrill of our lives."

Sammy was being kept busy as well. The short-lived sketch comedy show *Seven at Eleven* (named for having seven guests on at 11 p.m.) featured Sammy along with six other local comics, including the ubiquitous Herbie Faye. Two days after Martin and Lewis's Times Square shutdown, Sammy could be found at the Boulevard nightclub in Queens, billed as a "TV Comic Find." In July he appeared on the premiere episode of *Hold Everything,* a short-lived variety show on a local New York City station, WOR. He also showed up in August at the nearby Silver Edge

Sammy chews a thermometer and the scenery in a guest bit on the *The Colgate Comedy Hour* with host Eddie Cantor. June 17, 1951.

Tavern performing a solo act. In September Sammy was back with George DeWitt at a prestigious gig opening for Lena Horne at the Riviera in Fort Lee, New Jersey. The *Brooklyn Eagle* described Sammy's performance as "a Jerry Lewis type by nature and dint of hard study." *Billboard* harshly observed that "George DeWitt battled a mob for almost 35 minutes. His opening four-five gags lay there gasping. It wasn't until his take-offs that he managed to get going. His biggest laughs came from a Martin and Lewis carbon, where DeWitt did a Dean Martin and brought out Sammy Petrillo, a dead ringer for Jerry Lewis, to do the obvious. The surprise element made it funny."

In October, Sammy and dozens of entertainers paraded down the Grand Concourse in the Bronx along with the armed forces and veterans to celebrate the sixth anniversary of the U.N. and the opening of a new Winston department store. It was a three-hour trek that was carried live on WPIX-TV.

Sammy's nomadic lifestyle, one that would define his living situation for much of his life, began that November. His on-again, off-again partner

George DeWitt somehow scored a booking at the Flamingo and invited Sammy along. The Flamingo was one of the first upscale casinos to open on the Las Vegas Strip, and an appearance there could be a springboard to better things. In its review of the show, *Variety* noted DeWitt's "impressions and nimble gab," but suggested "that he might show more of himself instead of miming somebody else's somebody. Uses Sammy Petrillo, Jerry Lewis's double, to help carbon Martin & Lewis in what turns out to be a showstopper. Petrillo not only looks like the zany Lewis, but mugs and chatters on the button. Bit tops stint for peak huzzas." Freddie Bass, a well-known club booker on the coast, wasn't buying the huzzas, no matter how peak. "DeWitt would let Sammy roam around doing all kinds of undisciplined things," Freddie said. "This was not an act destined for greatness."

George and Sammy split up after an argument and with the remaining Flamingo loot, and Sammy hoofed it to L.A. and took up daytime residence at Schwab's Pharmacy on Sunset Boulevard. Schwab's was the West Coast equivalent of Hanson's, a malt shop that doubled as a feeding ground for industry wheelers and dealers. Penniless, Sammy hung out in front of the drugstore, cracking wise and making with the silly jokes. He was young and brash and looked like Jerry Lewis, so the world was at his feet.

Another Schwab's regular was the brusque burlesque comic Joe E. Ross, later treasured for his star turns on *The Phil Silvers Show* and *Car 54, Where Are You?* Known for his trademark phrase, "Ooh! Ooh!!", Ross would park himself in a booth, guzzle malteds, and hold court. A fortuitous meeting changed the trajectory of Sammy's career. Years later, Sammy would recall that Joe E. Ross "was a great guy (may he rest in peace). He said, 'Hey! This kid's funny!' and when he found out I was broke, he took me under his wing. I lived at his apartment with him and a fellow named Al Cook who was in the siding business. Joe E. used to give me some money so I could buy some food. He got me a job at a little place called the Toddle House in Culver City where he was the emcee. It was a little place that he used to call a 'pusbag.' It's a disgusting expression, but a lot of comics used to say that. 'I'm working in a real pusbag, you know?' He said, 'I gotcha this job, kid, and I know yer gonna be great in it! Heh, heh heh heh!' So he got me this job and I made $65 a week at that time."

It was obvious that Jerry wasn't going to be any help to Sammy. If anything, he was keeping this high-school dropout from making a living. Sammy was cast off and would have to find success on his own, albeit with someone else's face. "The Jerry Lewis thing threw me for a loop," mused Sammy years later. "I went into show business and suddenly I look like somebody else. I don't know whether to think of it as a dirty trick played by God or whether it helped me get in the business." Partnering with Duke Mitchell was the next logical step in achieving success as a Martin and Lewis knockoff act. It was a legendary pairing, one that would set the stage for one of the most infamous movies ever filmed: *Bela Lugosi Meets a Brooklyn Gorilla*.

CHAPTER 6 REALART

Universal Pictures was founded by Carl Laemmle, a five-foot-two émigré from Laupheim, a small, poverty-stricken village in Germany. In 1918 he transformed 230 acres in the San Fernando Valley in California into Universal Studios. Laemmle was responsible for hundreds of productions at Universal. Most were low-budget westerns, melodramas, and serials, along with a handful of prestige motion pictures that featured A-list names and large budgets. In 1928, Laemmle handed over control of the studio to his son, Carl Laemmle, Jr. Under Junior's reign, Universal conquered the switch from silents to talkies with highbrow fare like *All Quiet on the Western Front* and *Waterloo Bridge*. However, it was the horror movies that put Universal on the map.

Universal's productions of *Dracula, Frankenstein, The Mummy, The Invisible Man, Bride of Frankenstein,* and *The Old Dark House* were German Expressionist–influenced forays into the macabre that touched a nerve with Depression-era audiences. Boris Karloff (star of *Frankenstein* and *The Mummy*) and *Dracula*'s Bela Lugosi were middle-aged actors whose portrayals of monsters were so compelling that they remained in the horror genre, with varying degrees of success, for the rest of their careers. Scary, witty, and well-made, the movies were massive hits. They were the perfect confluence of commerce and pop culture and remain astoundingly engaging after almost a hundred years.

By 1946, after conjuring up a new monster (the Wolf Man) and countless sequels for the old ones, the horror craze at Universal had finally run its course. The studio's diet of westerns, serials, and Abbott and Costello comedies was going stale. Universal merged with the British-owned International Pictures to chase a new, upscale market exemplified by their upcoming productions of *Hamlet* and *Great Expectations*. Looking to shake off their lowbrow rep, Universal licensed off whatever they could.

Seeing no real value in their past successes, Universal leased their entire catalog from 1930 to 1946 to Realart Pictures, Inc. Realart held the exclusive rights on all Universal releases for a ten-year period (1947-1957) and that would be more than long enough for them to change the world. (Television rights, which would have made Realart a mind-boggling fortune, were not included in the deal, possibly because no one thought of it.)

Realart was the brainchild of Jack Broder, a Polish émigré who settled down with his family in 1920 in the tough streets of Detroit. Jack struggled, working odd jobs selling newspapers, running a pool hall, and recycling glass bottles, before opening a candy concession stand in the Colonial Theatre. Running a small business in Detroit in the 1920s had its own unique hazards that Jack and his new partner, his brother Paul, soon realized. Detroit was rife with crime, courtesy of a group of Jewish mobsters known as the Purple Gang, who peddled booze and death with impunity right up until the St. Valentine's Day Massacre in 1929. Staying on both the right side of the gangsters and the right side of the law proved to be a unique challenge for the brothers, who were getting an on-the-street lesson in the American Dream and all of its subtleties.

By the 1940s, Jack and Paul had sold enough candy bars to buy the Times Square Theatre and ended up owning a dozen more theaters in the greater Detroit area. With an eye on infiltrating the film-distribution business, Jack moved to Beverly Hills just in time to swing that deal with Universal in 1946. The timing couldn't have been better. Audiences, theater owners, and distributors had soured on Hollywood's latest crop of movies. Realart was able to pass off recycled, quality productions as new releases and at a deep discount for the movie theaters. Realart became one of the busiest reissue companies in the business, expanding their regional reach and filling theaters across the country. Most consequentially, Realart raised the repackaging of old westerns, Abbott and Costello comedies, and horror movies to an art form. Its slick posters and wild promotions were courtesy of Jack's latest hire as general sales manager, James Nicholson, known around the office as Jim or Jimmy.

Jim got a taste for movies first as an usher at the El Rey Theatre in San Francisco at age thirteen and then as a projectionist when he was sixteen. At eighteen, he owned his own theater in Omaha, Nebraska, before trying his luck in Tinseltown. By the time he was twenty-eight, Jim owned three movie theaters in L.A.: the Picfair, Marcal, and Cinema, which all specialized in films of the 1920s and 1930s. Appearing on a local talk show, *Editor's Round Table,* on NBC, Jim was brought in to respond to the burning question, "Are Movies Better Than Ever?" "If movies are better than ever," countered Jim, "what happened to all those patrons we had before the war?" It was true. There were fewer keisters in the seats for current movies compared to Realart's cavalcade of recycled hits.

Jim's passion for quality old movies was reflected in his creative zeal in marketing Realart's reissues. If the movie poster for the original release was good enough, he would simply paste a Realart logo over the Universal logo. For other movies with less compelling images, he'd swap it out with a poster from an entirely different movie. Corny or outdated names of movies would be replaced with attention-grabbers—*Ladies Courageous* became *Fury in the Sky,* the Olsen and Johnson comedy *See My Lawyer* was rereleased as *In a Padded Cell,* and so on.

Similar to Martin and Lewis's debut in *My Friend Irma,* Abbott and Costello were merely supporting characters in their first feature film, *One Night in the Tropics*. In order to give the budding comedy team more screen time in the reissue, Realart simply lopped fifteen minutes of romantic plot off the movie, making them appear to be the stars. Jim created intriguing double features that would have a theme, such as jungle pictures, Technicolor A-movies, the East Side Kids, and, crucially, horror movies. A double feature of *Dracula* and *Frankenstein,* with its tales of bloodsuckers and graverobbers, was bound to be an eye-opening day at the movies for the wee ones. Universal had had a similar, yet short-lived success with a *Dracula* and *Frankenstein* double bill in 1938. Renewed interest in horror movies resulted in *Son of Frankenstein* (1939) and *The Wolf Man* (1941), plus a few other spooky sequels, until the genre was quickly run into the ground again.

Realart expertly publicized these early horror movies as vibrant, roller-coaster rides into the eerie and unknown. The dead monster-movie industry, nickel by nickel, was finding new life in the hands of kids across the nation. Without intending to, Realart's creation of monster culture anticipated the dawn of the teenager in the late forties. It was something that belonged to the kids and no one else.

Taking a cue from Realart's success with their hand-me-down monsters, in 1948 Universal cooked up the genre-bending classic, *Abbott and Costello Meet Frankenstein.* It was conceived as an all-star monster affair with the comedy team mixing it up with the Frankenstein monster, Dracula, and the Wolf Man. Bela Lugosi returned to portray the world's most famous bloodsucker for the second and last time. The belly-laughs-mixed-with-scary-moments formula was such a success that in future films Abbott and Costello would go on to "meet" other notables (Boris Karloff, the Invisible Man, Captain Kidd, the Keystone Kops, and the Mummy), with diminishing results.

There were horror comedies before *Abbott and Costello Meet Frankenstein,* but only Bud Abbott and Lou Costello got to be chased by the officially licensed Mount Rushmore of movie monsters. However, all was not copacetic in Abbott and Costello land. They sued Universal and Realart for $5 million for not being informed of, nor cut in for profits on, the reissues of their old comedies. Abbott and Costello settled with Universal for 50% of the Realart profits, yet, nearing their twilight years, it might have stung the team to have to compete with their younger, funnier selves at the box office. In the end, Universal's noble leap into literary adaptations didn't pan out, and by 1950 they were back cranking out *Francis the Talking Mule* and *Ma and Pa Kettle* movies for the lowbrow crowd.

Meanwhile at Realart, Jack Broder was getting an itch to produce his own movies. After taking a stab at associate-producing the earnest runaway drama *When I Grow Up* for Horizon Pictures, Jack formed his own film company, Jack Broder Productions. Besides genuinely loving the business, now he would be able to charge distributors more if there was actually a new movie at the top of the double-feature bill. Jack ran an ad in *Variety* for an assistant who was willing to work for cheap.

Herman Cohen, another ex-Detroiter, got the job. Like Jim, Herman had begun his career ushering, first at the Dexter Theater and later co-managing the 5,000-seat Fox Theater (both in Detroit). Herman was involved in all aspects of the productions, learning on the job and boning up at the Cinema Department at UCLA for the nuances of the business that eluded him. "Jack Broder was a wonderful, wonderful guy," Herman recounted, "and I owe a lot to him. He wasn't too good with the bucks, but he certainly gave me all the titles, up to and including vice-president. Oh, he gave me a lot of titles!"

They set up shop first at the Hal Roach Studios in Culver City, then at the Samuel Goldwyn Studios in Hollywood, and finally at General Service Studios, also in Hollywood. Built in 1919, General Service was first known as Hollywood Studios and later as Metropolitan Studios. By the time that Jack Broder Productions moved in, all the other studios on the lot were being used for television productions, most notably *I Love Lucy,* which filmed in an adjoining studio.

Realart promotion. Circa 1952.

Jack Broder Productions' first movie was *Two-Dollar Bettor,* a postwar fable about a naïve "mark" whose escalating gambling debts plunge him into a life of crime. Starring John Litel, with an able assist from the always spectacular Marie Windsor, *Two-Dollar Bettor* is a fine B movie. It's a cheapie, but the writing and acting are better than they needed to be. The same can be said for *The Basketball Fix,* a ripped-from-the-headlines journey through the sordid world of corrupt college basketball. *Kid Monk Baroni* featured Leonard Nimoy, in his first starring role, as a former street-gang punk trying to navigate his way through the crooked underworld of professional boxing. When selecting this story, Jack was clearly mining his own unsavory experiences of running from hoodlums back east. As an afterthought, an anonymous gang of street thugs in the movie were rebranded in post-production as "the Billy Goat Gang" and were given an above-the-title billing. In possibly a nod to the Purple Gang, it was also an attempt to keep the door open for a sequel and franchise, à la the Bowery Boys.

Jack Broder was tough, and he patrolled the film sets with his hands tucked into his side pockets, Napoleon-style, barking out orders in his Polish accent. He carefully watched the budgets, and if a ten-day shooting schedule could be crammed into nine by cutting out some scenes, then so be it. Jack was also obsessed with gorillas and monkeys in general and would often try to fit simian references, or actual simians, into his movies. His grandson, the literary manager David Kopple, surmised that Jack's "obsession with the gorilla/ape/primitive man is a metaphor for his own transformation from European immigrant to Hollywood dream maker."

Ever the doting father, Jack would do almost anything for his six children. One of his favorite pastimes was driving the brood around L.A. in his light blue Cadillac convertible with the top down. Aside from giving some of his kids cameos in his movies, Jack depended upon their youthful instincts to sniff out a good script. His eldest daughter, Madelynn, remembered that Dad would put an ad in the daily *Variety* and the *Hollywood Reporter*: "Scripts Needed" and he'd give his home address. People would drive on over and drop off scripts, so we had scripts all over the house. All the kids were assigned to read them and the ones that we liked we put in piles and the ones we didn't like we put in another pile. His plan was to get two different scripts that could both utilize all of the same props and the same sets. He would film the first one for ten days and on day eleven the second director came on along with the new actors and everybody else.

One of the scripts that got the green light from the Broder kids was a horror movie called *The Face in the Water*. For Jack, changing the title to *Bride of the Gorilla* was an easy decision. With a title reminiscent of *Bride of Frankenstein, Bride of the Gorilla* was shot in ten days with indoor sets subbing for outdoor locations, the way that Jack liked it. The onscreen and real-life femme fatale Barbara Payton, on suspension from Warner Bros., was nabbed for the lead, along with Raymond Burr, Tom Conway, and Lon Chaney, Jr. Married to the movie star Franchot Tone, Barbara carried on an open affair during the ten-day film shoot with the B-movie actor and real-life lug Tom Neal, star of the film *Detour*. A jealous Franchot Tone sent a private eye to the set only to discover that Barbara was also making time with two co-stars: Tom Conway and the former L.A. Rams football star Woody Strode. After filming wrapped, Tom Neal pummeled Franchot Tone into next week in a beating that almost turned deadly.

Bride of the Gorilla was directed by Curt Siodmak, who, along with his older brother, the director Robert Siodmak, had escaped from Germany in the late '30s when antisemitism was reaching a boiling point. Curt Siodmak created one of the most popular Universal monsters right after *Dracula* and *Frankenstein*. Those two films were adaptations of pre-existing novels, while Siodmak's creation of *The Wolf Man* was the first Universal monster, complete with wolfbane/full moon tropes, written directly for the screen. After nearly fifty screenplays to his credit, including *Son of Dracula, House of Frankenstein, I Walked with a Zombie,* and *The Invisible Man Returns,* this was to be Siodmak's directorial debut. "He was from Europe," Herman Cohen said, "a very serious man—and when he did *Bride of the Gorilla* he thought he was doing *Gone With the Wind*."

Following the premise of *The Wolf Man,* in *Bride of the Gorilla* Raymond Burr transforms into the titular brute and runs amok. With the limited budget and tight shooting schedule, the technical wizardry of Lon Chaney, Jr.'s on-camera transformation into a wolf wasn't even halfway attempted on Raymond Burr, and it didn't matter. A stuntman, Steve Calvert, zippered up in a gorilla suit, aimlessly walking into rubber plants neatly summoned up the existential emotions that are usually involved when one turns into a gorilla. By making a horror picture, Jack Broder was able to express his longing for something else, a reinvention, a transformation, and an escape, and if it involved a gorilla suit, then all the better.

In all, Jack Broder Productions and Realart would produce about a dozen feature films, all Poverty Row productions to be sure, but all of them imbued with a sense of wonder and horror at man's follies. Realart's true claim to immortality still resides in its creation of an industry where one didn't exist before. Reissuing old Universal monster movies would have a monumental effect on popular culture across the globe. Without Realart, the presence of classic monsters in popular culture might never have happened. Imagining a world without Frankenstein, Dracula, the Mummy, and their pals at this point is unthinkable. Realart's late-'40s and early-'50s horror blitz was a wakeup call for future weirdos worldwide—inspiring novelty records, books, comic books, comic strips, cartoons, trading cards, the *Creature From the Black Lagoon, I Was a Teenage Werewolf,* the TV hosts Ghoulardi and Zacherley, the radio host the Mad Daddy, Hammer movies, TV shows such as *The Munsters, The Addams Family, Dark Shadows,* and *Buffy the Vampire Slayer,* punk bands such as the Cramps, the Misfits, the Damned, and the Mummies, Goth, Chinese hopping vampires, Ann Rice novels, *Famous Monsters of Filmland* magazine, custom cars, dark rides and haunted houses, Halloween costumes, model kits, candy, breakfast cereal, T-shirts, iron-ons, temporary tattoos, permanent tattoos, *Blacula, Young Frankenstein, What We Do in the Shadows,* and other parodies, endless remakes, countless sequels—Realart was responsible for generations of happy, horror-crazed fans who drew joy and inspiration from these almost-forgotten gems.

Most importantly, Realart produced *Bela Lugosi Meets a Brooklyn Gorilla,* starring Duke Mitchell and Sammy Petrillo.

The hairy precursor to *Bela Lugosi Meets a Brooklyn Gorilla,* and shot on the same sets. Newspaper advertisement, circa 1951.

THE CURSE OF A LUPINO!
To be the mistress...
and the BRIDE OF A GORILLA!
JACK BRODER
Productions
presents
Bride of the GORILLA
Starring
BARBARA PAYTON · LON CHANEY
RAYMOND BURR · TOM CONWAY
Written and Directed by CURT SIODMAK

CHAPTER 7

DUKE MITCHELL

Dominic Salvatore Miceli was born in 1926 in Farrell, Pennsylvania, a township nestled by the Shenango River and the Ohio border. Farrell, formerly known as South Sharon, was called "the Magic City," after the industrialist James A. Farrell erected a massive steel mill there in 1901. Escaping an industrial manufacturing future, the Micelis picked up and moved to New York when Dominic was eight. His father had already nicknamed him Duke, after John Wayne's horse in the movie *Ride Him, Cowboy*.

Raised streetwise in the East New York section of Brooklyn, Duke was inspired enough by the song stylings of Frankie Laine and Vaughn Monroe to change his last name to Mitchell and seek a career as a crooner. Working as an usher in a small theater's "swooners and crooners" contest, he kept submitting his own name to management until they let him sing. Duke aced the contest and won a wristwatch for his trouble. He graduated to better theaters and winning better wristwatches, which he promptly sold to his buddies waiting outside. By nineteen, Duke was polished and professional.

Billed as "Brooklyn's Newest Singing Sensation," in 1945 Duke vocalized for the orchestra Jimmie Valentine and His Boys at the Victory Inn, a nightclub located at the far end of Flatbush Avenue, down near the marina. Duke sang in various nighteries from the Club LeBistro in Chicago to the Flamingo in Vegas to the lounge of the Tropicana in Miami. On a tip, he took off for Hollywood so he could break into the movies during the day and snag singing engagements at night. Duke shared an apartment with James Dean, then an aspiring actor, at the Garden of Allah Hotel in West Hollywood. The Garden of Allah was legendary for its decades of hedonistic goings-on—booze parties, junk parties, sex parties—all routine business for Hollywood's actors, writers, directors, and producers. It also was the last stop for scores of has-beens and never-weres who enjoyed, and then couldn't survive, the nonstop debauchery. A drunk and destitute F. Scott Fitzgerald had once written a postcard to himself that read, "Dear Scott, How are you? Have been meaning to come in and see you. I have [been] living at the Garden of Allah. Yours, Scott Fitzgerald."

Duke crooned his way into a job singing at Larry Potter's Supper Club ("Intimate Vaudeville at its Best!"), where he was third-billed to the "Startling Show Stopping Singing Star" Joaquin Gray. James Dean got a gig as a parking-lot attendant at CBS Studios, collecting tips and scanning the trades for auditions. James Dean and Duke would go on the same auditions, which is how they both ended up in a Martin and Lewis movie. In *Sailor Beware,* they appear as corner men in the climactic boxing scene between Jerry and a generic brute. The boxing sequence is notable for being Jerry's directorial debut after he stepped in for the slapstick-impaired director, Hal Walker. Being a silent-movie nut, Jerry attempted to bring back some of that undercranked slapstick magic by working in a sequence where his character, Melvin Jones, runs several laps, at double speed, around the boxing ring. It was Jerry's first manipulation of the movie camera and it wouldn't be his last. Jerry insisted that his fee for choreographing the sequence go directly to the newly founded Muscular Dystrophy Association. James Dean had one line as the brute's corner man ("That guy's a professional"), while Duke mutely looked on as he stood behind Dino and Jerry.

Sometimes Duke, James Dean, and their pal Bob Romeo would convene down at Tabletoppers for drinks and a beatnik jam session, complete with the requisite flute and bongos. On one of those nights, someone ran a tape and it was released as a single after James Dean's death: "Dean's Lament" and "Jungle Rhythm." The Garden of Allah party ended with Duke kicking James out of the apartment after he found one of the method actor's male friends coming downstairs for breakfast one morning.

In November 1951, Duke was pulling a respectable crowd at Larry Potter's for $65 a week when his pal, Al Cook, showed up with his funny roommate who bore an unearthly resemblance to Jerry Lewis. It was obvious to everyone in the room what needed to happen now.

They vamped. Duke sang and Sammy interrupted. This might work.

There was an immediate understanding between the teenager and the young singer that this was an act where you didn't have to waste time coming up with material. Duke didn't have to do much—just hang back, good-naturedly chastise Sammy, and sing a couple of numbers. Sammy went all

The birth of an act. *Los Angeles Mirror*, December 18, 1951.

out, channeling and amplifying every Jerry Lewis mannerism and muscle twitch. Like Dean, Duke intuitively knew how far to let Sammy go in full-throttled nutzoid mode before reeling him back in. Duke was salt to Sammy's pepper, he was yin to Sammy's yang. Duke was Dean to Sammy's Jerry.

Sammy recalled that

> there was instant chemistry between us. Duke was eight years older than me, and he and his wife were like parents to me. We used to laugh almost all the time. We'd have a ball onstage and off. I was a dead ringer for Jerry. Duke looked like Dean when he stood next to me; when he was by himself [he] just sort of looked like him. But our act was much more than just being Martin and Lewis imitators; it had to be. When we hit the stage, we had to prove ourselves. I'm not saying we were better than Martin and Lewis, but we had to be better than just an imitation of Martin and Lewis because people in the audience would have one of two reactions: either it was "Oh, aren't they cute" or "What the hell are they doing here, trying to steal someone else's thunder? I hate these guys!" So what we had to do was give them that little spark of Martin and Lewis and then do a lot of other things that didn't smack of them.

In December, Mitchell and Petrillo headlined at the Toddle House, the Culver City "pusbag" where Joe E. Ross worked as an emcee. The show was provocatively titled "Girls A-Poppin'," and its ads promised "The Spiciest

Show in L. A.—Never a Dull Moment." The Toddle House was known for "its steak and delicious fried chicken, and also for the variety of potent cocktails which [could] be obtained at the mirrored bar."

Duke and Sammy were hired to be Martin and Lewis impersonators, and the raincoat crowd expected nothing less. For kicks, the boys would often switch things up. "We'd say, 'Now, ladies and gentlemen, the impression you've all been waiting for: Dean Martin and Jerry Lewis!'" Sammy recalled, "and we'd turn around and I'd say, 'Whatcha doin' there, Jer boy?' [and Duke would say,] '*Hehehe it's nice to be here!*' You know? It was kind of a tongue in cheek thing."

Sammy would also break out his Bela Lugosi, Walter Brennan, and Jimmy Stewart impersonations; however, it was his Johnnie Ray that was particularly manic. Sammy would tear his clothes off and work himself into a frenzy, mimicking the histrionics of the overemotional singer. Even with these comedic detours, their bread and butter would always be Martin and Lewis.

Sammy was philosophical about his limitations. "In comedy, when you can only do so many takes, so many looks, cross your eyes, there are only so many physical things you can do," he mused. "The difference between myself and other comics was that whenever I did them, I looked like Jerry anyway. So people figured I was doing Jerry even if I wasn't. I looked so much like the guy, I *had* to do him. I *had* to impersonate him. I looked like him no matter what I did. Like Duke Mitchell used to say—may he rest in peace—he'd say, 'You could hit Sammy with a truck and he'd still look like Jerry.'"

The Mitchell and Petrillo Toddle House shows were the talk of the striptease circuit. With "5 Solid Hours of Continuous Entertainment," Duke and Sammy were the headliners and performed several times a night. They'd hone their craft, iron out the rough spots, and remember the good ad-libs, all in between chatter from the "TV Star" Joe E. Ross and gyrations from the "Gorgeous Girls" Sheila Lind, Peggy Davis, Pat Flannery, and Mona Rae. With "Convenient Free Parking" and its "No Admission, No Cover" policy, the Toddle House was a hopping center of Culver City nightlife. As good as things were, they were about to get a lot better.

"One day, Duke and I were sitting in a restaurant," Sammy said, "and this guy named Jack Klass says to me, 'Aren't you Sammy Petrillo? I'd like you to come and meet somebody.' He brought us over to an agent named Maurice Duke, who said, 'This is the greatest talent I've seen in over forty years!'"

Maurice Duke's daughter, Fredde, asserts that it was her father who created the Sammy and Duke partnership: "Before Sammy and Duke Mitchell teamed up, my dad was the manager to each of them. Then [one] night in the club, Sammy heckled [Duke] as Jerry Lewis and it got so many laughs, my dad asked them to team up. Sammy told me this."

Born in the Bronx in 1910 and crippled by childhood polio, Maurice Duschinsky maneuvered through life with leg braces and a cane. "I had it before it was popular," he'd say. He taught himself to play harmonica when he was recuperating from surgery. Maurice won a few harmonica contests and joined Borrah Minevitch and His Harmonica Rascals. After touring the Loews Theater chain with the Rascals, he hooked up with the Cappy Barra Harmonica Ensemble on the vaudeville circuit and ended up managing the group when he turned twenty-one. Taking a stab at local politics, he formed the Maurice Duke Democratic Club of Brighton Beach, before turning his full attention to the managerial side of showbiz. He made up for his infirmity by developing a colorful, cigar-chomping personality that was described by the *Los Angeles Times* as "loud, coarse, insistent, self-promoting and irresistible." His son-in-law, the future *Tonight Show* writer Michael Barrie, described Maurice as "a force, a bigger-than-life Hollywood character . . . he was about five feet in height, but eight feet in personality."

Maurice had a knack for producing philistine entertainment that would exploit whatever fad was sweeping the nation. When the concept of teenagers came into vogue in the late 1940s, Maurice whipped up the *Teen Agers* series of films at Monogram. To cash in on the rise of Top Ten radio in 1951, he produced *Disc Jockey* for Allied Artists. Serving up a radioactive Mickey Rooney in *The Atomic Kid,* Maurice stoked the public's Cold War anxiety. Coasting on the backs of Martin and Lewis, the hottest comedy team in showbiz, Maurice shopped Mitchell and Petrillo around for a movie deal. As Michael Barrie says, "Maurice Duke wanted to make a Martin and Lewis picture, and the fact that he didn't have Martin and Lewis to make it with wasn't going to stop him."

Getting Duke and Sammy out of the Toddle House was the first order of business, so Maurice made a few phone calls and got the boys booked into the Club Bingo in Las Vegas for four shows nightly. Their familiar antics definitely caught the attention of a certain comedy team. As the syndicated Hollywood columnist Edith Gwynn wrote on January 7, 1952, under the headline, "Martin-Lewis Battle Alleged Copycats,"

> Martin and Lewis [have] consulted their attorney about one Sammy Petrillo, who, with his partner, Duke Mitchell, is doing a nightclub act in Las Vegas—and one so blatantly imitative of the things by which Dean and Jerry have risen to fame, that the originals are taking definite steps to curb the carbons.

They had gotten the attention of Martin and Lewis.

"[Maurice Duke] was like a father to me," Sammy said. "He was like a mother to me. So I was very close and it made me feel so great, you know, that he was so down to earth. [He] took us night after night after night to meet different producers. We went to the Beverly Hills Hotel. [They] brought the butler with the tray and poured us a drink and I flipped a half a dollar in the tray—'Thanks a lot, see you later.' We did all these kinds of things. And these kinds of people just loved it. Duke Mitchell and I were very natural off-the-street-type guys."

Jack Broder at Realart Pictures was next on the list of potential producers. Maurice convinced Jack, who wasn't much of a nightclub-goer, to come out with him to catch the best Martin and Lewis impersonators in town. Duke and Sammy must've been on fire that night because Jack loved them. He wanted to see what his right-hand man, Herman Cohen, thought of them. "Maurice sold Jack Broder on the idea to do a picture with these two boys, Mitchell and Petrillo," Herman said. "They had a cockamamie nightclub act imitating Martin and Lewis, and Maurice took Jack to some little club someplace, Culver City maybe, to see these guys. Jack thought they were hilarious." Herman went down to the Toddle House to see for himself. "I thought they stunk," Herman said. "Jack Broder was in hysterics over those two guys. We were at General Service Studios which is only a stone's throw from Paramount [laughs], and Broder thought he was looking at Martin and Lewis!"

Jack tasked his family with finding a script that would match the still-standing *Bride of the Gorilla* set. Something jungle-themed would work. Jack's older kids, Madelynn, Bobby, Billy, and, to a lesser extent, Richard, who was a little younger, scanned through the pile of scripts on the living room floor and pulled out a winner.

The April 26, 1952, issue of *Boxoffice* spilled the news:

> HOLLYWOOD—for distribution through Realart Pictures, Jack Broder Productions set to produce a musical, "White Woman of the Lost Jungle." It is scheduled to begin work next month, with the

nightclub comedy team of Duke Mitchell and Sammy Petrillo making their screen debut.

Mitchell and Petrillo weren't marketable names, so a meeting was called. "We all sat around the table and we tried to figure out who would be the one to play the lead in this picture," Sammy remembered. "We were thinking about [a] horror comedy. Herman and Jack said, 'We have to get a star name in this picture because you two aren't known yet.' They threw around several names, and somehow Lugosi's [name] came up. So they decided on him."

Another version of the story has Maurice walking around the studio one day when he ran into Bela Lugosi. "Maurice asked him if he wanted to be in this picture," Michael Barre says. "As you probably know, Lugosi would pretty much do anything for money, and he said, 'Sure.'"

CHAPTER 8

BELA LUGOSI

In the 1910s and '20s Bela Lugosi was a respected stage star both in his native Hungary and on Broadway. His iconic lead role in the movie version of *Dracula* rocketed him to the heights and just as quickly knocked him down to the depths of show business.

Born in 1882, only fifty miles away from the western border of Transylvania, Béla Ferenc Dezsö Blaskó left home at a young age to follow his passion for acting. Bela took his surname from his hometown of Lugos and landed a few bit parts. By 1913 he ascended to matinee-idol status in Budapest's National Theater Repertory. From comedies to tragedies, Lugosi was praised for his versatility in roles ranging from the lead in *Romeo and Juliet* to Jesus Christ in a passion play. Continuing film work in Vienna and then Germany, Lugosi cranked out another seventeen movies, including *Der Januskopf,* F. W. Murnau's 1920 knockoff of *Dr. Jekyll and Mr. Hyde.* Lugosi sailed to New Orleans in 1921 and then to Ellis Island in New York, where he became a naturalized U.S. citizen. Not knowing a word of English didn't stop Lugosi: he formed a stock company of like-minded Hungarian ex-pats and he performed his lines phonetically to rave reviews. In 1927, Lugosi lobbied hard and won the coveted lead in Hamilton Deane and John L. Balderston's authorized production of *Dracula* on Broadway. In the occult-crazed 1920s, the eerie tale of an undead gigolo seducing women with a bite on the neck was a sensation with the flapper set.

Still delivering his lines phonetically, Lugosi owned the role of Dracula, not just then but for now and forever. In the Bram Stoker novel, Count Dracula is a wretched nightcrawler, with pointy ears, a long white mustache, bushy eyebrows and hair growing out of his palms. Many of the tropes now associated with Dracula come directly from Lugosi's portrayal of the Count on stage and screen. Lugosi played him suave and he played him rough. He could be the Prince of Darkness in a top hat and

Lugosi's career defining role. Newspaper ad, circa 1931.

tails, strolling to a box seat at the opera, where his doe-eyed bride awaits; however, when angered or hungry, he's an unrepentant bloodsucker that attacks without mercy. Lugosi essayed both aspects with equal nobility.

When Junior Laemmle at Universal decided to take a crack at a movie version, Lugosi, strangely enough, was at the bottom of the list of potential Draculas. Universal refused to even consider him for the part, as Broadway actors rarely reprised their roles in movie adaptations. After their first choice, Lon Chaney, succumbed to throat cancer and others dropped out for one reason or another, Lugosi was finally awarded the role at the insultingly low salary of $500 per week for seven weeks' worth of shooting. Letting the studio walk over him financially had a devastating effect on his ability to negotiate for the rest of his career.

While *Dracula* is slow-paced and talky, Lugosi's suave Count from the Carpathian Mountains delivers a mesmerizing punch. As Lugosi's future co-star Carol Borland would observe, "Dracula is Bela Lugosi and Lugosi is Dracula. There is no separation between the two." Eschewing the fangs that were called for in the script, Lugosi created his own makeup, which bugged the Universal makeup legend Jack Pierce to no end. Agreeing to wear a hairpiece, he penciled in the now-iconic widow's peak, another Lugosi touch that superseded Bram Stoker's slimy creation. After portraying the Count nightly for two years, Lugosi was fully immersed in the character and believably inhabited the dead body and soul of the vampire.

Lugosi recalled,

> During those two years I did not speak a word to any person behind the scenes during the progress of the play. And since everyone knew the strain I was laboring under, no one spoke to me. . . . I was under a veritable spell which I dared not break. If I stepped out of my character for even a moment, the seething menace of the terrible Count Dracula was gone from the characterization and my hold on the audience had lost its force.

In his excellent book *The Monster Show*, David J. Skal spoke with Lugosi's co-star David Manners, who "recalled Lugosi as insufferably vain and pretentious, standing in front of a full-length mirror on the set, velvet cape wrapped over his shoulder, almost literally hypnotized by his own reflection. 'I *am* Dracula,' he would intone, parading up and down the soundstage."

Needing to reel in the stage version's hitting-the-last-row histrionics, Lugosi underplayed as much as he allowed himself to. A lover of traditional Hungarian folk tunes, there's a musical lilt in Lugosi's delivery—"I am . . . Drac-U-La . . ."—and that goes a long way in putting the lines menacingly across. It's a beautifully hammy yet on-the-nose performance, which retains its otherworldly power generations later.

The movie version of *Dracula* premiered at the Roxy Theater in New York City on February 12, 1931, and it was an instant hit with the public (not so much with the critics). In other cities, it was held over for weeks, and extra early-morning showings were held, along with some round-the-clock screenings. *Dracula* was Universal's top money-maker of 1931 and helped pull the studio out of a two-year downward spiral.

Lugosi's career short-circuited quickly, mainly due to Universal's insistence that he play the monster in the film version of Mary Shelley's *Frankenstein*. Lugosi envisioned himself more as the tormented Dr. Frankenstein type, complete with impassioned speeches about life and death, rather than a grunting monstrosity under a ton of prosthetics. He reluctantly submitted to a makeup test and everyone was disappointed with the results. Not having any dialogue wasn't exactly a selling point either, so he bowed out. The monster was eventually played by a middle-aged Englishman, Boris Karloff, who had acted in more than seventy movies but was still an unknown. Years later, Lugosi would take credit for Karloff's success.

"[Universal] said that they would let me out of the part if I would dig up someone to do it," Lugosi said. "So I looked around and found Boris

Karloff. He did the role and of course it was a hit. I created my own Frankenstein monster by turning down the part."

Invoking empathy and terror, Karloff's take on the Frankenstein monster was stunning, and he deservedly enjoyed a rewarding career in the horror genre because of it.

Lugosi's difficulty with English made dealing with agents and studio executives nearly impossible. He was no dummy, but he was headstrong, and, coupled with weak bargaining skills, better roles were out of his reach. Universal half-heartedly made good by casting him in *Murders in the Rue Morgue,* but it couldn't compare to the popularity of *Frankenstein*. Lugosi filed for bankruptcy in 1932, and his career nosedived almost immediately. While working for all of the major studios, he also accepted leading parts in a string of Poverty Row productions. World Wide Pictures, Mascot, Principal, Monogram, Victory, Republic, and PRC were but a few of the studios that snagged Bela Lugosi at bargain-basement prices. For personal appearances, he was billed as "Dracula himself" and "Bela 'Dracula' Lugosi." In the late 1930s, Lugosi was treated for excruciating lower-back pain with morphine and, after the war, doctors prescribed him methadone and Demerol. The multiple addictions took an inevitable toll on the actor's mental and physical health. He was still an in-demand character actor for the major studios—*Mark of the Vampire, Ninotchka* (both MGM), and *The Wolf Man* (Universal)—where his presence was always a welcome addition to the proceedings. On Poverty Row, he was leading-man material—*The Devil Bat, Bowery at Midnight, The Ape Man, Return of the Ape Man, The Return of the Vampire,* and a couple of comedies with the Bowery Boys. A few plum roles came his way, which brought critical acclaim, most notably playing the demented hunchback, Igor, in *Son of Frankenstein* (1939) and *Ghost of Frankenstein* (1942). With *Frankenstein Meets the Wolf Man* (1943), Lugosi was reduced to finally playing the lumbering Frankenstein monster, the role which initiated his decline.

By 1948, Abbot and Costello's careers were starting to circle the drain along with Universal-International's failing brand of highbrow entertainment. Inspired by Realart's success with reissuing their old Abbott and Costello comedies and classic monster movies, the studio heads probably held the world's shortest brainstorming meeting and commenced production of *Abbott and Costello Meet Frankenstein*. Lon Chaney, Jr., would reprise his Wolf Man character, alongside Glenn Strange, who had portrayed Frankenstein's monster in *House of Frankenstein* and *House of Dracula*. Lugosi's agent, Don Marlowe, later claimed that he had to beg Universal-International to cast Lugosi as Dracula, but studio records suggest that Lugosi was penciled in for the part well in advance. Lugosi relished his return to the screen as the famous Count and was relieved that the script was not "unbecoming to Dracula's dignity. All I have to do," Lugosi said, "is frighten the boys, a perfectly appropriate activity. My trademark will be unblemished." *Abbott and Costello Meet Frankenstein* turned out to be the second-most-successful Frankenstein movie in the series (after the original) and one of Universal-International's highest-grossing features of the year. It also was one of the funniest, if not *the* funniest, Abbott and Costello movie.

The success of *Abbott and Costello Meet Frankenstein* did nothing to resuscitate Lugosi's moribund career. There wasn't any talk of reviving the Dracula franchise or any other horror franchise at Universal-International, for that matter. After going for laughs over screams, the classic Universal monsters could no longer be taken seriously, and the genre was now in the hands of comedians. In a similar fashion, decades later, Zucker, Abrahams, and Zucker's *Airplane!* effectively wiped out the disaster-movie business, even forcing *The Concorde . . . Airport '79* to rebrand itself as a comedy on its second run. Parody, when done right, can be a genre killer.

In one of his last acts as Lugosi's agent, Don Marlowe put the word out that his client would star in a Rudolph Valentino biopic, but nothing ever came of it, and attempts to secure the lead in the comedy *Harvey* never left the talking stages. Lugosi had no choice but to stick with his professional "boogey man" status. Traveling with his fourth wife, Lillian, and tween son, Bela, Jr., Lugosi moved to New York City, where he occasionally turned up on network television shows—*Suspense, The Paul Winchell Show, The Red Skelton Hour,* and Milton Berle's *Texaco Star Theater*.

With zero movie offers coming in, Lugosi performed at midnight spook shows at movie theaters in the New York and New Jersey area. Billed as "The Bela Lugosi Horror and Magic Show," it was another rung down on the ladder of showbiz. Lugosi said, "Without movie parts I was reduced to just 'freak status.' I just couldn't stand it." The film historian William K. Everson, who knew Lugosi at the time, caught one of the shows, which consisted of Lugosi in a laboratory with a manacled girl and a gorilla. Heckled by the crowd, Everson said, "Lugosi knew it was a wretched act and hated doing it, but at the same time it was his only income."

Lugosi soldiered on. In the warm months, he toured the northeast, appearing in summer stock versions of *Dracula* and *Arsenic and Old Lace,* in which he played Jonathan Brewster, a role that had been written for Boris Karloff and which Karloff had played to accolades on Broadway. From Bridgeport, Connecticut, to Saratoga Springs, New York, from Litchfield, Massachusetts, to the Steel Pier in Atlantic City, New Jersey, Lugosi hit the straw-hat circuit, usually producing more giggles than scares.

Lillian, Lugosi's long-suffering fourth wife, was his personal assistant, costumer, registered nurse, and chauffeur. She would help with his daily injections and puff on his cigar for him, keeping it alive while Lugosi was a few feet away onstage. His wife for twenty years, and thirty years Lugosi's junior, she was also getting fed up with his jealous rages, which were bordering on the psychotic. Her comings and goings were scrutinized by the ever-incensed Lugosi. Lillian couldn't even go to the dentist without Lugosi calling to check to see what time she arrived. He was driving her batty.

At a production of *Arsenic and Old Lace* in Sea Cliff, New Jersey, Lugosi met two brothers who would have an incalculable effect on the rest of his career. Alex and Richard Gordon were British émigrés writing about American entertainment for fanzines back in England. However, they were also looking to break into the film business. They befriended Lugosi and his family after a performance, and, learning that Lugosi didn't have an agent, they promised to help him. For a couple of years, they tried and then finally arranged a twenty-six-week tour of *Dracula* in the English provinces which was supposed to culminate with a run in London's prestigious West End. It was a dream project of Lugosi's to return triumphantly to Europe, accompanied by his own silk-lined coffin.

When *Dracula* opened in try-outs at the Theatre Royal in Brighton, it was a disaster. The amateur cast couldn't remember their lines and were thrown off by Lugosi's presence. The tour was canceled before it reached London, which was, perhaps, his best career move in a long time. Stranded in England with no income, Richard Gordon salvaged the expensive trip by getting Lugosi a movie deal with Renown Pictures, which produced a series of comedies starring the music-hall team of Old Mother Riley and Her Daughter Kitty.

One of the first and most successful drag acts in twentieth-century British entertainment was Arthur Lucan, who had been dressing up as an Irish washerwoman named Old Mother Riley since 1934. With his wife, Kitty McShane, they conquered music halls, theater, radio, and movies with their musical-comedy shenanigans. They had starred in fifteen cheaply made, yet lucrative, Old Mother Riley movies, and Lugosi was there just in time to star in the sixteenth. Arthur and Kitty were hopeless drunks and weren't on speaking terms by that point, so she was fired just before filming—a move which gave Lugosi more screen time.

Mother Riley Meets the Vampire did fair business in England, but American distributors weren't interested. The title was changed to *Vampire over London* and still no one wanted it. A plan to edit out all of Old Mother Riley's scenes and then add new footage of Lugosi under the new title *King Robot* didn't work out either. It was finally released in the States as *My Son the Vampire* in 1963 with the title sung over the credits by the comic singer-songwriter Allan Sherman. Arthur Lucan had already drunk himself to death in 1954, depriving the world of what was to be his next movie, *Old Mother Riley's Trip to Mars*. Lucan's understudy, Roy Rolland, continued the Old Mother Riley character in cabaret and on television into the 1980s.

Things were not good on the home front for the Lugosis. Moving from New York to an apartment in the Baldwin Hills section of Los Angeles was a cost-saving measure, but at least they were back in Tinseltown. Unable to make ends meet while waiting for the phone to ring, Lillian did the unthinkable—she got a job. The stubbornly proud Lugosi was not happy with this option, but they had little choice. Lillian got work as the character actor Brian Donlevy's personal secretary and bookkeeper. Donlevy was producing and starring in *Dangerous Assignment,* a syndicated television series which he distributed to several markets across the country. The following year, Lillian would divorce Lugosi and, thirteen years after that, she would marry Brian Donlevy.

Often left to his own devices, Lugosi wandered the streets of Hollywood to pick up his daily newspapers. From the 1990 fanzine *From Bela Lugosi: Then and Now,* Lisa Mitchell remembered seeing the Prince of Darkness on his daily jaunts to the Midnight Delicatessen on Hollywood Boulevard:

> He was quite tall and Ichabod Crane-thin. He wore loud printed sport shirts, open at the throat, sandals and Bermuda shorts which revealed how painfully skinny his long legs were. Winter or summer, I don't think I ever saw him in anything but shorts. His hair, no longer really thick, was steel gray and combed straight back from a high forehead. And he was never without a cigar.

"I look in the mirror and I say to myself, 'Can it be you once played Romeo?'" Lugosi confessed to the fan and Bram Stoker biographer Harry Ludlum during this period. "Always, it is the same. When a film company is in the red, they come to me and say, 'Okay, so we make a horror film.' And so that is what we do. I always do."

CHAPTER 9

THE STOOGE

Success was not making Jerry Lewis a happier person. *Sailor Beware* had opened to terrific reviews, the first Muscular Dystrophy telethon had raised over a million dollars, *The Colgate Comedy Hour*, now broadcasting from the El Capitan in Hollywood, was more popular than ever, and Martin and Lewis could now turn down a month's worth of shows at the prestigious Copa because they felt like it. They had just signed a better contract with Hal Wallis, where they only had to deliver one movie a year to Paramount, instead of two. Most importantly, their comedy chops were at their peak. Martin and Lewis catchphrases were being repeated across the country from classrooms to barrooms. Jerry recorded his catchphrase "I like it! I like it!" as a best-selling single for Capitol Records. Once during a skit when Dean went off-script and asked Jerry what his name was, Jerry responded, "*Melvin!*" with such a sing-songy inflection that the printed page can't attempt to describe the hilarity of that delivery.

Asking Jerry's name and getting "Melvin!" in response became a running gag of the highest order, and a week didn't seem to go by without a "Melvin!" gag. Desperate for any new material, newsreel interviews of the pair were being advertised as full-fledged movies and even their recently canceled radio show had been renewed. They were about to begin shooting their sixth motion picture, *Jumping Jacks*. *Modern Screen* reported that "there's a telepathy between the pair that could put Western Union out of business." Martin and Lewis were the jolt of manic energy that post-war America desperately needed.

The Lewises moved into a twelve-room ranch house in L.A.'s elite Brentwood neighborhood. It was the whole movie-star deal: orange and lemon trees, swimming pool, butler, maid, and cook—the works. However, family life coupled with showbiz shenanigans was taking its toll on Jerry. Six-year-old Gary was perplexed by the man who would entertain anyone at the drop of a hat and then transform into a holy terror at home. It didn't help when Gary was traumatized for weeks after seeing a ventriloquism sketch on TV in which Dean tore Jerry's arm out by the socket and tossed it across the stage. Things were generally frosty between Jerry and Patti. "Jerry used to tell me that every person was really two people," Patti wrote in her autobiography, *I Laffed Till I Cried*. "He certainly was—the husband and father who was solicitous one day and vindictive the next."

Worn out from making the same movie over and over and running out of branches of the military to ridicule, Jerry fought for, and won, approval to appear in what was essentially a drama. *The Stooge* is a maudlin affair that's allegedly based on the real-life story of the 1920s comic Sid Silvers, who made a career of an act in which he heckled the accordionist Phil Baker from the audience. It's an uncomfortable look into the world of an egocentric performer (Dean), and the schmuck partner (Jerry) he abuses and takes for granted until the last reel. *The Stooge* was held back from release for a year and a half while its producer, Hal Wallis, pondered the implications of this bleaker version of the team. Jerry studied Charlie Chaplin's movies, looking to augment his zany persona by adding a modicum of pathos, a formula that secured the Little Tramp's international success. For the first time, Jerry appeared as the naïve victim, faithful yet helpless, pining for the audience's sympathy in between pies in the face. Pathos was an emotional setting that Jerry felt comfortable with, and it was the missing ingredient in his quest to be the ultimate artist. *The Stooge* was eventually released to positive reviews, and Jerry's ascension to actual acting, as opposed to his usual buffoonery, did not go unnoticed. Jerry would always rank *The Stooge* as his favorite Martin and Lewis movie.

At twenty-six, Jerry had become a multi-hyphenate, especially when filming on the Paramount lot. Zipping around the soundstages on a bicycle or golf cart, he became fascinated with the behind-the-scenes machinations that created the final product. As a kid, to fill up the lonely hours, Jerry had turned to gadgets and anything with moving parts. He loved cameras and radios and would take them apart and then piece them back together just to see what made them tick. While filming the *Irma* movies, he was working towards his goal of being the total filmmaker by being a total pain in the ass, pestering the crew with endless questions and peering through the cameraman's viewfinder. Jerry's fascination with film and photography led him to open his own camera store in 1950, steps away from the Brown Derby. The Jerry Lewis Camera Exchange only lasted a year, but it gave him a taste of running a business.

Jerry's next hobby was accumulating high-end movie cameras and sound and editing equipment so he could produce his own professional-looking home movies starring Hollywood buddies such as Tony Curtis, Janet Leigh, Jeff Chandler, Vince Edwards, John Barrymore, Jr., Shelley Winters, and others. From storyboards to shooting and editing, Jerry produced a series of shorts that were parodies of the current movies and some of the funniest work of his career, though, sadly, unreleased. Named after his sons Gary and Ronnie, Gar-Ron Productions held its catered, black-tie premieres at Jerry's home, complete with klieg lights and a hired film crew to document the red-carpet entrance, newsreel-style. Some of the titles included *How to Smuggle a Hernia across the Border, Fairfax Avenue, The Re-inforcer,* and *Come Back Little Shiksa*. Jerry also took an interest in guns and for kicks would shoot them into the woods with his pal Danny Kaye. Around the same time, Jerry started sleeping with a gun under his pillow.

It's never a good time in your career to find out that someone is angling to steal your livelihood. Jerry thought that he had put an end to his Sammy Petrillo problem, but it was back like the common cold. Sammy's handful of TV appearances made Jerry crazy, but now the kid was working Vegas with a Dean Martin knockoff. Hearing that Sammy and his fake Dean would be starring in a movie was more than Jerry could bear. And on top of that, his pal Jack Broder, whom he knew from the Friars Club, was producing it. Herman Cohen continues the story:

> The rumor got around that we were gonna do a movie with these two guys Mitchell and Petrillo . . . One day at the office, this guy came dashing in and he said [in an angry voice], "Where's Jack Broder?!" I said, "Well, he's in his office, right there—" It was Jerry Lewis. . . . and he was furious about this [the Mitchell-Petrillo movie]. And Jerry Lewis and Jack had a screaming session and what have you. I didn't go into the office, I stayed out. I didn't want any part of it. Then when Jerry Lewis walked out, they were still calling each other names: "You fuckin' asshole," "You this," "You that," and what have you.

Act-Alikes?

The comedy team in a new film, *Bela Lugosi Meets a Brooklyn Gorilla* — reminded many of Martin and Lewis. Their names: Sammy Petrillo and Duke Mitchell.

Jerry Lewis

Sammy Petrillo

Martin and Lewis

Mitchell and Petrillo

Quick News Weekly connects the dots. November 1952.

Jerry and Hal Wallis threatened to sue Jack Broder Productions. On May 13th, it was announced on the wire services that "Bela Lugosi has been signed by Jack Broder Productions to star in 'White Woman of the Lost Jungle.'" Seventeen-year-old Sammy Petrillo appeared in the paper that day as well, under the headline "Court OK's Film Pact":

> Sammy Petrillo, 18 year old Bronx comic who looks like Jerry Lewis of Martin and Lewis fame, today had approval of a five week movie contract with six month options starting at $250 weekly (with recently acquired partner Duke Mitchell, 23).

Sammy felt vindicated. As he later explained, "Jerry Lewis was gonna give me my own show. . . . He was gonna take care of me, take me under his wing, all that show business and all that glory, and this man was gonna back me, and all he did was sign me up and kept me in the background for months and months. He wasn't very nice."

As far as everyone knew, the plan all along was to make a fake Martin and Lewis movie. Sammy, it turns out, had other ideas. "I thought we could cultivate ourselves as a new team without having to trade in on the Martin and Lewis imitation," he said. "I even dyed my hair blond and combed it differently in an effort to play down our similarity to them. But when Hal Wallis and Jerry Lewis sent us a threatening telegram, we got mad and decided to do the imitation anyway."

According to Sammy, another offer showed up which could have stalled or killed *Brooklyn Gorilla* before the cameras even turned over. Sidney Skolsky, a Hollywood insider who wrote a syndicated gossip column from his headquarters at Schwab's drugstore, was writing and producing an Eddie Cantor knockoff of *The Jolson Story*. Sammy took a meeting with Sidney and Eddie Cantor. Sammy recalled, "[We] had this meeting and they asked me, 'If you don't make this Bela Lugosi movie, would you consider starring in *The Eddie Cantor Story*?' [I said] I'd consider it if you had a big role for Duke. But I wound up turning down their offer and doing *Brooklyn Gorilla*."

The role of Eddie Cantor went to Keefe Brasselle, whose unremarkable portrayal of Cantor was blamed for the film's failure. Brasselle later directed and starred as himself in 1975's *If You Don't Stop It . . . You'll Go Blind!!!,* a series of smutty blackout gags strung together to make a feature-length film. It was a midnight-movie hit with the college crowd. With the Eddie Cantor biopic hiccup out of the way, the Martin and Lewis knockoff movie could now commence production.

CHAPTER 10

THE GORILLAS

On May 15th, *Variety* reported that "'Bela Lugosi Meets the Gorilla Man' is the new tag for Jack Broder production previously tagged, 'White Woman of the Lost Jungle.' Film rolls today at General Service Studios under direction of William Beaudine, with cast headed by Lugosi, Duke Mitchell, and Sammy Petrillo, new comedy team, Charlita and Muriel Landers." *White Woman of the Lost Jungle* would be retitled *White Women of the Lost Jungle* before being released under its now-iconic title.

The script was a straightforward stranger-in-a-strange-land affair. The movie opens with Duke and Sammy waking up after parachuting into an exotic South Seas island. Duke falls in love with a beautiful native girl (Charlita) and Sammy runs away from her overly amorous sister (Muriel Landers). Lugosi as a mad scientist tries to kill both of them.

According to Herman Cohen, it was ten-year-old Bobby Broder's idea to put Lugosi's name in the title. "I became very friendly to Bobby to keep him on my side—Bobby could talk his dad into anything, his dad loved him so much," Herman said. "I had no trouble with Bobby, because I won him over with ice cream! Bobby was the pride of Jack because he was the first and the oldest son. He was a good-looking young kid, smart as a whip, and he actually was the 'king' behind the scenes of his dad—his dad would discuss everything with Bobby." Bobby would be known one day as Bob Broder, of the top Hollywood talent agency, Broder-Kurland-Webb-Uffner. For Lugosi, this was better than having your name above the title—it *was* the title. In 1949, Universal-International had released *Abbott and Costello Meet the Killer, Boris Karloff,* but Lugosi needed no such qualifier, no "killer," to describe who and what he was. Bela Lugosi was Bela Lugosi, and now he was going to meet the Gorilla Man.

An obviously tickled Lugosi was asked by Bob Thomas for his syndicated column, "About Hollywood," if, after playing everything from Shakespeare to Byron, he ever objected to being typecast. "No, not at all," Lugosi replied. "The main thing for an actor is to keep working. And I have managed to do so for a good many years. It is a kind of security, this being a horror man. I have just returned from playing 'Dracula' in England for eight months. I also made a picture over there . . . I have appeared on television with Milton Berle and a dozen other shows. Now I am filming 'Bela Lugosi Meets the Gorilla Man,' which is not bad publicity. I am to return to England for another picture, and I am talking about a television series. So you can see I have been busy."

Though the Gordon brothers were still in close contact with Lugosi, Richard stayed in New York to pursue a career in film distribution, while Alex moved to Hollywood, where his roommate was fellow movie buff, the writer, director, actor, and visionary Ed Wood, Jr. Lugosi asked Alex if he would chauffeur him to the set since Lillian, busy working for Brian Donlevy, could rarely drive him. Alex was also asked to be Lugosi's right-hand man, someone to keep him company on the set and fetch newspapers for him. This request put Alex in an awkward position since he had recently accused Jack Broder of plagiarism. Not long after arriving in Hollywood, Alex had submitted a script, co-written with Ed Wood, as a starring vehicle for Lugosi. It was called *The Atomic Monster,* and Jack, or more likely one of his children, had passed on it. Whether deliberately or accidentally, Realart reissued Universal's *Man-Made Monster* as *The Atomic Monster*. *Man-Made Monster* was Lon Chaney, Jr.'s 1941 horror-movie debut and it was the cheapest movie that Universal produced that year. Seeing the title of his script being sold as the latest name for an old Lon Chaney movie crushed Alex, and he asked his friend and entertainment lawyer, Samuel Z. Arkoff, what he could do about it. Arkoff knew that Alex didn't have a case, because you couldn't copyright a title, but he offered to go down to Realart with Alex to discuss it with Jack Broder. Pleading innocence, Jack pulled his young sales manager, Jim, into the meeting. Jim was responsible for retitling the old Universal clunkers for the kiddie circuit. Jim said that he never even saw the script for *The Atomic Monster*. "I'm thinking up new titles all the time," he said, "and when I came up with *The Atomic Monster,* it was an original." After some back and forth, to Arkoff's surprise, Jack offered to settle the matter by paying Alex $500, an offer which was gladly accepted.

This fairly uneventful business meeting would have reverberations that would revolutionize the film industry, ushering in a new generation and a new way of doing business. It was at this meeting that Samuel Z. Arkoff and Alex Gordon met the wunderkind behind many of Realart's more creative marketing ploys, James H. Nicholson. The three became fast friends and Jim and Arkoff would go on to form the American Releasing Company, which served up low-budget double features for the incipient teenage market. With the addition of Alex and the up-and-coming filmmaker Roger Corman, they launched American International Pictures (AIP). AIP was notable for being the first movie studio to hold focus groups and poll teenagers about their likes and dislikes. This led them to correctly identify their target audience as nineteen-year-old males.

By the end of the 1950s, Herman Cohen had joined AIP as well and produced his most popular movies, *I Was a Teenage Werewolf* and *I Was a Teenage Frankenstein*. Corman became the first distributor to publicize the works of such foreign directors as Akira Kurosawa, Ingmar Bergman, François Truffaut, and Federico Fellini. The writers and directors Francis Ford Coppola, Peter Bogdanovich, Ron Howard, Martin Scorsese, Jonathan Demme, John Sayles, James Cameron, and Joe Dante all got their starts under Corman's tutelage, as did actors such as Bruce Dern, Jack Nicholson, Diane Ladd, Dennis Hopper, William Shatner, and Peter Fonda. With the inception of AIP, Realart's hidden influence resulted in a sweeping change in American culture: the popularization of classic monsters.

Alex agreed to be Lugosi's valet, even though he felt that his presence wouldn't be welcome at the studio. On May 15th, the first day of shooting, he picked up Lugosi in his beat-up Pontiac and drove the thirty minutes up to General Service Studios. "When we arrived, Herman Cohen greeted us very nicely," Alex said. "I've always been friendly with Herman, I've known him for umpteen years, and I thought he was a nice person and a good producer, someone who knew what he was doing. He had no objections to my being Lugosi's 'butler,' which is what I was there for, to act like Lugosi's valet, which I had done before at functions—hold his cigar and all that. Herman said that, as long as I didn't get in the way of the shooting, I could just wander around and do whatever I wanted."

Alex was glad to see the legendary director William "King of the B-Movies" Beaudine attached to the project. Also known as "One-Take" or "One-Shot" Beaudine, he entered the business as an actor before becoming D. W. Griffith's assistant on *Birth of a Nation* (1915) and *Intolerance* (1916). Beaudine directed several silent short comedies starring Bobby Vernon and Snub Pollard and became an in-demand feature director who was noted for expensive-looking movies done on the cheap. Two of Mary Pickford's most expensive-looking features, *Little Annie Rooney* (1925) and *Sparrows* (1926), were directed by Beaudine, as well as talkies starring Jean Harlow and W. C. Fields. In addition to scores of Poverty Row cheapies—with the East Side Kids, the Bowery Boys, Charlie Chan, Torchy Blaine, the Shadow, and more—Beaudine directed the most popular sexploitation movie of the 1940s, *Mom and Dad* (1945), for Hygienic Productions. By the end of his career, he had directed an astounding 179 movies and television programs, ending with *Billy the Kid vs. Dracula* and *Jesse James Meets Frankenstein's Daughter* (both 1966). His last credit was a posthumous collection of *Green Hornet* TV episodes released in movie theaters in 1974 to cash in on the recent death of Bruce Lee, who had played the Green Hornet's sidekick, Kato.

Beaudine took a realistic approach to his art. "These films are going to be made regardless of who directs them," he said. "There's a market for them and the studios are going to continue to make them. I've been doing this long enough, I think I can make them as good or better than anyone else." Lugosi had worked with Beaudine on *The Ape Man* (1943), *Ghosts on the Loose* (1943), and *Voodoo Man* (1944), so he was accustomed to an easy shoot by a man who knew how to bring in movies on time and under budget. On the set, Beaudine would act out scenes for everyone, except Lugosi, whom he trusted to come up with his own bits of business. "We needed somebody who was *fast* . . . who was not too bright or intelligent, but who knew *film*," Herman said. "I went over to Monogram and I watched him work on several things, and I said, 'Jack, this is the director for this movie. He knows comedy, he knows crap.'"

In his introduction to a MaltinFest screening of *Brooklyn Gorilla* held at the Egyptian Theatre in Hollywood in 2019, the film historian Leonard Maltin remarked, "I was talking to a friend last week and he said, 'You know, [*Brooklyn Gorilla*] was actually not a badly made movie.' No, it's not! William Beaudine was a very experienced director, who for some reason I cannot fully explain, found himself in the B-movie rut for [most of] his career. He made literally hundreds of movies and television episodes, so he was an old pro."

The cameraman Charles Van Enger was no slouch, either. From shooting all of Ernst Lubitsch's silent movies in the '20s to grinding out episodes of *Gilligan's Island* forty years later, Van Enger amassed a staggering eighty-four TV and movie credits. He also shot *The Hunchback of Notre Dame* (uncredited), *The Phantom of the Opera* (both starring

Lon Chaney, Sr.), a few Sherlock Holmes mysteries, the *Lassie* series, and *Abbott and Costello Meet Frankenstein*. Herman used him for several more movies. "This guy was terrific," Herman would say, "and we were lucky to get him. There was nothing that he didn't know about lighting—*nothing*. And he was fast—God, he was fast!"

The original music Richard Hazard wrote for *Brooklyn Gorilla* is quite good—not rehashed B-movie schlock. His first score was for Herman Cohen's debut feature for Allied Artists, *Disc Jockey*, in 1951. Hazard played keyboards on the soundtrack of *Soylent Green* and orchestrated Jerry Lewis's *Way . . . Way Out* with Lalo Schifrin. Working under Schifrin, Hazard also conducted the scores for the TV shows *Mission: Impossible* and *Mannix*. His later credits include *Terms of Endearment, The Right Stuff,* and *The Wiz*.

Generally speaking, the crew assembled by Herman Cohen, who did the lion's share of the producing work, was exemplary. Each person either had a rich history in Hollywood where his expertise could help the production or was bound for greater achievements.

The editorial supervisor Philip Cahn worked at Universal for decades, including editing a half-dozen Abbott and Costello movies and 1944's *House of Frankenstein*. *Brooklyn Gorilla* benefits from Cahn's brisk cutting, especially in the second half of the film, when the action bounces between the castle and the jungle. The art direction by James Sullivan is about as realistic as one could hope for when creating a tropical paradise out of a hundred potted plants on a Poverty Row soundstage.

The script for *Brooklyn Gorilla* was by Tim Ryan and Edmond G. Seward, who had co-written several Bowery Boys features, many of them directed by William Beaudine. Tim and his wife Irene Noblitt, also known at various times as Noblett, Noblette, or Ryan, had one of the more successful "Dumb Dora" acts of the 1930s, very similar to Burns and Allen's routines. Tim and Irene starred in several two-reelers for bottom-of-the-barrel Educational Films, which touted itself as "The Spice of the Program." Tim's henpecked catchphrase "*Will you stop*?" captured the country's imagination, and they were able to coast off that punchline for several years. After divorcing Tim in 1942, Irene Ryan found fame as Granny on Paul Henning's rural sitcom *The Beverly Hillbillies* from 1962 to 1971. Tim usually played dumb bartenders and cops and co-starred with Mickey Rooney's father, Joe Yule, in a series of Maggie and Jiggs comedies. He also worked as a screenwriter, with over forty credits to his name.

Edmond G. Seward, who contributed additional dialogue, was another writer and actor known for adapting Jonathan Swift's satirical novel *Gulliver's Travels* into a screenplay for the Fleischer Brothers animated feature. Additional dialogue was also offered up by Leo "Ukie" Sherin, a former Borscht Belt comic and gag writer at Vitaphone's Brooklyn studios (credited as a "dialogue director"). Ukie served as Bing Crosby's on-air foil on the radio and wrote a B side, "Don't Forget Tonight Tomorrow," for Frank Sinatra in 1945. He also appeared on an episode of Spade Cooley's TV show *The Hoffman Hayride* along with Bela Lugosi and Stepin Fetchit. Entertaining in Dallas in the '50s, he befriended the club owner Jack Ruby who, in a 1963 jailhouse visit after Ruby had assassinated Lee Harvey Oswald, told Ukie (in Yiddish) that he had had nothing to do with John F. Kennedy's assassination. Ukie's association with Ruby earned him a few mentions in the Warren Commission Report (volume XXIII).

The men's costumes were designed by Wesley Jeffries, so if there's anyone to blame for Duke's odd way of wearing a Hawaiian shirt—with the shirttails tied into a knot, teenage-girl-style—then it would probably be Jeffries. Duke and Sammy also sport Levi's, which according to Sammy, makes Mitchell and Petrillo one of the first teams to work in jeans. "People wouldn't do that in the '50s," Sammy said. "Also, if you look closely, you'll see that I was wearing those pointy 'Beatles' boots ten years before the Beatles!" Jeffries also did the wardrobe for Lugosi's last real movie, *The Black Sleep,* and was a costumer for *The Manchurian Candidate* and wardrobe coordinator for the Elvis Presley period piece *Frankie and Johnny.*

Esther Krebs designed the women's wardrobe, which mainly consisted of sarongs for Charlita and Muriel Landers. Charlita played Duke's love interest, Nona, while Muriel Landers, as Nona's comically overweight sister Saloma, chased Sammy around the jungle. Charlita's low-slung sarong got *Brooklyn Gorilla* flagged by the National League of Decency for "Suggestive Costuming," classifying the movie as being "Morally Objectionable" for "Adults and Adolescents." Charlita was a public advocate for nudism and thought that women should go topless at the beach "because that is the most beautiful part of a woman's body—why hide it?" In a press-baiting interview, she claimed that she "wanted to go topless in her current jungle epic, *Bela Lugosi Meets the Brooklyn Gorilla*, but the censors trembled at the thought."

Born to Portuguese parents, Clara Isabella DeFreitas moved from New Hampshire to Hollywood to pursue showbiz and its spoils. Adopting the stage name Charlita, she worked as a model and led the musical outfit Charlita and Her Men of Rhumba at local dine-and-dance joints, opening for Lawrence Welk and His Orchestra. Despite her Boston accent, she was described in the press as a "Mexican Pepper Pot" and parlayed her exotic beauty into a handful of small movie roles. Unfortunately, Charlita was usually typecast as hot-headed vixens: Chiquita in *Brimstone,* Raquelita in *The Brave Bulls,* Rosina the Fortune Teller in *South of Caliente,* and small floozy roles in *Ten Tall Men* and *Rancho Notorious.* A two-minute walk-on as Princess Papoola in 1951's *Let's Go Navy!* didn't further her artistic arc, but at least it was fun to film. "Leo Gorcey and Huntz Hall kept looking at me cross-eyed while I did a hula number," laughed Charlita. "I was in stitches." The 1951 James Cagney melodrama *Come Fill the Cup* afforded Charlita a little more screen time as a nightclub singer, but she played the same hot-tempered minx. She accentuated her exotic side by arriving on the set accompanied by an enormous Persian cat on a leash with a rhinestone collar.

Charlita's swimsuit-modeling career never flagged; however, in her thirty-first year, she was photographed burning her bikini in protest. "Cheesecake art helped me get noticed in Hollywood," she said, "but now those Bikini pictures are hurting me. Producers just can't believe that a Bikini model can act. Producers always want to cast me in Mexican roles. I can play Jewish, Irish, or Italian girls as well."

In Erskine Johnson's syndicated column "Hollywood Notes," Charlita conceded that she was "just a mid-riff actress." "Honey, it's a problem," she told the columnist. "I'm looking my leading man straight in the face and he keeps taking peeks at my stomach."

Charlita told the press that she needed a "good girl" role soon or her family would disown her. "They're Portuguese," she explained. "And very strict . . . the only jobs I can find in Hollywood are painted-lady parts. And all my relatives that see me on the screen are horrified." Her next feature-film role would turn out to be her largest and would not require her rhumba, hula, or singing skills. Charlita would get that good-girl role that she always wanted, and it would involve being Duke Mitchell's love interest and working closely with Ramona the Chimp.

"Ramona the Chimp was really Cheeta the Monkey," Sammy said. "It was *the* Cheeta at the time of Tarzan fame. . . . This was the current Cheeta and it actually was a boy. And we named the monkey Ramona because we wanted a girl monkey in *Bela Lugosi Meets a Brooklyn Gorilla* to fall in love with me."

With all due respect to Sammy's memory, there is no simian way possible that Ramona in 1952 was the same chimp as Cheeta from twenty years earlier. Ramona is not Cheeta and this anonymous (and very

Charlita Meets a Brooklyn Gorilla, 1952.

talented) chimpanzee (not a "monkey," as Sammy called him; chimpanzees are apes) will heretofore be referred to by his screen name, Ramona. According to Herman Cohen, "We got [Ramona] from a company in Saugus that had chimps and apes and what have you. He was smart."

The chimp that wasn't Cheeta discussed his experience on the *Brooklyn Gorilla* set in his as-told-to 2009 memoir, *Me Cheeta: My Life in Hollywood* (actually a piece of pseudonymous fanciful auto-fiction)—"Petrillo's impersonation of Jerry Lewis was uncannily accurate. He was every bit as unfunny as Jerry . . ."—while also claiming to have co-starred with Ronald Reagan in *Bedtime for Bonzo* and Rex Harrison in 1967's *Doctor Dolittle*. In a business where everyone is pretending to be somebody else, even the chimp has a fake résumé.

Ramona and Sammy, 1952. Courtesy of David Kopple.

The rest of the cast had just the right amount of acting chops to counterbalance the top-heavy talent that propelled *Brooklyn Gorilla*. Pepe Bordo, the tropical island's constable, was essayed by the journeyman character actor Martin Garralaga. A familiar face in *Casablanca, Treasure of the Sierra Madre, Jolson Sings Again,* and *Bride of the Gorilla*, Garralaga appeared, mostly uncredited, in nearly 300 movies, usually as a hotel desk clerk or a cop.

Lugosi's henchman, Chula, was played by the veteran character actor Mickey Simpson. According to Sammy, they couldn't come up with a name, so Sammy suggested "Chula." "The joke is that Chula is a Greek term for prick," Sammy said.

An ex-boxer and one-time chauffeur for Claudette Colbert, Simpson would notably torment Shemp Howard in 1952's *Gents in a Jam* and clobber Rock Hudson to a pulp in the climax of James Dean's last movie, *Giant*.

Looking like a bad-acid-trip version of *Sesame Street*'s Big Bird, Milton Newburger's turn as Bongo the Witch Doctor early in the picture is abrasive and shrill, setting the tone for the comedy to follow. Newburger's only other role was an uncredited appearance as a deputy in the Mickey Rooney western *The Twinkle in God's Eye*.

The Hawaiian-born Al Kikume was cast as Charlita's father, Chief Rakos. Kikume was a warrior in 1933's Poverty Row serial *Tarzan the Fearless,* starring Buster Crabbe, and spent his career mostly playing ethnic cops and head waiters. He had recently appeared as a head waiter in *Sailor Beware*.

Muriel Landers portrays Nona's love-starved sister Saloma, whom Sammy refers to throughout the movie as "Salami." Landers had studied acting in New York City, but, at five-foot-two and weighing in at 200 pounds, conventional roles weren't an option. Herman recalled, "We also had a fat little broad named Muriel Landers—*she* was funny. In the picture, she was in love with Sammy Petrillo and was chasing him all around. I remember Bela Lugosi laughing at her—he also thought she was funny." Landers honed her comic timing and became an in-demand comedienne who found work with A-listers such as Frank Sinatra, Jack Benny, Jimmy Durante, and Ray Bolger. She would eventually show up in the Three Stooges short *Sweet and Hot*, where she sings "Let's Fall in Love" to a cow, and a couple of Jerry Lewis movies: *Who's Minding the Store?* and *The Disorderly Orderly*. One of Landers's last roles was in 1967's *Doctor Dolittle,* where she co-starred with the aforementioned not-Cheeta. *Bela Lugosi Meets a Brooklyn Gorilla* was Muriel Landers's first feature-film appearance.

While the five native warriors in headdresses and checkered beach towels resemble William Frawley on laundry day, a couple of the actors are actually of South Seas descent. They had hundreds of onscreen appearances between them; however, only Jurado Decordovier, an American Samoan, would appear twenty-five years later as a senator in Tom Laughlin's answer to *Mr. Smith Goes to Washington, Billy Jack Goes to Washington*.

Spoiler alert: there are two gorillas in *Bela Lugosi Meets a Brooklyn Gorilla* or, more accurately, two performers in two gorilla suits—one who was definitely in the movie but preferred to remain anonymous and one who was among the most famous gorilla-suit performers ever but who might not have actually set foot on the set at all.

Sammy, Steve Calvert, and presumably Bobby Kaye in a posed shot on the *Brooklyn Gorilla* set, 1952.

The gorilla-suit legend Raymond Benitz was born in Milwaukee, Wisconsin, in 1902. Benitz began his career in MGM's 1932 *Tarzan the Ape Man* and went on to become the dependable gorilla go-to from prestige studios down to Poverty Row productions. After appearing as an "orangopoid" in the first Flash Gordon serial, he starred in a watery knockoff serial for Republic Pictures, *The Undersea Kingdom.* In a savvy showbiz move, Benitz took his character's screen name as his own: Ray "Crash" Corrigan.

He became a bigger-than-life figure in the stuntman community and a physical-fitness trainer for movie stars. While on a hunting trip with Clark Gable in 1937, Corrigan decided to buy a plot of land, name it Corriganville, and rent it out for location shooting. The movie ranch opened to the public as a western theme park in 1949, complete with stuntmen shows and pony rides. (In 1966 Corrigan sold the property to Bob Hope, who renamed it Hopetown, one year before Charles Manson and his followers moved down the road to the neighboring Spahn Ranch.)

Corrigan's leading-man status was short-lived, and soon he was playing gorillas again in *Three Missing Links, The Strange Case of Doctor Rx, The Ape, Captive Wild Woman, Nabonga, White Pongo, The White Gorilla, Killer Ape, Dizzy Detectives,* and many more movies too numerous to mention. In the late '40s, looking to cut back on his gorilla work, Corrigan walked into Ciro's on the Sunset Strip, struck up a conversation with the head bartender, and found his successor.

William Seeger was a movie extra, a stuntman, and a stand-in at various Hollywood studios in the 1930s and '40s. He was getting a decent amount of work, but he never quit his main gig, which was bartending at Ciro's—the main hangout for Hollywood's stars and the gossip columnists that fueled their careers. In Seeger, Corrigan found a similar spirit, a fellow traveler who, if trained correctly, might carry on the rich tradition of portraying gorillas in the movies. More to the point, Corrigan had an extra gorilla suit he wanted to unload and would Seeger be interested? Seeger glanced at a bottle of Calvert Blended Whiskey, changed his name to Steve Calvert, and never looked back.

It was a weighty, eighty-five-pound commitment of a gorilla suit and Calvert had to get into shape fast. The headpiece was a furry bucket that couldn't be worn for more than five minutes at a time without the human inside passing out. Corrigan taught Calvert all the tricks and nuances—the walk, mannerisms, and general psychology of the great ape. Calvert's first job was chasing a forty-four-year-old Johnny Weissmuller through a backlot in the first Jungle Jim picture. He took home $200 for nine days' work but still kept his shift at Ciro's.

Wearing the recognizable "Crash" Corrigan gorilla suit caused some confusion among the historians of such things, both then and now; however, it's safe to assume that any movie with a "Crash" Corrigan–like gorilla made after 1948 really was Steve Calvert under that ape head. From *Bride of the Gorilla* to *Bride and the Beast,* from chasing after the Bowery Boys to pursuing Hope and Crosby, Calvert was very good at what he did, what one might call a natural. Calvert went on to be a sought-after television gorilla, scaring the bejesus out of Ed Wynn, Tennessee Ernie Ford, and Johnny Carson as well as playing an inspired, improvised game of ping pong with Buster Keaton.

For all of his accomplishments, Calvert was a professional who toiled anonymously. "The studios kept up the misconception that the gorilla was real, and I never insisted on screen credit," Calvert said. "It would've spoiled the illusion." It was believed for many years that "Crash" Corrigan appeared in *Brooklyn Gorilla* as the second gorilla. Since both suits had that distinctive Corrigan look, it wasn't an absurd assumption. The administrator of the Facebook group "Ape Suit Cinema," Craig Scott Lamb, has the most detailed and credible answer, so far:

> Though it has been reported by some that Corrigan played the second gorilla in this film I personally have serious doubts about that because the "second gorilla" does not move or act like Corrigan at all. I strongly suspect that the second gorilla was actually played by Calvert's long time friend Bobby Kaye aka Robert Smiley (sometimes erroneously called Bobby Small). Bobby Kaye is known to have played the second gorilla in *The Bride and the Beast* (1958) and the acting style leads me to believe that it was Kaye NOT Corrigan that played the second gorilla in *Bela Lugosi Meets a Brooklyn Gorilla* as well.

Herman Cohen was very happy with his selection of Steve Calvert to play the gorilla. He also never paid for a drink at Ciro's again.

Depending on who's telling the story, *Bela Lugosi Meets a Brooklyn Gorilla* cost either $50,000, which was Alex Gordon and Sammy's account, or $130,000 (including Lugosi's salary) according to Herman, whose recollections might be more accurate, since he was closer to the accounting department. "Jack Broder would come onto the set a few times during the day," Herman recalled. "Jack was a very short guy, and he had a habit of putting his right hand in his belt—he'd walk like Napoleon. He'd say, 'Herman. You tell dem if dere behind schedule, I pool the shwitch. I pool the shwitch!' Then when Jack would leave the soundstage, Maurice Duke would get up and repeat Broder: 'Herman! If dere behind schedule, pool the shwitch! Pool the shwitch!' That used to be our running gag every night! Oh, Maurice Duke had a *great* sense of humor."

Jack Broder's second-oldest child after Bobby was Madelynn, then ten years old. In an interview with the author sixty years later, and after a successful career as a Santa Monica criminal defense attorney, she recalled her days visiting the set:

> I remember that there was a guard at the gate, but there was no security issue. We could walk around anywhere. It wasn't a major studio like Warner Bros. I would bring my wagon and my Girl Scout cookies. Herman Cohen, my father's right-hand guy, who would go on to greater things, escorted me around to the various sets to sell my cookies. We couldn't come back until all of the cookies were sold.

> Herman didn't care for it too much, but he was a good sport about it. I also remember a lot of people dressed up like natives in colorful outfits. It was a fun experience. It was a happy set. It wasn't like we were going out to dinner or lunch at fancy Hollywood restaurants. They brought in sandwiches from some deli. Cookies and chips and stuff like that. I vaguely remember Bela Lugosi. I think he was very fragile at the time. He was a larger-than-life-type person. Everyone was in awe of him because he was so famous.

Lugosi was only needed on set for four out of the nine shooting days, and that was four days of aggravation for Herman. He was habitually missing from the stage when a shot was ready for him, and it was Herman's job to chase him down. "I thought he was going to the bathroom or something," said Herman. "I didn't realize, young *pisher* that I was, that he was taking morphine."

Alex Gordon, who had clocked in long hours traveling with Lugosi in England, was seemingly oblivious to the monkey on Dracula's back. "I had no idea that Lugosi was on any drugs at the time," Alex said. "I never saw him with a needle in his hand or anything like that. And I was at his house *so* many times, Ed Wood and I, or I alone. We knew he had a liquor problem; he was never drunk in our presence, but we knew he liked to knock 'em back. But I had absolutely no knowledge of [Lugosi's morphine addiction] until much later, when I saw the headline in the *Herald Examiner* that he had entered a hospital for drug treatment."

Herman remembered Lugosi as "a nice old guy and he was happy just to be working. They brought him there, they told him what to do, he did it for the money—that's my recollection of Bela Lugosi."

On the Marc Maron podcast WTF in 2017, Martin Landau, who had won an Academy Award for his portrayal of Lugosi in Tim Burton's *Ed Wood,* recalled his prep work for the role:

> Tim [Burton] kept sending me Bela Lugosi movies, including one that I became a huge fan of. . . . It's got Martin and Lewis look-alikes—one sings and one does spastic humor and they're on an island running in muumuus and there's a castle on the island and there's a mad scientist on the island, Bela Lugosi, who's injecting serum into monkeys that overnight become actors in terrible gorilla suits and it's called *Bela Lugosi Meets a Brooklyn Gorilla* and it makes Ed Wood's movies look like *Gone With the Wind.* I'm not kidding. It's . . . you gotta see this movie because Lugosi

is working his ass off playing this part in this piece of trash. My heart went out to him.

Despite Lugosi's infirmities, *Brooklyn Gorilla* was, according to Herman, "a fun set. There were lots of visitors, because they wanted to see Bela Lugosi. Not Mitchell and Petrillo—Bela Lugosi. General Service was like a family in those days."

Ramona wasn't crazy about Sammy and tried to bite him in a scene. "The trainer suggested, 'Why don't you take the chimp out for an ice cream cone and maybe you'll get closer?'" Sammy recalled. "I bought this chimpanzee an ice cream cone and we're walking through the lot and all of a sudden I hear this laugh, 'Eh, eh, eh, eh, eh, eh,' and then I hear a guy say, 'Deez ez thee funniest *theeng* I've ever seen!' and I turn around and it's Desi Arnaz and he says, 'You must come here to meet my wife Lucy! She must see this!' And Lucy saw us and fell down laughing!" Burns and Allen, Shelley Winters, and Vittorio Gassman, and, according to Herman, "Ozzie and Harriet and their two little sons [David and Ricky Nelson] came on [the set] and, oh God, this one gal I *loved*, Joan Davis, who was then doing her TV series *I Married Joan*. . . . In those days, everything was fun."

"Duke and I thought that we would become big stars," Sammy said, years later. "We used to get up at 5:30 in the morning for makeup. We had stand-ins that would stand under the lights for us. It was a little bit ridiculous, but it made us feel like, 'Oh, we've made it. We're in Hollywood. We're stars.'"

Sammy said that Beaudine not only allowed ad-libbing but encouraged it. "He was the most easygoing guy; when he was directing, it was almost like he wasn't there. He was of the philosophy that if you let a comic run wild, you'll get something great out of it. So I would suggest a joke to Beaudine and he'd let me go with it."

Alex Gordon disagreed. "This annoyed Bill Beaudine *very* much . . . [Sammy] would improvise on his line, because he always thought that he could do better than the lines that were written for him. He didn't tell anyone ahead of time—no one would know until they were actually shooting. He'd say [about the script], 'This is *rubbish* that you got here.' Petrillo was even more obnoxious than Jerry Lewis in person, and that's really saying something if you knew Jerry Lewis. [Sammy] was never ready when they called him, never on the set—he was always doing something else or in his dressing room or whatever, and they had to drag him out. Petrillo was in all respects really trying to *do* a Jerry Lewis. Everybody hated Lewis at Paramount . . . and Petrillo was hated by everybody at Jack

Broder Productions! I have seldom encountered people like this, people who are *that* obnoxious and *so* egomaniacal—except, of course, the original [Jerry Lewis]! Mitchell and Petrillo never spoke their proper lines—they were all over the place and making fun of Lugosi and so on—but he stoically spoke his lines and did his stuff."

Like any gig that Lugosi took in his long career, when signed onto a project, he was on board 100%. With the help of his son, Lugosi studied the *Brooklyn Gorilla* script at home, incessantly trying out different approaches to the dialogue. "Dad used to rehearse lines at home," Bela, Jr., said, "and he'd take one line at a time and he'd dissect it, and put an emphasis on a different word each time, until he got that sentence just the way he liked it and then he'd move on to the next sentence." Lugosi had memorized the plays of George du Maurier and William Shakespeare, so why not the works of Tim Ryan with additional dialogue from Ed Seward and Ukie Sherin? No stranger to the world of comedy, Lugosi could hold his own masterfully, as long as everyone else stuck to the script. With his lack of English skills, drug addiction, and advancing age stacked against him, there was no chance that Lugosi would ever be able to add improvisation to his bag of acting tricks. "But he was a nice man—oh, golly!" Herman remembered. "I used to break up talking to him, because he always was playing Dracula. 'Herrrman! Herrrman, I vant to talk vith yyyooouuu . . .!' I used to break up!"

Herman Cohen remembered that "On the set, Mitchell and Petrillo were funny guys. Duke Mitchell was much more classy than Sammy, but Sammy was the Jerry Lewis character and Duke thought he was Dean Martin. They were easy to get along with . . . we told 'em what the *fuck* to do and they *did* it. . . . Petrillo was a nutty kid. Duke Mitchell was much more serious. Petrillo, as they say in Yiddish, was *meshuggah*—he was crazy. And he was funny. But he was insecure."

"People don't realize that I was playing an adult part as a seventeen-year-old kid," Sammy said in hindsight.

Throughout the ensuing decades, Sammy would have nothing but positive things to say about working with Lugosi. "He had a *great* sense of humor," Sammy would say. "During the making of the picture he'd say to me, 'And so, Jerry . . .' He knew who I was, but he'd call me Jerry as a joke. So I'd say to him, 'Listen, Boris . . .' He was just beautiful. May he rest in peace."

The feeling might not have been mutual, according to Huntz Hall, who struck up a friendship with Lugosi on the set of the East Side Kids comedy *Spooks Run Wild* in 1941. "Bela took his work very seriously and did not

Duke, Sammy, and Charlita. Halcyon days, 1952.

like to clown around on the set," Huntz said. "But Bela had a great sense of humor! He loved to laugh, but not to be laughed at. That would make him more angry than anything!" In an interview in *Filmfax* from 1990, Huntz recalled visiting Lugosi in his *Brooklyn Gorilla* dressing room. "I heard that Petrillo and Mitchell were putting him on a lot," Huntz said, "trying to make a jerk out of him. So I said, 'How are you getting along with the boys?' And he said, 'They're *scum!*' You couldn't make a jerk out of Bela Lugosi. He was brilliant. You know, he was a European matinee idol before he came to this country. I loved him. All those guys who play monsters are always nice guys."

During Sammy's 1991 appearance on the idiosyncratic New York City public-access TV show *Beyond Vaudeville,* the simmering Huntz Hall controversy stirred up by *Filmfax* was addressed: "Huntz Hall, may he rest in peace [Huntz would live another eight years], recently said something very derogatory about my relationship with Lugosi, which I won't go into, but whatever he said was not true and I might sue him."

Sometimes Sammy would refer to Lugosi as an old Jewish gentleman. Michael Townsend Wright, the versatile character actor who famously appeared on *The Uncle Floyd Show* and in several movies, including a hilarious turn in the Owen Kline comedy *Funny Pages*, met Sammy in the

’70s at a burlesque show in New Jersey. Sammy performed schtick and projected a 16mm print of the Marx Brothers movie *Duck Soup*. “I was mystified by Sammy’s recollection of Lugosi,” Michael recalled. “He said that Lugosi was an old, tall, Jewish man. He was in denial. I remember that because even back then I was aware that Lugosi was not Jewish, but Sammy was [Jewish], of course.”

Further muddying the waters are stories of Sammy denying his Semitic background. The impressionist Will Jordan told the comedy historian Kliph Nesteroff, “I didn’t understand why he always said he was Italian. I said, ‘Sammy, your mother was Jewish. Doesn’t mean to say you’re not Italian, but shouldn’t you say you’re *half*-Italian?’ For some reason he wanted it known that he was Italian and not part-Jewish. There must have been a reason.”

CHAPTER 11

BELA LUGOSI MEETS A BROOKLYN GORILLA

Bela Lugosi Meets a Brooklyn Gorilla is better than any Martin and Lewis film for the simple reason that Bela Lugosi is in it. Lugosi doesn't even show up until a third of the way through the movie, yet his commanding presence casts a shadow over the scenes in which he doesn't appear. He's the B-movie Harry Lime, where the anticipation of his inevitable arrival is powerful and palpable. And when Lugosi does arrive, he walks away with the picture.

"When shooting began, everybody was in awe of Bela," Herman said. "The set became quiet the minute he arrived and the kibitzing and joking sort of stopped. He seemed to command a lot of respect whenever he talked to anyone, but he could be quite talkative and charming."

Brooklyn Gorilla is, at its core, a comic reworking of *Bride of the Gorilla*. Raymond Burr as a plantation manager, Barney Chavez, and Duke Mitchell as Duke Mitchell are each punished for going after the wrong girl. In line with Jack Broder's penchant for simian-themed movies, those punishments involve them being turned into gorillas. In *Bride of the Gorilla,* Barney kills his boss to hook up with the widow, played by the slinky Barbara Payton. A native witch catches him in the act and casts a spell that transforms Barney into a bloodthirsty gorilla every night. Deep in the jungle, a chastisement such as this appears reasonable. Barney prefers being a gorilla, anyway. Duke's transformation into a singing ape at the hands of Lugosi's Dr. Zabor seems harsh by comparison. However, there's no sense in jumping ahead. The beginning is usually the best place to start.

"This is the jungle, the vast wilderness of giant, lush foliage," the unseen narrator in *Brooklyn Gorilla* intones as the movie opens with grainy stock footage of wild animals. The camera moves in on Duke and Sammy sprawled unconscious on the ground, wearing shredded tuxedos, bearded and mop-topped. "And here? What have we *here*?" asks the narrator incredulously. "Who *are* these men? What could they *possibly* be doing in this cruel tropical wilderness?"

Native warriors bring the passed-out duo back to the village and jungle-talk gibberish ensues between Chief Rakos, his daughter Nona, and Bongo the witch doctor. Sammy immediately addresses the Martin and Lewis elephant in the room by saying in a Jerry Lewis voice that "You got us mixed up with two other guys." When Sammy is told that the native men in the jungle carried them to safety, he cracks, "Yeah, whadda we owe them for carrying charges?" and laughs uproariously at his own joke. "Get it? Carrying charges? Funny one! Let's laugh it up here, lady! [realizing his joke bombed] Ohhh . . ."

The bad jokes continue, and after almost every one of them Sammy screws up his face, purses his lips, and looks downward in shame. He deals with embarrassment as a child might, or specifically, as Jerry Lewis imitating a child might. After Sammy goes off-script to insult Chief Rakos ("Well, gee, you sure look super, chief. Superchief! Get it? Ha ha ha ha ha . . ."), Duke reprimands Sammy: "You know, someday I'm gonna let you fry in your own grease?" "Can you make it chicken fat . . . *maybe*?" Sammy asks querulously.

In a native dance sequence, choreographed by Lee Scott, who also was working on *I Love Lucy* on an adjoining stage, Sammy ramps up his first in-your-face Jerry Lewis impression. Running away from the amorous Saloma, a shirtless Sammy unexpectedly finds himself in the middle of a native dance routine. Trying to match the dancer's moves, Sammy dances like he's on a hot plate. He twirls and leaps in the air with a dedicated frenzy that only a teenager like Sammy might possess. Three months earlier, *Sailor Beware* had been released, with an almost-identical sequence in which Jerry disguises himself as a South Seas dancer in order to elude his commanding officer. Jerry tries to fall in with a native dance, but he's hopelessly out of step. As wacky as Jerry is, dancing with natives or creating havoc in the Navy, Sammy's version of Jerry might not be funnier, but it is wackier. His voice is higher-pitched. When he bugs his

Sammy, Duke, and the Chimp That Wasn't Cheetah, 1952. Courtesy of David Kopple.

eyes, they're a little bigger. When he opens his mouth, it's a little larger. His Jewishness is more Jewish. Sammy is a Silly Putty image of Jerry that's just stretched thinner. What Sammy is doing is almost as much a parody of Jerry as it is a steal. And none of this could have made Jerry very happy.

After the dance, Sammy tries to entertain the natives with stale jokes, which they don't understand. He bombs. Sammy runs the gamut from "A fella told me that he hadn't had a bite in three days, so I bit him" to "Did you take a bath this morning? Why—is there one missing?" Saloma throws Sammy over her shoulder and carries him away while Sammy screams, "Ahhhh . . . Dukey! Dukey!" When asked to dance, Duke says, "Well, I don't dance, but I'll do eight or ten tunes for ya."

Jack Broder's daughter Madelynn was on the soundstage the day this was filmed. "I remember the set and I remember the hula dance," she said. "There were a lot of people dressed up like natives in colorful outfits. I remember the scene when Sammy Petrillo was doing some goofy stuff

54 CONTINUED:

NONA
Do you think perhaps she is too rough?

DUKE
Guess she doesn't know her own strength.

NONA
(turjs toward Saloma)
Saloma! Saloma!

55 CLOSEUP - SAMMY AND SALOMA

She is swinging him around. She hears Nona - turns - lets go of Sammy. He flies out of scene.

56 AT PALM TREE

Sammy flies into scene, hits palm tree. Four cocoanuts fall on his head (accompanied by xylophone sound effect and finish of music).

57 CLOSEUP - SALOMA

She looks from Nona to Sammy. Runs to him. Sammy is out. She picks him up like a baby.

SAMMY
(groggy)
Did anyone get the license number?

Saloma carries Sammy out of scene.

58 GROUP - NONA, DUKE, ETC.

Saloma carries Sammy in. Nona and Duke are amused. Sammy is groggy and cuddling up to Saloma. He slowly opens his eyes - sees her - does a "take" - starts yellin

59 CLOSEUP - CHIEF

He barks at Saloma.

RAKOS
Saloma! Toma - Dundar - Vita!

and I think that Duke Mitchell was singing, and he sang great. He sang like Dean Martin."

Herman also conceded that Duke "had a pretty good voice." Alex thought that Duke "was certainly not an actor. I understood that he was sort of a nightclub singer, but on a very small scale, one who appeared in some small places around town. Not many people that I talked to seemed to have heard of him. He was very *vague* about everything, and haphazard. He sort of went through the motions of everything, probably thinking he was another Dean Martin. But he certainly was not. He didn't *look* anything like him and he didn't have that kind of voice, and he had no personality whatsoever."

Duke tears off a swinging version of "'Deed I Do," an old chestnut of a song that Ruth Etting and Johnny Marvin had top-ten hits with in 1927. The co-writer, Fred Rose, composed over a dozen iconic songs with Hank Williams and created the first Nashville-based music publishing company, Acuff-Rose. Lyrics were courtesy of Walter Hirsch, who also co-wrote "Who's Your Little Who-Zis!", which Dean sings in *The Stooge*.

In a scene in which Duke has a makeout session with Nona, Sammy gets an opportunity to unleash another impression. "It's getting awful sticky around here!" Sammy says in a nasal Groucho voice, staring into the camera. Sammy's eyebrows maniacally go up and down, forcing his crew-cut hairline to go up and down with it. Even Sammy's Groucho is over the top.

Unafraid to steal from the best, in a gag lifted from the "Help is on the way!" sequence in the Marx Brothers' *Duck Soup*, Sammy gestures frantically at stock footage of steer, giraffes, and leaping gazelles as he screams, "Run for your lives! Run for your lives! G'wan, *get outta here—* run for your lives!" Sammy looks at the camera. "Maybe I should run for mine, too, *no*?" Sammy's Yiddishisms abound throughout the movie, from the repeated exclamation of "oy gevalt" to inflections that go up in pitch on the last word of the sentence, *yes*?

We first set sights on Lugosi as he portrays Dr. Zabor, hard at work in his laboratory, wrestling with a mortar and pestle and surrounded by a maze of beakers and test tubes. Lugosi is in his happy place, and this is one of his last roles as a full-on evil genius, fueled by jealousy with a dash of

The four coconuts falling on Sammy's head gag that never made it to the screen. Courtesy of David Kopple.

revenge. Entering the lab with Duke and Nona, Sammy breaks Dr. Zabor's studious experimentations.

"It looks like the monkey house at the Bronx Zoo," Sammy says, spying a cage bearing two capuchin monkeys. He snatches a test tube from the table and asks what's in it. "Streptococci," replies Zabor.

"Hello, Strepta! Hello, Cockeye!" Sammy blurts out, to no one's amusement.

"I'm performing a series of experiments in evolution," Zabor explains. "Scientists have proven that all living things originated in a process of evolution. They also know that there is a growth force that tends to make genetic changes, physiologically and morphologically. Chimpanzees and gorillas are the highest members of the ape family and are the ancestors of men. Darwin, in his provisional hypothesis, assumes that every living cell contains a genus, which is a hypothetical granular. I have found the chemical formula that stimulates the growth force. Where nature takes years, I can, in a matter of hours, make a complete embryonic metamorphosis, both physiological and morphological. Do you understand?"

Sammy semi-memorized the speech and in his later years would recite most of it at the drop of a hat. "He did that whole speech in one take," Sammy said. "We couldn't believe it. Everybody just froze. . . . The whole crew applauded at the end. It was like a standing ovation. That's how great he was."

In the center of the movie, there's an inspired bit requiring the combined talents of Lugosi, Sammy, and Ramona the Chimp to put it over. Ramona lets himself out of his cage. Lugosi, settled in a chair and enjoying some serious drinking, is oblivious as Ramona walks upright behind him and up the stairs. It can't be overstated what a masterful job Ramona is doing in this scene. Still walking upright, Ramona's explorations in the upstairs hallway as he looks for Sammy come off as thoughtful and deliberate. Even though the scene was likely shot without sound with the trainer yelling commands, the chimp's naturalness is engaging. Ramona hops into the bed and cuddles up with Sammy. "Ramona the Chimp," Sammy said, "grew to dislike me as filming progressed and bit me whenever the trainer wasn't looking." Sammy and Ramona are working eyeball to eyeball here, and doing it well, despite the documented on-set friction between the two.

Sammy carries Ramona downstairs like a baby, passing a stewed Dr. Zabor. (In the original shooting script, Dr. Zabor threatens to whip Ramona as Sammy pleads for mercy for the chimp. Thankfully, a looser and funnier scene replaced it.)

"Take her back in her cage!!" the doctor commands. Working off-script, Sammy asks, "What?"

"Take her back in her cage!" He yells again, more of an angry Bela Lugosi than a drunk Dr. Zabor. In a precursor to Jim Carrey's *Ace Ventura* catchphrase, Sammy glides to the door, still holding Ramona, and ad-libs, "Allllllll riiiiiighteee!" Sammy gets in the cage and rocks Ramona to sleep.

In a luau dinner scene, the main characters sit cross-legged on the ground. Chief Rakos is in the middle, flanked by Bongo the witch doctor, Dr. Zabor, Duke, Nona, Sammy, and Saloma. Duke and Nona are romantically feeding each other slices of papaya with Zabor shooting daggers at them, silently chomping down his own slice of papaya. Lugosi nails the look of intense jealousy as he glares at the two young lovers. It's the face of a person that, in real life, has stared down his own evil half and lost, leaving him seething with useless envy. Maybe it's not "method acting" by definition, but it might be in the same ballpark.

The papaya-eating scene stood out to young Alex because of Lugosi's discovery of the sticky fruit. "Lugosi was apparently unfamiliar with papayas," Alex said, "but when he first tried it, he ab-so-lute-ly *loved* the papaya. In fact, he became such an addict that he deliberately fluffed his lines several times so that they would do another take and bring fresh plates of papaya! There must have been something about them that appealed to Lugosi . . . Maybe they were unknown in Hungary! He kept eating 'em and eating 'em and eating 'em, which was very funny!"

Unfortunately, Lugosi doesn't fare as well in a subsequent sequence that was entirely improvised. "Hullo! Hullo, hullo, hullo! Good morning!" Sammy yells upon entering the doctor's lab. He gives Zabor a whack on the back. "Hiya, pops!" Sammy shouts into Lugosi's presumably one good ear. Wincing, Lugosi reflexively puts his hand to his ear and mutters, "Good morning." Years later, Sammy admitted to ad-libbing the slap and chalked it up to the fact that he was just a kid and didn't really think about what he was doing.

"How about a little strep-ta-cockeye?" Sammy asks, reviving an earlier, half-baked joke. He gives Zabor another hard slap on the back.

To his credit, Lugosi rolls with the ad-lib and counters with one of his own. "Never mind that!" Zabor snaps back. Sammy sticks his tongue out at Zabor behind his back. "When you're finished with that," Sammy says to Nona, as she mixes chemicals in a test tube, "will you make me a malted?"

A highlight of the movie is the scene in which Duke, now turned into a gorilla by Dr. Zabor, has to convince Sammy that he's really Duke.

"Look, look, look, look, whaddaya tryin' ta tell me? I can't understand a word!" Sammy says, his voice pitched higher than usual. "What am I, dumb or somethin'? *Don't answer that!* Oh, if only Duke were here. He'd figure it out. He's the smart one."

At this point, Duke the Gorilla belts out a credible version of "'Deed I Do" in a gravelly gorilla voice. Sammy, who had been pacing around the room, slowly turns around in shock.

"Dukey! What have they done to ya?" Sammy screams. "We gotta get that screwy doctor to change you back again. What if he doesn't have the combination?" Sammy facepalms himself. "Oy vey!" He tries to console his hairy partner.

"Don't worry," Sammy says. "We can get a nice apartment by the Bronx Zoo and you can come over to visit anytime you want."

A visibly upset Duke the Gorilla starts pounding his chest with both hands. In the same gorilla suit that he had worn portraying a tormented Raymond Burr in *Bride of the Gorilla,* Steve Calvert is now playing it for laughs. Apart from the requisite chest-thumping, the human qualities—pacing the floor, shrugging his shoulders, sitting like Rodin's *Thinker* when he's in deep thought—are all gags that solidly land because there's almost nothing in the world funnier than an ape acting like a human or a human in a gorilla suit.

Outside, a random gorilla hears the commotion and climbs in the window while Sammy is looking in a closet for clothes that might fit Duke. Mistaken-identity gorilla hijinks follow, with Sammy yelling and slapping the random gorilla until Duke the Gorilla pokes his head out from behind the door.

"Here—now put it on 'cause we gotta get out that door!" Sammy looks in the direction of Duke the Gorilla offscreen and then does a whiplash-inducing double take.

What follows is the movie's single funniest scene. The moment that Sammy realizes that he's in a room with two gorillas is as comical as anything that might happen in any other like-minded comedy. In an underplayed, comedic tour de force, Sammy, ever so slowly, turns his head towards the Gorilla That's Not Duke Mitchell with his eyeballs following suit five seconds later.

Sammy chatters nervously away while the random gorilla plays with Sammy's bow tie, tilting his head inquisitively, as a child might.

"Dukey . . . Dukey, please. Tell me it's you, wontcha, Duke? Aw, c'mon, sing, dance . . . do somethin', will ya?"

Duke the Gorilla, still standing just outside the door, sings "'Deed I Do" and Sammy responds with an exasperated, "Oy *gevalt*!"

In Sammy's next big scene, he's trying to save Duke from getting shot. As Dr. Zabor takes aim with his rifle, Sammy stands in front of Duke and catches a bullet. He grimaces, clutches his gut, and melodramatically hits the studio floor. As a child of thirteen in an Arizona home movie, merely four years before this was filmed, Sammy pretended to get shot and fell to the ground in an almost identical fashion. Duke the Gorilla bends down and cradles Sammy's head in his hairy paws. The scene dissolves to Sammy lying on a couch while Human Duke shakes Sammy awake. They're backstage in a nightclub. Sammy is delirious. He stands up and weakly asks, "Where am I?"

"Where are ya?" Duke yells. "You're in our dressing room at the Jungle Hut in Passaic, New Jersey, and we're on next!" Everybody that was in Sammy's dream now appears to be working at the Jungle Hut. Lugosi gets in one last salvo as the Jungle Hut manager when he threatens Sammy with an ultimatum before he and Duke go onstage: "You better get some laughs this time, or you will be collecting unemployment insurance!"

An offstage announcer says, "And now, ladies and gentlemen—those two Fireballs of Fun—Duke Mitchell and Sammy Petrillo!"

Duke and Sammy run out to a microphone in a spotlight. The band plays a quick vamp. Duke grabs the mic.

"Good evening, ladies and gentlemen, and welcome to the—"

Sammy interrupts him with a tortured joke about an "Ooo-Aah bird." "It's a bird that lays square eggs and it goes"—Sammy clutches his stomach and doubles over—"*Ooo! Aah! Ooo! Aah!*"

"Play, boys!" Duke instructs the band as he flips the mic stand away and casually grabs it on the way back to him. Dukes sings the last chorus of "'Deed I Do" as Sammy pretends to conduct the orchestra. Putting an arm around Sammy, Duke pulls him in until they're nose to nose. The camera dollies in on the team and "THE END—A Jack Broder Production" is superimposed over their smiling faces. Fade to black.

Five weeks after filming wrapped, there was another title change. According to the June 20th issue of *Variety*, *Bela Lugosi Meets the Gorilla Man* would now be known as *Bela Lugosi Meets a Brooklyn Gorilla*. It was an ingenious move putting the real name of a cult movie star and a location-themed punchline into the title of a movie. (In England it was released as the generic *Monster Meets the Gorilla* and in Singapore as *Gorilla Capers*.) It might seem inconceivable in a post-hipster world that Brooklyn used to be perceived very differently from the way it is today. Before the first Gen-X-er named their daughter Brooklyn, and before the first latté shop broke ground in Bushwick, Brooklyn, was known as a bustling metropolis of good-natured, working-class slobs of the *dese, dems,* and *dose* variety. In other words, a punchline for everything that was amiably dumb-ass. It was the "other" borough. The skewed subway conversations in Thomas Wolfe's 1935 *New Yorker* piece, "Only the Dead Know Brooklyn," helped to solidify the forgotten borough's identity as the ungainly stepsister to Manhattan's wry wit and sophistication. Lugosi's second-most-popular summer stock play, *Arsenic and Old Lace,* takes place in that funny borough of Brooklyn. When Realart sold *Bela Lugosi Meets a Brooklyn Gorilla* to television, the movie was retitled to the seemingly more commercial-sounding *The Boys from Brooklyn*. Brooklyn endures. Lugosi, not as much.

Is it a fool's errand to make the case for the caliber of *Bela Lugosi Meets a Brooklyn Gorilla*? There are lots of movies that are worse, so that's not a bad place to start. Insincere, pretentious, pandering, middlebrow movies are worse. And usually movies that don't have Bela Lugosi are worse. As the film historian Leonard Maltin noted, "This movie will only take an hour and a quarter of your life. You can watch this twice and *The Avengers* will still be running!" While obviously showcasing the new comedy team of Mitchell and Petrillo, the movie is a star turn for Lugosi.

"Bela is a little older here, but he brings such gravitas to his scenes," Maltin went on to say at MaltinFest. "He's not playing comedy here. He's playing it straight, and that's why it works in the context of the movie. Because he is still the imposing Bela Lugosi that we remember. A little older, but he's still delivering that wonderful intonation of his."

Bela Lugosi Meets a Brooklyn Gorilla documents the intersection of two unique talents—one not that successful, the other one less so. In 1952, Lugosi and Sammy were both looking through the same funnel of fame, but from opposing ends, Sammy was not yet eighteen and just beginning decades of imitating Jerry Lewis. Lugosi, a bad sixty-nine and at the end of a lengthy career, longed to play serious roles but was resigned to wearing a vampire cape, even to his grave. Lugosi and Sammy each embraced and were revolted by two of the most distinct cult personalities of the twentieth century: Count Dracula and Jerry Lewis.

A month before *Brooklyn Gorilla* was set to open, the trades were alive with talk of a possible lawsuit from the Martin and Lewis camp. In Aline Mosby's syndicated column, she reported that Mitchell and Petrillo didn't see "any resemblance" to Martin and Lewis:

Sammy impersonates the Ooh-Aah bird. Courtesy of David Kopple.

"They're the greatest comedy team in the business," shrugged Mitchell. "We're not trying to take anything away from them. We plan to continue in this business, and we think the public accepts us on our own talent."

Mitchell, the singer, claims his hair "just happens to fall on my forehead—I can't help it." And Petrillo, the comic, says he's worn a butch haircut since he was eight years old, and was doing his act on a Phoenix, Arizona, radio station years before he first saw Lewis in a New York theatre. Everybody in show business, they added, is a "combination of everybody else, anyway.

"Chaplin is the only original comic," said Petrillo, and hid his face in his arm like Lewis does.

"If it wasn't for Minosha Skulnic [the Yiddish comedian Menasha Skulnik], Harry Ritz and Gene Bayless [Gene Baylos], Jerry Lewis wouldn't have an act. And that trick he does with his upper lip he got from Huntz Hall."

"I'm a combination of Billy Daniels, Billy Eckstine and Sarah Vaughan," put in Mitchell. "Sometimes I get up to sing and I feel like Vaughn Monroe. Nothing's original in show business. Who do you think Martin is? Crosby. Mel Torme's like Sinatra, and he did all right."

Jack Broder and Maurice Duke were loving the publicity. Herman Cohen was embarrassed. And last time anyone checked with Dean Martin, he couldn't be reached for comment, but probably didn't care one way or the other about Mitchell and Petrillo. Jerry was ready to eat a table. Hal Wallis wasn't happy with this impending fake Martin and Lewis movie either, especially with the next picture set for release being the long-delayed showbiz drama *The Stooge*. (Wallis didn't have to worry—it was a hit.)

Jack and Maurice figured anything that Dean or Jerry could possibly say about Duke and Sammy could only translate into ticket sales. In Dorothy Manners's syndicated "Hollywood" column, she elaborates on the "legal fireworks," if the film were to be released:

> Jack Broder, producer of the "infringing impersonations," has been notified by Martin and Lewis' agents that a restraining order will be clamped on if he so much as takes the covers off the cans of film.
>
> Broder says "phooey." The fight's on.

Jerry sounded off in Louella Parsons's syndicated column:

> "I met with Sammy when he was just a punk kid of sixteen," Jerry told Louella. "And we had him on one of our TV shows as a gag. He looks like me and so he went and hired a partner and had him cut his hair just like Dean's. You can't create something and have people swipe it right from under your nose without doing something about it."

Duke Mitchell got involved.

> "Sammy looks like Jerry—it's an act of God," Duke told the press. "But I should be the one on the other end of the lawsuit. I should be suing Dean Martin because he went out and got a nose job to look like me!"

Dean and Jerry's independent production company, York Pictures, along with Hal Wallis, contracted the law firm of Wright, Wright, Green and Wright to serve Jack Broder Productions with a warning that if they "show, exhibit, sell, distribute . . . *Mr. Lugosi Meets a Gorilla From Brooklyn* . . . you will do so at your own risk . . . and our client . . . will hold you personally responsible for any and all resulting loss, injury or damage." The more coverage Mitchell and Petrillo got, the more it was perceived that Martin and Lewis were appearing uncharacteristically like the heavies, looking to squash the livelihood of a couple of nobodies. The Paramount and MCA lawyers weren't interested in suing Mitchell and Petrillo for the same reason. They figured that it would be better for the imitators to fade away on their own, rather than giving them any more free ink. Paramount smooth-talked Jerry just long enough to tell him that they were prepared to buy the negative of *Brooklyn Gorilla* and then destroy it. Herman Cohen was right in the thick of it and had a unique perspective on the fracas.

"People have speculated that Jack Broder made the picture planning not to release it," Herman said, "that he made it figuring that Hal Wallis would pay him off not to release it. That's not true. However . . . Jack did have a meeting with Hal Wallis, to see if Wallis wanted to buy the film. Wallis knew Jack Broder and was pissed off at Jack [for producing it]. Jack figured, 'Hey, if he wants to buy the negative, I'll make a lot of money!' Wallis wanted to buy the negative and burn it. I was in on that meeting, but I don't remember how much money they were talking. (We made the picture for three cents!) But Jack couldn't get what he wanted from Wallis, and he decided he was going to release it. [Wallis] never talked to Jack Broder again at the Friars Club—that should tell you something!"

Maurice Duke's son-in-law Michael Barrie saw actual legal documents. They were:

> cease-and-desist and stealing-of-intellectual-property documents. Which is funny in and of itself. Then Maurice fantasized, "Hey, maybe I can make more money by selling this negative to burn than I can actually make releasing this picture." Paramount had demanded to see the film and Maurice refused to show it to them, but then he was out of town or something and Jack Broder had screened it for Hal Wallis and Jerry Lewis. Once they saw it, I guess they realized that it wasn't really going to be a problem. That fantasy about selling them the negative to burn disappeared. Broder had shown them a screening of it without [Maurice] Duke's knowledge or permission.
>
> Jerry Lewis never held it against Maurice Duke. They would see each other occasionally. Jerry Lewis was always friendly with him. There was a story where I think Jerry and Maurice Duke and another guy may have been in France. Three of them were in a cab. The cab

> pulls up on the street and Duke gets out first and he had a brace and a cane. He had this side-to-side crab-like walk that he did. He's the first one out and he starts up the street like that, and a couple of attractive women stop to watch on the sidewalk. Then Jerry and the other guy get out and they start to walk up the street in the same way. It was probably before the Muscular Dystrophy telethon. [It wasn't.]

"Astounding days," Sammy recalled, about filming *Brooklyn Gorilla*. "They were the glory days. *They* were the golden days. There *were* problems. First of all, we made the picture and somebody said to us it's not gonna be released, and they're deciding whether to release it or not, and I'm living in a five-dollar-a-week boarding-house room with Duke Mitchell, and we're shivering and I'm praying. We're both praying all the time that this picture will be released, and finally we got a call one day that it *was* being released and I was so excited and happy."

Sammy was upset that Jerry insisted on seeing the movie in advance. It was simply an impersonation that came naturally, Sammy felt, just like impersonations he did of other people. Sammy did concede that Jerry had "a very funny line while watching it. Toward the end, when I get shot . . . when he saw that, he yelled, 'Thank God!' I thought that was pretty funny."

Bela Lugosi Meets a Brooklyn Gorilla opened at the Rialto Theatre in New York City on Wednesday, September 3, 1952. The Rialto was a 1,960-seat movie palace built in 1935, complete with Greek columns and winding, ornate staircases. It was located at the corner of 42nd Street and Seventh Avenue, the heart of the beast. The outside of the theater was bedecked with plastic palm trees and large cardboard cut-outs of Duke and Sammy, along with a blow-up of the UPI journalist Aline Mosby's article "Martin, Lewis May Sue Pair Who Look and Act Like Them."

In a "Reporter at Large" piece in the *New Yorker,* Lillian Ross describes Charlie Chaplin's trip to New York on the eve of the release of what would be his last Hollywood movie, *Limelight,* a semi-autobiographical tale of a comic who wasn't funny anymore. She accompanied the dapper, sixty-three-year-old Chaplin on a walking tour through Times Square while he regaled her with anecdotes about the ghosts of New York's past. They stopped in front of the Rialto Theatre on 42nd Street. "'Bela Lugosi Meets a Brooklyn Gorilla,'" Chaplin read from the marquee. "This used to be *the* showplace," he said. "It [used to be] called the Victoria."

Free promotional passes for the premiere were printed up featuring a photo of Duke, Ramona, and Sammy, all making funny faces with their

A free pass with conditions. September, 1952.

respective signatures below. (Ramona had a delicate penmanship.) Deals were brokered concerning personal appearances at select movie theaters, but, as Sammy explained:

> Duke and I jumped the gun. We couldn't wait—we *ran* to New York. It was playing at the Rialto Theatre . . . we stood outside and signed autographs. We also sat in the theater and watched the movie. Duke pointed out that as I watched myself, I was making the exact same faces I was up on the screen. Because we were talking out loud in the audience, a guy turned around in front of us and said, "Shhh! What's the matter with you two? I paid to watch these guys on the screen!" Duke and I laughed so hard we just couldn't get over it.

Sammy's younger brother Marvin also saw the movie at the Rialto. Due to their ten-year age difference, Marvin hadn't spent much time with Sammy growing up. "Sammy was always on the road," Marvin said. "Traveling, living in other states. What I do remember is when he made that movie with Bela Lugosi. I just sat there watching the movie in the movie theater and I was very proud of him. I was like, 'This is my brother!'"

A few weeks after *Brooklyn Gorilla* opened and closed at the Rialto, Sammy stopped by his boyhood theater, the Zenith, down on Jerome Avenue and 170th. He paid his two bits, settled down into the back row, and gazed upon the enormous screen to enjoy *Bela Lugosi Meets a Brooklyn Gorilla*. A few years earlier, amid the sticky floors and darkness, Sammy had hooted and hollered with the other kids at the second-run westerns and horror movies.

"Someday I'm gonna be sitting here, and I'm gonna look up on the screen and I'm gonna be on it," Sammy used to say in those days. "I went down there and lived out my fantasy."

APTER 12

BELA LUGOSI MET A BROOKLYN GORILLA

"Imitators of 'Lucy' are crawling out of every crevice, cottoning to the theory that nothing succeeds like success. . . . It's impossible to duplicate the success of 'I Love Lucy' merely by paraphrasing the formula . . . Carbon copies rarely pay off. Amos and Andy celebrated their 25th anniversary, their 10,000th broadcast. What became of Molasses and January? Burns and Allen are still doing fine. Where are Block and Sully? Everybody has tried to copy the so-called 'Bing Crosby formula.' Dean Martin and Jerry Lewis will still be great when Duke Mitchell and Sammy Petrillo are just two names in the telephone book."

—Jack Hellman, "Light and Airy," *Variety,* November 17, 1952

Unsurprisingly, *Bela Lugosi Meets a Brooklyn Gorilla* opened to mediocre reviews. Columnists felt a loyalty to Martin and Lewis, who had kept the entertainment industry sizzling along for the previous five years, with enough gravy to go around for everyone. There was no reason to stab Dean and Jerry in their collective back even if *Brooklyn Gorilla* was actually a good movie. You were either on board with a Martin and Lewis rip-off or you weren't, and almost none of the critics were going along with it. *Bela*

The Springfield, Illinois, *State Journal-Register*, November 9, 1952.

Lugosi Meets a Brooklyn Gorilla would also signal the birth and demise of the comedy team of Mitchell and Petrillo.

The *Yale Daily News* declared that *Brooklyn Gorilla* "poses as a 'comedy,' using the very loose definition. It features a poor man's Martin and Lewis. They don't dance, they don't sing, they aren't funny—they just look stupid."

"Foolish and dull," was how the *Miami News* summed up *Brooklyn Gorilla*. They called Sammy "singularly unfunny, his idea of humor consisting of grimaces and plaintive yells. Mitchell can neither sing nor act . . . the plot of the film is merely a string of tired gags loosely strung into a tedious 75 minutes of non-entertainment."

Variety wrote that "This low-budgeted, long-titled comedy-horror pic is destined for a quick demise," singling out Sammy as "the Lewis carbon . . . an amazing duplicate. He's got Lewis's manner down pat including the maniacal laugh and the occasional Yiddish inflection. Also alike are haircut, facial contortions and gestures. It's all good for a five-minute nitery turn, but wears in the 74-minute pic . . . It's doubtful, however, if the team will be able to make any noise in pix, niteries or TV by cashing in on Martin and Lewis's thunder."

The Syracuse, New York, *Post-Standard* spoiled the ending with their not-horrible review: "The hocus-pocus of changing folks into monkeys and monkeys into people gets rare treatment. . . . The ending is a complete surprise and everybody joins in to enact a double role."

"Undiscriminating neighborhood and small-town audiences will get some laughs," *Boxoffice* decided.

The *Los Angeles Times* had a thoughtful take: "Sammy's face, with its India rubber mouth, and horse teeth, gives him a head start as a comedian . . . he has a chance to wisecrack, mug and romp to his heart's content. Time will probably tone down his tendency to try so hard to be funny."

Harrison's Reports wrote that, "At the theater where this picture was previewed, many people walked out when Duke Mitchell, imitating Dean Martin, started to sing."

The *Exhibitor,* an industry newspaper, advised that it was "Okeh for the exploitation spots and lower half," meaning that hiding *Brooklyn Gorilla* on the bottom half of a double feature might be a wise move.

Another industry periodical, the *Independent Film Journal,* advised that "This film will take plenty of exploiting and drumbeating, but if handled wisely will do a fair share of business in houses that specialize in exploitation films." They also went on to skewer Sammy, who "most of the time misses the boat," while praising Ramona the Chimp as "outstanding in the film, providing laughs with her almost human antics." This viewpoint was shared by other news outlets. "Ramona the chimp was the only authentic actor among the crew," pronounced the *Daily News* in its one-and-a-half-star review.

The *Wisconsin Jewish Chronicle* printed its mixed-up assessment: "Another Italo-Jewish combo starting to click is the vaude team of Duke Mitchell and Sammy Petrillo. . . . Mitchell, who is Jewish and a singer, resembles Dean Martin, who is Italian, and Petrillo, who is Italian, gives out with the comedy just like the Jewish Lewis."

The newspaper ads for *Brooklyn Gorilla* jumped off the printed page, with Sammy and Duke's leering mugs alongside screaming taglines that promised action, thrills, and hilarity. "A Horror Film That Will Stiffen You With Laughter" and "Brooklyn Chumps Become Island Monkeys in a Jungle Full of Laffs & Girls" sold the general zaniness. Other blurbs latched onto the water-cooler fodder: "Duke Mitchell and Sammy Petrillo Look So Much Like Martin and Lewis That They Are Being Sued for $300,000.00" and "See the Two Comedians Who Look Like Martin and Lewis and Roused the Ire of Hall Wallis."

The *Brooklyn Gorilla* ads were sometimes placed near or right next to ads for Martin and Lewis's latest movie, *The Stooge,* which was released on New Year's Eve 1952. Some ads just went for it—with copy that read, "SEE Lewis at his best . . .! Jerry Lewis in The Brooklyn Gorilla," next to a photo of Jerry Lewis swiped from *Sailor Beware.* One could see how this might have led to some confusion on movie night. Audiences looking for nutty shenanigans might've been better served by *Brooklyn Gorilla* than by the downbeat proceedings of *The Stooge,* anyway.

Curiously, it seems that no other motion picture in recorded history was cursed with as many misspellings and mistakes in its print ads. The blunders were as numerous and as stupefying as they were moronic. Some were typos, but other times you had no idea what they were thinking. A few of the craziest were *Lugosi & Jerry Lewis "Meet a Gorilla," Bella Lugosa Meets Gorilla, Frankenstein Meets Brooklyn Gorilla, Boris Karloff Meets Gorilla,* and so on.

Mangled names of the actors were rife as well: Sim Petrillo, Danny Petrillo, Sammy Petrilli, Jerry Petrillo, Luke Mitchell, Roy Mitchell, Bella Lagosa, Belgi Lugosi, and Ramona Chim. Even in a promotional ad that Jack Broder took out, he misspelled poor Bela's name as Bella.

Jerry's nightmare double-bill. *Lansing State Journal*, June 21,1953.

Brooklyn Gorilla made its $130,000 budget back, but not much more than that—certainly not enough to warrant another Mitchell and Petrillo comedy. Still, the movie scraped in the nickels and dimes at second-run houses across the land, where it was paired with other Realart reissues for months and even years afterwards.

No one's career was exactly hurt by their association with *Brooklyn Gorilla*. Charlita's playing against type went unnoticed, and soon she was swaying her "atomic hips" to the sounds of the mambo king Pérez Prado at the downtown Paramount Theatre in Los Angeles. Shortly after *Brooklyn Gorilla* was released, it was announced in the trades that Charlita had changed her name to Clare Regis, and a few months later she showed up on Dick Powell's *Four Star Playhouse* TV show as Rena Regis.

Aside from bumping Mitchell and Petrillo into better club dates, *Brooklyn Gorilla* marked a brief resurgence in Lugosi's popularity. Several items in *Variety* celebrated Lugosi's return to the zeitgeist: "Jack Broder's *Bela Lugosi Meets a Brooklyn Gorilla* was a distinct triumph for Bela, but he will need the help of Frankenstein, Boris Karloff, and Abbott and Costello if he meets the Brooklyn Dodgers," and "Jack Broder's *Bela Lugosi Meets a Brooklyn Gorilla* is not a sequel to 'Casey Stengel Meets the Brooklyn Dodgers.'" *Variety* also reported that, "After winning a decision over the *Brooklyn Gorilla*, Bela Lugosi is ready to meet all comers, human, simian or mechanical. His next opponent is 'The Atomic Monster.'"

Ironically, *The Atomic Monster*—the movie title that Alex Gordon accused Jack Broder of ripping off from him—was rewritten by Alex's roommate Ed Wood, Jr. Soon to be known as *Bride of the Atom,* and, later, *Bride of the Monster,* it would feature Lugosi in his last juicy mad-scientist role. Alex's attorney Samuel Z. Arkoff financed *Bride of the Monster* and used the profits as seed money for the creation of American International Pictures with Alex and Herman Cohen.

Before *Bride of the Monster* began production, Ed Wood shot his magnum opus, *Glen or Glenda,* in four days, using Lugosi as the onscreen scientist, narrator, and observer of the human condition. Wood, as the titular character, imbues the exploitative goings-on with a sincere plea for acceptance, which gives the wacky mélange of stock footage and stilted performances its heart. Lugosi's speeches are superb ("*Pull da string!*"), even though they barely have any relevance to the plot about transvestism, other than detailing what little boys are made of, as opposed to little girls.

Lugosi's unrealized dream was to star in a Technicolor, 3-D remake of *Dracula*. A few weeks after *Brooklyn Gorilla* was released, Arch Oboler, producer and writer of radio's *Lights Out,* hit theaters with the movie that would kickstart the 3-D craze: *Bwana Devil.* Filmed in a process known as Natural Vision, the promotional material promised "A Lion in Your Lap" and "A Lover in Your Arms." The audiences ate it up and, for a brief spell, 3-D movies were expected to replace 2-D movies, just as sound had replaced silence twenty-five years before.

The closest Lugosi got to a 3-D movie was attending the Hollywood premiere of the Vincent Price schlockfest *House of Wax.* Dressed in vampire garb and sunglasses, newsreel footage shows Lugosi clearly enjoying himself as he escorts Steve Calvert in a gorilla suit down the red carpet on a chain. Lugosi acted in as many gorilla movies as he did vampire movies (about five apiece), so it's a special moment for Lugosi fans to see him combine his two distinctive trademarks.

In early 1953, Lillian Lugosi moved out, taking Bela, Jr., with her, and by July the Lugosis were divorced. Auctioning off most of his furniture, Lugosi moved into a smaller apartment near the Hollywood Freeway and pursued what was left of his career. Attempting a nightclub comedy act, Lugosi teamed up with Wally Vernon, a deadpan comic known for his Damon-Runyon-esque delivery. Vernon had previously appeared with Lugosi in *The Gorilla* and with Eddie Quillan in a series of incredibly violent two-reel comedies for Columbia in the '40s. Lugosi and Vernon never got beyond their initial outing at Top's Nightclub in San Diego. Lugosi came to the inevitable conclusion that he needed to leave comedy in the capable hands of comedians.

For the first two weekends after *Brooklyn Gorilla* opened, Duke and Sammy appeared at Frank Nocella's El Mombo club in Franklin Square, Long Island, for a series of "farewell parties." Newspaper ads boasted that this was the last time that one could see Mitchell and Petrillo before they "return to Hollywood for their next picture."

Despite the dismal reviews for *Brooklyn Gorilla,* Sammy was optimistic. *Variety* reported that the team was signed by "the William Morris Agency for theatre-nitery representation," and that helped to buoy his spirits.

"There were only a handful of comedy teams at the time," Sammy would later say. "There was plenty of room at the top for another team, especially a couple of guys that were young and really funny."

The day after their final show at El Mombo, Duke and Sammy were playing the Town Casino in Buffalo, New York, conveniently located across the street from the Greyhound bus terminal. Billed as the "Most Howlarious Act in Show Business," they shared the bill with "Her Nibs,"

Miss Georgia Gibbs, a Russian Jew who based her career on copycat versions of Black rhythm-and-blues hits. After rebranding Etta James's "The Wallflower" as "Dance with Me, Henry," Gibbs swiped "Tweedle Dee" from LaVern Baker and had a bigger hit with it. Not long afterwards, Gibbs covered Baker's "Tra La La," effectively shutting down those sales as well. An exasperated Baker took out a life-insurance policy on herself before a trip to Australia and named Gibbs as beneficiary. "You need this more than I do," Baker wrote to Gibbs, "because if anything happens to me, you're out of business."

Less than two weeks after the Town Casino, Duke and Sammy headlined a live revue, *Broadway Brevities of 1953: A Lavish Musical-Comedy Extravaganza,* at the 2,500-seat Carman Theatre in North Philly. Supporting them were the dance team of Harry Joyce and Ginger; "Direct from Chicago Theatre in Chicago, Hal Sands Manhattan Rockets"; the comedy star of "Meet the Dames," Harry Savoy; and the lovely Neptune of the Sea performing her act in an "800 gallon water tank." Duke and Sammy's matinee and evening appearances at the Carman were in conjunction with the first Philadelphia showing of *Brooklyn Gorilla,* an event whipped up to provoke controversy. Blazoned across the advertisements was the disclaimer, "THE PUBLIC IS ENTITLED TO KNOW That Any Similarity Between the Characters on Our Stage to Any Persons, Living or Dead, is Positively Coincidental."

The hyperbolic blurbs boasted of their magic: "Most Sensational Comedy Team of the Year," "The Greatest Comedy Discovery Team of the Year," and "Never a dull moment these nights at the Club Castle with this famous movie and TV Comedy Team rocking the place with laughter twice a night in the most sensational show ever to appear in Orange County."

Abandoning Duke altogether and singling out Sammy and his unique talents was also considered to be more than enough to sell tickets. During this period, Sammy was routinely referred to as "The Jerry Lewis of Burlesque," "The Today Comic with All the Experience of Yesterday," "Real Funny Guy," "Italian Comedian," and "A Refreshing New Comic." One ad went so far as to ask, "Who is Sammy Petrillo? He is Jerry Lewis now."

The second coming of Martin and Lewis hit Allentown, Pennsylvania, in mid-November for seventeen performances a week at the 745-seat Midway Theatre. Between showings of *Brooklyn Gorilla,* Duke and Sammy were joined onstage by a local celebrity, Monstro the Gorilla. Halfway through the engagement, the team showed up at the Hess Brothers department store, where reporters caught them cavorting with a large stuffed gorilla in

Newspaper advertisement, circa 1952.

the toy department. When interviewed for the local paper, Sammy turned pensive: "I can't help it if I was born to look like someone else. This is my face and I do not intend to wear a mask because Jerry Lewis resembles me. My life blood is the theater, and I hope to continue entertaining the public."

Some of the reviews for Duke and Sammy's stage act were just as bleak as those for the movie. Performing with Martha Raye and the Kirby Stone Quintet at the Five O'Clock Club in Miami, in what should have been a triumphant return for Duke Mitchell, instead raised questions about the necessity of a Martin and Lewis "carbon." Under the *Miami Herald* headline, "Big Laugh Backfires; Double Apes Comedian," the "Night Life" reporter George Bourne pondered that "it must be annoying to have a pair of unknowns prove that they too can get belly laughs with the same physical grimacing, and fumbling off-key delivery, which have won fame, fortune, and the dubious flattery of imitation for Jerry Lewis and Dean Martin."

A review of the team's appearance in the Flamingo Cavalcade of 1952 at the Flamingo Casino and Hotel in Las Vegas read:

> Mitchell & Petrillo hit big during opening moments, then begin to lose grip as they flounder in wads of poor material. Sammy Petrillo brings gasps with his positive aping of Jerry Lewis, but without a strong partner to bat screwball gags back and forth, resorts to flip antics for attention. Duke Mitchell hasn't the hang of forcing his straight lines over, thus plenty of jokes go into oblivion. Petrillo has a funny mugg, and is a wild man on stage, yet must latch on to something more stable than his present Lewisian kowtows.

Bela Lugosi was approached to prop up the act. "I pitched the idea of us together with Lugosi," Sammy said. "We'd come out onstage singing, 'It's Mitchell! It's Petrillo! And Lugosi!' And then the lights would flash and thunder, like a Frankenstein-type thing, and here'd be Lugosi in a white coat, performing surgery. '*Give me the suture!*' And sound effects, you know. And he'd say, 'Ahh, congratulations, my friends. You no longer look like those other two comedians. No longer will people bother you and stop you and ask you if you are . . . Abbott and Costello!' And we would do all kinds of other bits too. But the William Morris Agency wouldn't buy it."

What William Morris was buying was choice gigs at legitimate nightclubs for the suit-and-tie crowd. In mid-December 1952, Mitchell and Petrillo graced the stage of the legendary 1,500-seat Latin Casino in Philadelphia. For a scant few months, the team would come as close to the perimeter of mainstream success as they ever would. Duke and Sammy's collective star was shining brightly and, for that moment, they were the very best at being second-best.

Two days before Christmas, Sammy was called upon to appear solo on America's other favorite comedy program, *Texaco Star Theater*, starring the man whose arms Sammy had jumped into two years before, Milton Berle. Mimicking the punchline from Sammy's debut on *The Colgate Comedy Hour*, once again Sammy would impersonate Jerry Lewis for the blackout gag.

The skit opens in "The Year 1751" where a ship's captain, "Horatio Hornberler" (complete with Cap'n Crunch hat), is engaged in a sword fight with a little person, no more than three and a half feet tall, also in a Cap'n Crunch hat. Berle wins the duel and, as a henchman carries the pocket-sized pirate offstage, Berle yells after them, "Take him back to Phillip Morris!" The comedian Milton Frome appears for some schtick, as well as the diminutive Arnold Stang, who brings his own putz energy to the proceedings. For many triumphant decades, Stang was the bespectacled, nebbishy go-to for roles that required Jerry Lewis geekiness with none of the insanity. Basil Rathbone is at his silliest best as a shipmate sword-fighting with Berle, and the sloppy fun is infectious. Berle breaks up the both of them when, as an aside, he refers to Rathbone as "Bathroom." Stang announces that a female stowaway has been discovered on board and escorts onstage a very skinny Sammy Petrillo, wearing high heels, a checkered dress, and a veil hanging from a hat to hide his face. Sammy's left knee is bent at a provocative angle while his hand rests lazily on his hip.

"Leave that woman alone," shouts Berle. "It's Lady Gwendolyn—she's gonna be my wife!"

Sammy drapes his arm around the front of Miltie's neck and comes in close to him.

"And now, Gwendolyn," Berle continues, "I come to you, my darling. My darling, you and I are all alone. You can share my castles in Spain, my villas in France—you can have pearls, emeralds, and diamonds. Would you like it? Tell me—*would you like it?*"

In a medium two-shot, Berle lifts Gwendolyn's veil to reveal Sammy in a blonde wig, cross-eyed and smiling idiotically. His mouth is agape. The top row of teeth are so blindingly bright that it looks like Sammy may already be wearing the dentures that would define his future look.

"I like it! I like it!" Sammy, as Jerry, screams.

Berle takes a beat, then feigns shock, facepalms himself, and shouts, "Oh, no!" The camera lingers for five seconds, the audience erupts into shrieks, and the screen goes to black. After gales of applause, a sweaty Miltie is in front of the curtain, where he brings out and introduces by name his co-stars, Milton Frome, Arnold Stang, and Basil Rathbone. Sammy remains backstage.

If anyone could've gotten the real Jerry Lewis for a five-second cameo, it would be Milton Berle, who conveniently shared a network with Jerry. However, after "discovering" Sammy at Nova Studios, why shouldn't Berle partake in some of that fake Jerry Lewis magic for himself? In addition to stunning the audience into peals of laughter, there lies the possibility that, just for kicks, Uncle Miltie might've been using Sammy to get under Jerry's very thin skin. It didn't help that *TV and Radio*'s Michael J. Hayde gushed in his column that "the chap [Sammy] out-Lewised Lewis."

Sammy surprises Uncle Miltie on *Texaco Star Theater,* December, 1952.

Sammy appeared to be persona non grata back at *The Colgate Comedy Hour*. There were rumors that Jerry had put the kibosh on any further Sammy appearances on the show.

"Sammy didn't have any enemies," Rick Saphire, Jerry and Sammy's future manager, observed. "Sadly enough, you're in show business and you find that your only enemy is the person that you admire the most, and the person whose face you're stuck with. It was the Jerry camp that was adamant about putting a stop to the film. Dean didn't care."

Sammy was pals with the egg-shaped comedian Joe Besser, who later famously replaced Shemp Howard in the Three Stooges and who played the overgrown brat Stinky on the Abbott and Costello TV show. While hanging out at a deli in Ventura Valley, Joe suggested that he might be able to sell the concept of bringing Mitchell and Petrillo onto an Abbott and Costello–hosted *Colgate Comedy Hour* as Stinky's "nephews."

Plans, quickly arranged, unraveled just as fast. Allegedly, Lou Costello flipped out on the set in front of Besser and his collaborator Sid Fields: "They're like Dean and Jerry! You want us to start a feud? Things are bad enough!" Another variation of the story has Sammy noticing "one of Jerry's cronies—one of the guys that worked for him—at the rehearsal. And he looked at us and he walked out of the room. I turned to Duke and I said, 'That guy just went to call Jerry. We're off the show.' And then Lou Costello walked over to us and he says, 'Fellas, I hate to tell you this—NBC will not allow us to put you on the show, but we're gonna pay you anyway.' He said Jerry Lewis did it. That really happened. We were blackballed in nightclubs. We were blackballed here and there."

The Poverty Row studio Allied Artists pitched Mitchell and Petrillo a chance at another movie. They couldn't come to terms. "Federal Films offered a TV series of fifty-two episodes. We turned it down," Sammy said. "I don't know why we did that. We must've been real jerks. We thought we were flying high, anyway. We then found that Dean Martin was behind that offer."

"Dean's a wonderful guy," Duke concurred. "He don't want no trouble. He used to tell Jerry, 'Leave the kids alone, let 'em make a buck.' I'm sure Dean never, *never* bum-rapped us once."

"Oddly enough, Dean liked us and was always very nice to us," Sammy said.

Maurice Duke's son-in-law Michael Barrie has an objective take on the situation. "Dean, wisely, I'm sure, saw these guys as no threat whatsoever," says Barrie. "The fact that Jerry Lewis thought [Sammy] was stealing his act? The question is, did he even have an act? First of all, it's a copy. It's someone doing an impression. It's like Kirk Douglas being afraid of Frank Gorshin."

Nick Tosches, author of *Dino: Living High in the Dirty Business of Dreams,* his comprehensive and dazzling biography of Dean Martin, was asked in 2019 if he thought that Dean might have exerted some effort to help Mitchell and Petrillo, possibly at the expense of Jerry's sanity. Dean had a subtle sadistic streak and Jerry, being thin-skinned and paranoid, was an easy target. Tosches, being the expert on all things Dino (among other topics), responded with his usual wit and aplomb:

> To me, the Jerry end of this story sounds plausible, but the Dino end has to it a resonant tinny ring of jive, doesn't even cut it as apocrypha. I don't believe Dean would expend the effort even if he cared. But I think it's sweet, in a tragic and oh so human sort of way, that Sammy enjoyed feeling a personal affinity, a kindredness, with Dean.

In January 1953, Sammy Petrillo took his first bride. Sammy and Lucille Beell were married on January 18, 1953, in Mexico. They divorced October 20, 1955, in Minnesota. In between, one of their early addresses was 2 Fifth Avenue, a tony apartment building across the street from Washington Square Park. Lucy's father owned the Flame Cafe, a hot spot for steel-guitar-driven country music back in Minneapolis. Sammy and Lucy had a son, Clark Sammy Petrillo, who was said to be named after Clark Gable, but Lucy's brother was a more likely namesake. Later, when Lucy married Gaylord Gladwin, she changed her son's name to Clark Gaylord Gladwin. There's also the possibility that Sammy and Lucy had another child as well.

Another version of the marriage comes from Sammy's cousin Martin Jackowe. "Their marriage was annulled," Martin said. "She was young. She was seventeen and Sammy wasn't a hell of a lot older—maybe he was nineteen. She was from Minneapolis and her family was well off. They told Sammy he could be comfortable for the rest of his life if he'd give up show business. He would never have to worry about working again or anything like that. He refused. He loved the business so much. He didn't wanna give it up. That was his life." Martin's wife Nancy disagrees. "I don't think [Sammy and Lucy] were ever married," she says. "Sammy always told me that it was common-law."

In chronicling Sammy's life, names, dates, and places can be difficult to verify. Onstage, he was outgoing, brash, and confident, ad-libbing, going wild, and generally tearing it up with full abandon—a motormouth under the arc lights—but offstage Sammy afforded himself the luxury of keeping his private matters private. By many accounts, he was affable and well-liked. Sammy had plenty of buddies. He could turn on the charm with total strangers and offer up corny jokes and puns in any situation. Throughout the years, close friends and family members noticed that at times he could also be a cipher, infuriatingly vague when pressed on subjects he preferred not to discuss. Sometimes he found it easier to simply disappear. The gaps and misdirections in tracing Sammy's story are numerous, many of them placed there by Sammy himself, in an effort to free himself from accountability. Call it survival instinct in the cutthroat jungle of showbiz—Sammy lived like the nomadic, carny-talking joke salesman that he was, looking forward to the next big thing and dismissing any part of his past that held no worth for him.

Next up for Duke and Sammy was a spot on Spade Cooley's live TV show *The Hoffman Hayride*, which was broadcast weekly from the Santa Monica

Pier, locally on KTLA-TV in Los Angeles and nationwide on the fledgling Paramount Television Network.

In a story reminiscent of Sammy barging into Milton Berle's rehearsal so he could be introduced to Jerry Lewis as his doppelgänger, Spade Cooley, in the 1930s, sneaked onto the Republic Studios set where the "singing cowboy" Gene Autry was filming his latest western. Autry was struck by Cooley's resemblance to Roy Rogers and brought him to Rogers, who ended up using Cooley in dozens of movies as his stand-in and stunt double. Cooley led one of the most popular western-swing bands in California, had several hit country records and rebranded himself as the "King of Western Swing," even though Bob Wills had referred to himself as that before Cooley even picked up a fiddle. Cooley's Emmy-winning variety show managed to rope in Frank Sinatra, Dinah Shore, and other urban tenderfoots with great success.

It should be noted that Spade Cooley was not a good man. He was a deranged psychopath whose deepening dependence on booze and Thorazine only heightened his obsessively jealous behavior. For many years, Cooley suspected his wife Ella Mae of infidelity and threatened her life and those of their kids on more than one occasion. In 1961, word got to Cooley that Ella Mae had cheated on him with Roy Rogers, and Cooley went haywire. He tied up Ella Mae and tortured her to death in front of their fourteen-year-old daughter, a heinous act for which he was convicted of first-degree murder. Paroled after serving nine years, Cooley dropped dead of a heart attack after receiving a standing ovation for a performance at a benefit concert for the Alameda County Sheriffs' Department.

"Spade Cooley didn't do comedy like Milton Berle, but he was the Milton Berle of western swing," Sammy said. "He was very nice to me and Duke. We did forty minutes on his show! It was unbelievable! We went out to do our act and got lost. We never did a thing like this in our lives. We were really a little freaky. We were supposed to have a small spot—this was an hour show. And when we got through, Spade Cooley cursed us up and down and hated our guts and screamed and said, 'I never saw anything like this in my life!' I didn't blame him for being upset. A few weeks later we played a place called Larry Potter's Supper Club. Spade Cooley showed up and apologized and said that he picked up a lot of sponsors because of that show!"

Larry Potter's Supper Club, the venue which had midwifed the birth of Mitchell and Petrillo just two years earlier, was now ready to cut them loose. There are varying accounts of the night that finally got them canned.

One story involves a drunken woman sitting near the stage with three mobsters who started heckling Sammy. Sammy retaliated by dumping a full salad bowl on her head before racing out of the club with the mobsters in pursuit. Sammy refuted this version of the story: "I picked up a bowl of salad to use as prop and stumbled, and the salad flew on some of the kids' formal clothes. I apologized, gave them money to pay for the cleaning, and the show went on." All versions agree that Larry Potter personally tore up their contract that night.

Good gigs were still within reach. They played a week in February at the Club Oasis in Los Angeles on a bill with the rhythm-and-blues singers Linda Hayes and Little Caesar. Linda was the sister of the Platters' lead singer, Tony Williams, and was promoting her new song "Yes! I Know," an answer record to Willie Mabon's "I Don't Know." Several singers referred to themselves as Little Caesar. This Little Caesar had recently had a hit novelty record about a murder-suicide ("Goodbye Baby"), a subject which must have made for a visually compelling closing number.

March found the team performing at two of the most iconic spots in Vancouver, British Columbia, an area starved for Martin and Lewis and willing to settle for the next-best thing. The Fillipone brothers' Penthouse Nightclub was the epitome of cool—stylish and hip for the in-crowd, often with late-night entertainment from the likes of Sammy Davis, Jr., Ella Fitzgerald, and Louis Armstrong. The illegal booze that flowed under the radar at the Penthouse was Vancouver's worst-kept secret and it only made the club that more exotic. There's a beautiful photograph of Duke and Sammy posing with the co-owner, Ross Fillipone, inside the club. Duke and Sammy are both sticking out their tongues while stretching their mouths apart with their left and right pinkies. For good measure, Sammy is cross-eyed and his bow tie is askew. Kilroy (Was Here), Harpo's "Gookie" face, the toothless Papa-Oom-Mau-Mau guy on Ghoulardi's TV show, the stunned expression of the Operation board game's naked patient, Ben Turpin doing anything—these mugs all rightly belong on the Mount Rushmore of Stupid Faces. The crossing of the eyes, sticking out of the tongue, mouth pulled apart by extended pinkies—this look belongs up there as well. It's a classic funny face, one which Sammy used to great effect in *Brooklyn Gorilla* in the scene where he climbs to the top of a totem pole while trying to escape from lovesick Saloma. Ross Fillipone, standing between Duke and Sammy, his huge mitts draped over their shoulders, looks tickled to be in the business that he's in.

Penthouse owner Ross Filippone flanked by Sammy and Duke.
Vancouver, Canada, March, 1953. Courtesy of Danny Filippone.

The Cave Supper Club was another Vancouver mainstay where the boozing was discreet. Burlap and plaster stalactites hung from the ceiling. Duke and Sammy were booked on a bill with "Frenchy" Manning, "King of the Tight Wire" (sometimes billed as "Crazy Cowboy"), and Ellis and Winters "Dance Creations." After the first week, advertisements offered "YOUR MONEY BACK if you don't Laff and Laff and Laff at the Craziest, Zaniest, Nuttiest Comedy Team Ever To Play Vancouver . . . No Wonder Martin & Lewis Are Suing Mitchell & Petrillo And no wonder we're holding them for a second week. Honestly folks they are terrific, so come on down and chase your blues away with our sensational show."

The *Vancouver Sun* had little difficulty summing up the appeal of the show: "[Mitchell and Petrillo] do a good job of what they set out to do, which is imitating Martin and Lewis." In a sweet bit of synergy, no doubt coordinated by their manager Maurice Duke, *Bela Lugosi Meets a Brooklyn Gorilla* was set to open in Vancouver to coincide with the club dates. Another Vancouver paper, the *Province,* called the movie "a jumble of corn and creeps with Bela Lugosi looking absolutely ashamed of meeting Duke Mitchell and Sammy Petrillo."

During their run at the Cave, *Variety* reported that "Mitchell & Petrillo have signed with Joe Glaser's Associated Booking Corp." On March 27th, 1953, Duke and Sammy were called on to present the Quigley Award plaque to Ivan Ackery, beloved owner of Vancouver's Orpheum Theatre. Ackery won the coveted prize for creativity in the industry, citing the time he dressed a man up as a gorilla to publicize a movie.

Also on March 27th, almost three thousand miles due east, the *Brooklyn Eagle* announced that "Mitchell and Petrillo (they're the comics that look like Martin and Lewis) have called it a day."

Jack Wasserman in his "After Dark" column in the *Vancouver Sun* reported that Duke and Sammy completed their engagement at the Cave but were blowing off "a four-week contract for the 'Say When' in SF but Petrillo didn't have the fare . . . He blew his loot in expensive living. The 18-year-old comic and his pretty blonde wife finally got out of town Monday . . . Mitchell left on schedule April 5. Sammy told me before he left that he hopes to go on the road as single, if and when he gets straightened out with the AGVA [American Guild of Variety and Artists], because of the broken contract. He's got talent. Now all he needs is a keeper."

The *Vancouver Sun* made it appear that Sammy left before the complete run by saying that Sammy was replaced at the Cave at the last minute by "America's Newest Television Comedian," Lennie Russell.

Two months later, Sammy triumphantly returned to Frank Nocella's El Mombo in Franklin Square, Long Island, for two shows nightly every Friday and Saturday for five "smash weeks!" Mysteriously, and without any fanfare, Duke Mitchell appeared to be out of the act. The ads show Sammy and a Duke-alike both adjusting their bow ties, while the copy screams, "2 Names That Are Destined To Go Down In Show Business History!: 'Mr. Mood,' Ric Marlow 'A Singer Who Warms Your Heart,' and 'Mr. Madness,' Sammy Petrill [*sic*], 'A True Master of Comedy.'"

The team of Marlow and Petrillo did not last much longer than the five smash weeks at the El Mombo. In the revolving door of post–Duke Mitchell partners, one of the most successful in his post-Sammy life was the crooner Ric Marlow. Born Sanford Phillip Schafler, the twenty-eight-year-old Marlow, like Sammy, hailed from the Bronx, but that's where the similarities end. Starting out as a café singer, by the late '50s Marlow was an in-demand thug and bad guy on *Bonanza, Death*

Birth of a short-lived comedy team. *Brooklyn Eagle,* June 19, 1953.

Valley Days, and other TV shows. Later, in 1960, on a lark, he helped his former pianist Bobby Scott compose the song "A Taste of Honey" for a Broadway adaptation of a play also titled *A Taste of Honey*. The song took five minutes to write, won four Grammy Awards, and eventually sold millions of copies of covers by Martin Denny, Lenny Welch, Acker Bilk, Herb Alpert and the Tijuana Brass, the Beatles, Barbara Streisand, Tony Bennett, Bobby Darin, the Supremes, and the Four Tops. Marlow was married five times, once, in the late 1950s, to the actress and activist Leslie Parrish, who portrayed Lawrence Harvey's fiancé in *The Manchurian Candidate* (1962) and Jerry Lewis's love interest in *Three on a Couch* (1966). Marlow himself returned to acting in 1965 with back-to-back roles in Albert Zugsmith's sleazeball classics *The Incredible Sex Revolution* and *Psychedelic Sexualis*.

By November 1953, Duke was back. The reasons for the breakup and reconciliation with Sammy were never made clear. Years later, Sammy cryptically said that the "splits were always amicable—we'd just want to pursue other things." Duke's son, Jeff, remembered that "When I was a kid I was told that if Sammy ever called I was to tell him that he had the wrong number and hang up. My dad didn't really like him very much. I don't know what happened between them—I can't speak on that—but I tell you that he wasn't held in high esteem."

They shared a bill at the Say When in San Francisco with the "Sepia Marilyn Monroe," Tamara Hayes, who was promoting her new Decca record "Hold Me, Hold Me, Hold Me." This was a "make good" for the four-week engagement which they had flaked out on the previous spring. The Say When ads asked in huge letters, "Is it MARTIN and LEWIS," and then in much smaller type, "or Mitchell and Petrillo?"

Duke and Sammy played the entire month of December at the Club Castle in Santa Ana, California. Finality was in the air. The ads noted that this was "your last chance to see Duke Mitchell and Sammy Petrillo" and that they were headed directly to the Flamingo in Las Vegas. Whether they ever made it is unknown. Their New Year's Eve show, complete with "Noise Makers" and "Favors," was advertised as "the laugh of your life."

New Year's Eve 1953 was a special night in New York City and the tri-state area as well. Just five minutes past the new year, homebound revelers who could afford TV sets were treated to the television debut of *Bela Lugosi Meets a Brooklyn Gorilla* on *The Big Show*. It was a bold move on the part of the CBS affiliate, Channel 2, with *Brooklyn Gorilla* going up against Channel 4's *New Year's Eve in Times Square with Bob Wilson* and a New Year's Eve party for the disc jockey Martin Block on Channel 7.

Back on the West Coast the following Monday night, Duke and Sammy dropped in for a surprise number at the Winter Varieties of '54 dance party to benefit the senior class of San Pedro High School in L.A. The benefit was poorly attended. However, the *San Pedro News-Pilot* reported that Duke and Sammy "created spontaneous eruptions of laughter during their appearance."

Two weeks later, Duke and Sammy showed up at Fresno's Redwood Inn in Fresno. The club took an aggressive approach to their advertising campaign by warning patrons that they had "Better Make Reservations Right Now To See Duke Mitchell & Sammy Petrillo Because Most of the Chairs and Tables Were Broken Last Night and You Will Stand!" Another

America's Zaniest Comedy Team. *Santa Barbara News-Press*, February 23, 1954.

ad screamed, "WANTED!! People Who Have The Courage To Come To The Redwood Inn Because Those Two Crazy Mad Characters Will Scare You To Death!"

A "Limited Engagement!!!!" was advertised in early February for Duke and Sammy's turn at the Club Samoa in L.A.'s Boyle Heights neighborhood. Finishing up a two-week stay at King's Supper Club in Santa Barbara, it was reported that Duke and Sammy would host "a special farewell party appearance."

In what would appear to be their last engagement together, the boys returned to the scene of their earlier success at the Cave in Vancouver. Paired with the Capitol recording star Ella Mae Morse, the team presumably provided an advertised "60 Laffs a Minute." The final show was Friday, March 26th, 1954. They were replaced the following week by "Bill Kenny and His Famous Ink Spots." Kenny, the lead high tenor, had disbanded the influential singing group a couple of years earlier and was now touring with a pickup version of the Ink Spots.

From this point on, Sammy would be, essentially, Duke-less, destined to continue either as a solo act or with a conga line of replaceable Dean Martins. Sammy would never again star in a Hollywood movie, but he was savvy enough to know which of his strengths to exploit. Sammy understood that he was the best Jerry Lewis impersonator in the business and no one could take that away from him. Prepared to work almost anywhere, he would be wherever you wanted him to be. Sammy was nineteen and ready for it.

APTER 13

WAIT FOR THE LAUGH

"I got a gag about Martin and Lewis. Goes like this: Guy says 'Martin and Lewis get $50,000 a week' and I say 'Yeah, but it's not steady.' Cute gag, y'know?"

—Sammy Petrillo, *Pittsburgh Press*, March 23, 1955

With the glory of *Bela Lugosi Meets a Brooklyn Gorilla* receding into the past, Sammy settled into the life of a nomadic journeyman. In the ensuing years, his travels would reach beyond the old neighborhood in the Bronx, into the vast suburbs and remaining boroughs of New York City. Stretching eastward towards the counties of Long Island, Sammy plied his trade at a diverse selection of lounges and strip joints. The Full Moon in East Patchogue, the Continental on Old Country Road in Hempstead, and the San Su San in Mineola all bore witness to the antics of a Jerry Lewis at budget prices. Sammy stood in the spotlight at the Castle Night Club, the Gold Key Supper Club, and the Forum Lounge, nightspots situated on or near Sunrise Highway in West Babylon. The Club Safari in the College Point neighborhood of Queens and the Music Lounge in South Farmingdale relied upon Sammy's emcee skills to keep the nights running smoothly, as well as the Misty Mood Lounge in Ronkonkoma, located in the heart of Long Island. Overlooking Lake Ronkonkoma stood the Old Suffolk House, where broiled sirloin steak, lobster tail dinners, and go-go girls were the nightly offerings. Sammy worked there also, cracking jokes and keeping the businessmen sated, seated, and knocking back overpriced hootch between strip acts. B-girls with bouffant hairdos and long fingernails sat at the bar, taking in Sammy's act several times a night.

Pittsburgh Sun-Telegraph, March 20, 1955.

Headed back west from the island, nightclubs dotted Manhattan's neighboring boroughs, and there were scores of them. There was Crocitto's in the South Beach end of Staten Island, Moulin Rouge in Mariners Harbor, also on Staten Island, and the Hi Hat Cafe up in Morris Park, a predominantly Italian section of the Bronx. Brooklyn would provide a solid home for Sammy's talents over the years, with gigs at the China Lantern in Canarsie and Club 82 and the Parakeet Club in Bay Ridge. Sammy entertained at what was billed as "America's First Comedy Club," the Crazy Country Club in Bay Ridge, which boasted "Warm beer and lousy food" on its marquee. Sammy yukked it up on the dark wooden stage in the center of the room at the Airport Club, way out on Flatbush Avenue and Avenue U. He performed between the bump-'n'-grind acts at the 46th Street Theater in Borough Park, the Interlude in Gravesend, and underneath the elevated subway tracks at the Club Illusion in Bensonhurst.

Just four Fridays after his last show with Duke, Sammy was arrested in Manhattan for indecent exposure while strolling down Eighth Avenue and 53rd Street at four in the morning. Sammy and his roommate, Jerry Knapp, fortified by multiple scotch and sodas, were nabbed wearing "shorts, shoes, socks and nothing else," according to an account in the *Brooklyn Eagle*. "It was dark but the cops had no trouble spotting the loud polka-dot shorts of one of the men," the *Eagle* went on to report.

Sammy and Jerry Knapp lived in Manhattan Beach, an Italian and Ashkenazi Jewish enclave located to the west of Brighton Beach and Coney Island. An aspiring actor and piano player, Jerry Knapp hailed from St. Louis and worked as a shoe salesman. They were booked on violation of Section 435 of the Administrative Code (indecent attire on a public street) and fined $10 each in Lower Manhattan Court later that morning. They both claimed that they didn't know what happened to the rest of their clothing. Knapp was advised by Magistrate Louis S. Wallace to go back to St. Louis. That night, Sammy kicked off a three-night stand at Frank Nocella's El Mombo—two shows a night.

King Broder (real name: Irving Broder—no relation to Realart's Jack Broder), was Sammy's agent in the '50s and '60s. A tough-as-nails yet charismatic figure in the local circuit, King Broder was a small-time operator. He handled the bookings and sometimes drove his clients to gigs in the Catskills and other regions. Italian singers, amateur magicians, housewife strippers, and aspiring comics comprised King's stable of talent. Although King had some success early on with the Jerry Vales and the Al Martinos, he didn't make real coin until he sued Eddie Murphy in 1987 for breach of contract. After nailing an audition for *Saturday Night Live* in 1980, Murphy allegedly ghosted King even though he was under a three-year contract with him. After a week in a Mineola courtroom, Murphy settled for $1.1 million, explaining that he was busy filming *Beverly Hills Cop II* and admitting that he "always liked King."

In 2013, still in the business and operating out of an office at a strip mall in Hicksville, Long Island, a ninety-year-old King reflected upon his working relationship with Sammy.

"I was a pretty big club-booker at the time," King recalled. "If you had to work on Long Island, in Brooklyn, or the Bronx, you had to reach out for me. And we had a lot of the bungalow colonies and places up in the mountains and resorts like that. When Sammy was available and I needed a comic to fit the bill, I called and I'd give him a job.

"Sammy auditioned for me and then I started playing him in a lot of these venues. He was a funny guy. I don't really recall his act. I do remember—he had a face like Jerry Lewis, you know? He had that same quality of Jerry Lewis prancing around the stage when he was younger. And he was funny. He did his job and went home. The interesting thing is that at that time a lot of the comics were Jewish, you know? And to find Italian comics to play some of these nightclubs were hard to come by. There weren't that many Italian comics around. I knew he was Jewish, but he had the Italian name and that made it interesting, and so if you have an Italian club owner you say, 'Hey, I have Sammy Petrillo.' They thought he was Italian because of his name.

"He had other agents he worked with. There was a guy by the name of Johnny Martinelli, who had some rooms in the Bronx and Westchester. Nice guy, but we were competitors and he booked several of the rooms and sometimes Sammy worked for him and sometimes he worked for me. In those days, you had different families of wiseguys who controlled a certain amount of rooms. He had certain connections and I had certain connections. If a new room came up, then there was a bumping of heads, but basically it was sort of 'these are my people and these are your people.'

"Sammy went through a lot of partners. He was looking to be another Martin and Lewis. I used to tell him, 'Sammy, you're a funny guy! Be yourself!' He'd always revert to doing his routines like Jerry 'cause he had Jerry's face. If there was no Jerry Lewis, he would have been Jerry Lewis."

In 1954, Sammy took his cousin Martin along to one of his runs in the Catskills. "I'm nine years old and I remember the hotel," Martin recalled. "It was the New Edgewood Hotel and the reason I remember that name is that he would say, 'Here we are at the New Edgewood Hotel. So this is the New Edgewood? I'd like to see the Old Edgewood,' and that was the joke and the audience went nuts. It was a packed house because the entertainment came with a week at the hotel and after his act they actually stood in line to get his autograph. He signed all the autographs and then he put his arm around me and then we'd go off, and I thought I was just the luckiest person. They were waiting in line for his autograph and I have Sammy."

Not long after Sammy's twentieth birthday, Hicksville, Long Island, hosted the October 29th opening ceremonies for the sprawling Nassau Farmer's Market, a twenty-three-acre slab of shopping space touted as the "largest and most modern in the world." The festivities were broadcast live over CBS-TV and featured "A Galaxy of Prominent Stage-Screen-Radio and TV Stars," including the singer Libby Dean and the comedian Phil Foster, along with a twelve-piece orchestra led by Long Island's own "Hot Lips" Phil Lianzo. Prominently displayed in the full-page print ads, Sammy was described as the "Hilarious Comedy Star . . . of Monogram Films, stage, nite clubs and television! You'll howl as millions have before!" and "The zany who keeps you in stitches with his crazy antics!" Sammy was friends with the formidable tough-guy actor Lawrence Tierney, also appearing at the Farmer's Market and billed as "Broadway's Bad Boy" due to his offscreen brushes with the law.

Sammy scored a prestigious gig in early January 1955 at the Latin Quarter in Boston, the same venue where Martin and Lewis had followed up their 500 Club debut in Atlantic City almost ten years earlier. For the revue *Gotta Getaway!* Sammy was hired to play the "morbid son" to Lulubelle Clarke's "zany mother" in a musical travelogue that transported them to Miami, New Orleans, Las Vegas, and Paris in their quest to "getaway" from it all. Specifically hired for his Jerry Lewis vibe, Sammy lamented to the *Boston Daily Record* several of the issues that come with looking like Jerry Lewis. He said that people often mistook him for the real Jerry Lewis, and when they found out he wasn't they would get angry. "His managers," the article reported, "and he's had a succession of them, find it hard to get him work." Distancing himself from Jerry Lewis was futile: "I've let my hair grow, everything to try to get away from it, but [it] won't work." Sammy drily suggested that he was contemplating "getting his face changed" by the world-renowned plastic surgeon Veraztad Kazanjian.

There were problems with *Gotta Getaway!* The *Boston Daily Record* noted that "Main beef at the opener lies in the comedy sequences with Sammy Petrillo, aping the antics of Jerry Lewis, spilling his lines so rapidly that the impact is lost on the ringsides." After one week, Sammy was replaced by the comedian Georgie Johnston and the story was retooled as a boy-meets-girl, boy-hates-girl, boy-gets-girl romp.

Titter, slugged as "America's Merriest Magazine," showcased busty gals in various states of undress among a plethora of gags, giggles, and humorous captions. Geared towards the discerning buyer who was tall enough to reach the top rack at the newsstand, *Titter*'s February 1955 issue was made even more special by featuring a two-page spread on Sammy Petrillo. Accompanied by "bouncy" Toni Allen, a towering and buxom pin-up model wearing a white top hat, fishnet stockings, and not much else, they engage in a series of heavily retouched photos of their slapstick shenanigans. Parodying the Martin and Lewis movie *That's My Boy,* the layout was titled "That's My Girl," complete with Sammy chasing Toni with a baseball bat, Toni grabbing Sammy by his head, Sammy squirting Toni on the ass with a seltzer bottle, Toni singing off-key while Sammy comically sticks his fingers in his ears, and so on. Sporting a variety of checkered and striped outfits, Sammy is cross-eyed and screaming in all of the shots.

Oddly, the photos were authentically snapped in a real nightclub, with an audience listlessly staring at something more engaging that's happening off-camera. The patrons' ennui is palpable and is in stark contrast to the hijinks of Sammy and Toni's "Zaniest Act in Show Business." Burlesque was

Stepping into the world of men's magazines with statuesque Toni Allen.
Titter: America's Merriest Magazine, Vol. 11 #4, February 1955.

YOU'VE heard of the movie "That's My Boy!" Well, here we introduce the new nite club act That's My Girl! Talented comedian Sammy Petrillo, who bears an amazing resemblance to Jerry Lewis, teams up with tall and terrific Toni Allen in the craziest act in show business!

Bop! But not be-bop! Toni belts Sammy on the noggin, and the audience loves it! →

This is *singing*? Toni has the curves, but not the voice, and Sammy suffers!

35

on life-support at this point, but if you were casually flipping through an issue of *Titter,* you would never know it.

In April, Sammy was at the Copa in Pittsburgh billed as "The Boy Everyone Thought Was Jerry Lewis." Sammy took the opportunity to once again vent his vexations to the local paper, this time the *Pittsburgh Press*:

> Conservatively clad in a pink cashmere jacket, a rich maroon silk vest with gold buttons and a blue shirt whose collar flared like the top of a heart, Sammy outlined yesterday what it's like to resemble a celebrity. "I've had a lot of frustrations and setbacks," he said. "I know I have my own talents—I do other impressions besides Jerry, but all through my act I look like him. It's an act of God, y'know?
>
> "People walk up and say, 'Ah, you're just an imitation.' Before they've even seen my act, y'know? It's kind of frustrating, but Jerry Lewis is a great talent and I'm kind of proud of it, too.
>
> "Funny thing—I get taken for Johnnie Ray an awful lot, too. More even than I get taken for Jerry. Let me show you." He leaped to his feet and showed a mouth-open profile shot in the Johnnie Ray manner . . .
>
> "I can't seem to get a face of my own," Sammy continued. "It's a weird thing, y'know, sort of a setback, yet it's an advantage, too."

The article goes on to mention that "his wife Lucille resembles the late Jean Harlow . . . though this has not proved a source of public confusion yet."

Starting in the 1940s, Pittsburgh was a fertile stomping ground for top-shelf singers and comics. The Twin Coaches and the Holiday House were two of the biggest clubs on the circuit, seating roughly 1,000 patrons each, at New York City prices. Orbiting the major venues was a smorgasbord of smaller lounges downtown and in the suburbs that would happily throw their doors open for a Jerry Lewis look-alike. In the spring of 1955, Sammy typically worked every night at Pittsburgh's Hollywood Star Bar with Bunny Glenn, a tap dancer, and Lovely Grandy, a stripper.

A new comedy and singing team was unveiled on May 5, 1955, at Rudy's Blue Star in Meadville, about ninety miles north of Pittsburgh: Tom Cozzi and Sammy Petrillo. They were advertised as "Better than Martin and Lewis" and most likely this was their first and last appearance. That summer Sammy put in a week-long engagement at the family-friendly West View Park amusement park, twenty minutes north of Pittsburgh.

On July 25, 1956, Jerry Lewis and Dean Martin performed their last show together at the Copa in New York City. In Martin and Lewis lore, this date was chosen because it was exactly ten years to the day since their first appearance together. The split had been a long time coming. Dean and Jerry's not-so-secret contempt for each other was obvious to their co-workers, the press, and, more significantly, their fans. Two movies a year, a punishing TV schedule, and endless club dates would wear down any partnership, and it's a small miracle that Martin and Lewis stayed together as long as they did.

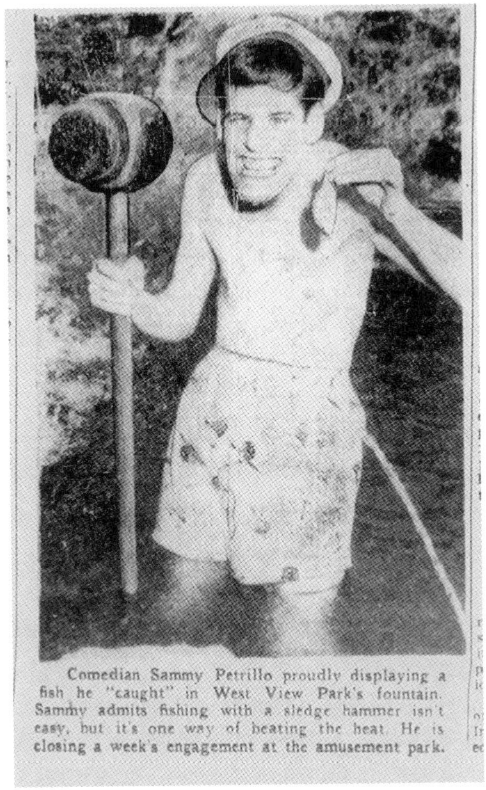
Comedian Sammy Petrillo proudly displaying a fish he "caught" in West View Park's fountain. Sammy admits fishing with a sledge hammer isn't easy, but it's one way of beating the heat. He is closing a week's engagement at the amusement park.

Sammy makes a splash in the Pittsburgh suburbs. *Pittsburgh Sun-Telegraph*, July 6, 1956.

Dean in particular, at age thirty-nine, had lost patience with the whole setup. Fed up with the stale movie roles written for him, the usually punctual Dean would show up late for shoots, just daring Jerry to pick a fight with him. As an extra flip-off to his partner, Dean missed important gigs, sending a henchman bearing the bad news to Jerry at the last minute. Jerry, in turn, lashed out at Patti and the kids, making their lives so miserable that at one point they had to move out of the house for a week. Unraveling, Jerry surrounded himself with eager yes-men, while still driving himself and everyone else around him crazy. In an abrupt and vindictive act, Jerry fired his favorite writing team, Norman Lear and Ed Simmons, after *TV Guide* revealed that, at $10,400 an episode, they were the highest-paid writers in television. *The Colgate Comedy Hour* was losing the ratings war to Ed Sullivan anyway, so it was a good time to wrap things up television-wise. As far as everything else was concerned, both partners knew that the roller-coaster ride had come to an end and it was time to hop off. After the breakup, Ernest Glucksman ended up managing Jerry as a solo act for another eight years. His autobiography, *You Can't Cure a Ham,* about his days as Jerry Lewis's manager, was announced in 1978 but, sadly, never published.

One day after Martin and Lewis's last show, Sammy was "Packing the House!", according to an ad for the Arcade Club in Sioux Falls, South Dakota, where he appeared with the musical group the Nicolettes. Returning to L.A., Sammy spent his days at Coffee Dan's on Hollywood Boulevard, a high-powered schmoozing hangout. It was time to look for a new partner. Possibly the loss of an actual Martin and Lewis might have opened the door for a new Martin and Lewis–like team to take its place. Or maybe the public was finally through with Dean and Jerry and were on to the next diversion. The burgeoning rock 'n' roll industry was ensnaring kids with a force unseen since bobby-soxers were paid to faint at Sinatra concerts. Sammy would have to find out for himself.

Skelly and Anna, along with their kid brother Marvin, traveled west to visit Sammy in October 1956. "We stayed in some hotel garden apartment," Marvin remembered. "We watched Don Larsen pitch a perfect game in the lobby of the hotel. I remember that there were a lot of guys trying to get into show business and they were actually sleeping in the hotel lobby."

Looking for work, Sammy rang up Kirby Allan, a moderately successful crooner, producer, and bongo player with whom he had struck up a friendship while filming *Brooklyn Gorilla*. Kirby took an interest in Sammy's career and let him live in the back of his office. Daytimes, they would confer at Coffee Dan's and plot out their next move.

Born Sidney Allen Pittman in Prescott, Arizona, Kirby Allan was a fascinating character who would soon be known as the guy that made exotica music go pop in a big way in the western world. His collaboration with the percussionist Leon Johnson, a.k.a. Chaino, from Philadelphia, resulted in a series of mesmerizing LPs which presaged and heavily influenced a wave of tiki culture that's still thriving today. Promoting Leon as orphaned from a lost African tribe, Kirby retrofitted the tribal sounds for western ears by tightening up drum solos and adding tropical sound effects. Kirby's Americanization of so-called primitive sounds created a new genre of music and gave the recording industry a much-needed kick in the ass.

Kirby, at twenty-eight, was a show-business veteran. He had scored a moderate hit in 1952 with the Sinatra-esque "Roamin'" and was running his own label, Maze Records. Kirby was still young enough to be full

Sammy playing the Black & Tan circuit in L.A.
Newspaper advertisement, circa January, 1957.

of ideas, and one of them was to pair Sammy with Bill Norman, one of the singers on his label. Kirby recommended Sammy to a pal, whom he referred to as "the biggest comedy writer in Hollywood," Rocky Kalish. Sammy remembered Rocky from the *The Colgate Comedy Hour*.

"I don't remember him being on the show," Rocky said in 2014. "In his memory, I'm sure that it was a big moment, but it wasn't a big moment for me." Rocky was one of the sharpest writers in the business, with an award-winning career penning scripts for everyone from Abbott and Costello to *All in the Family*. Above all, Rocky Kalish was a mensch and decided to help Sammy out "for gratis."

"I wrote a premise for a pilot that I would be involved in, in the long run, if it was picked up. The pilot had to do with Sammy and his partner being [theatrical] agents and Sammy would get crazy acts. He would get balloon acts and a dog that could howl 'Take Me Out to the Ball Game.' He would get these wild ideas. It was called *The Ten Percenters*."

Sammy and Bill Norman made an appearance at the Hollywood Christmas Parade in a car with "Norman & Petrillo" emblazoned on the side. There was even talk about them recording a novelty comedy record together for Maze. "We filmed a demonstration reel from Rocky's script," Kirby said. "It wasn't very good cause these guys didn't gel." At one point, even Kirby got into the act, briefly appearing onstage as Sammy's singing straight man.

The brief pairing of Norman & Petrillo. Promotional photo, circa 1963.

Fondly looking back on his days knocking around with Sammy, Kirby recalled that Sammy "was a rare bird indeed. He was funnier with his friends than onstage. He would frequently hail a taxi on Vine Street two blocks from Coffee Dan's and he and his friends would pile in and pile out a couple minutes later."

One of Sammy's more interesting encounters in Los Angeles involved the eccentric, long-haired "Nature Boy" composer eden ahbez. Born in Brooklyn as George Alexander Aberel, eden ahbez was living under one of the Ls of the HOLLYWOODLAND sign when he refashioned an old Yiddish song, "Shvayg mayn harts (Be Still My Heart)," into a chart-topping hit for Nat King Cole (and countless others). Anticipating the hippie movement by at least ten years, the deeply spiritual ahbez ate only fruit and vegetables and was often seen perambulating bearded and barefoot down Hollywood sidewalks. Kirby was present for some of Sammy's run-ins with ahbez. "One time when he and I went to Coffee Dan's," Kirby recalled, "Sammy opened the door and almost bumped into eden ahbez. He jumped back yelling, 'Jesus!'" It's likely that this gag was repeated on more than one occasion, with Sammy intentionally bumping into the barefoot hermit and yelling out some version of either "Jesus!" or "Jesus Christ!" Another anecdote involves Sammy catching the notoriously ascetic ahbez sneaking a late-night piece of chocolate cake at Googie's Diner, a hipster hangout on Sunset and Crescent Heights. Sammy snatched the cake away from ahbez and lectured the waitress that the "Nature Boy" could only be served "leaves, twigs, and dirt."

Kirby booked Sammy into the December holiday show at the Middle-Eastern-themed Club Oasis. On a bill with the singer Yvonne Pratts, the acrobat Iron Jaw Wilson, and Chaino, Sammy shared emcee and comedy duties with the comic, songwriter, and impressionist Slick Slavin. Born Howard Trustin Slavin in Chicago, Slick was a self-assured comic, whose various impressions included a Larry Parks, silently miming, a dig at Parks's voice dubbed in by Al Jolson in *The Jolson Story*. The versatile Slick would later appear in the Elvis Presley movie *King Creole* as an emcee and sing the crazed rockabilly song "Speed Crazy" in the Poverty Row movie of the same name before rounding out his career as a writer for *The Joey Bishop Show*.

Three weeks into 1957, Sammy was still at the Oasis, this time with a switched-up roster that included the "lovely" Miss Pat Sides, Big Bertha Henderson, and the Don Strong Dancers. The popular South-Central club featured the R&B pioneer Johnny Otis and his talent show every Thursday night and a "big breakfast show" every Sunday morning. The Club Oasis would be one of Sammy's last professional appearances in California.

In May, the *Pittsburgh Post-Gazette* ran an interview with the peripatetic Sammy, who announced that "the nightclub business is dead on the West Coast . . . top-grade acts are being peddled for as little as $100 a week." While "weighing a number of local cafe offers," Sammy took a gig at the New Nixon Restaurant and Supper Club. At the Talkie Temple amphitheater in West Park, Pennsylvania, four weeks later, Sammy was on a family-friendly bill which also featured Frank Jarema's orchestra and the aerialist Betty Paso, performing "atop a high, swaying pole with no safety device." Back home in the Bronx that summer, the *New York Post* reported that "Petrillo is . . . trying to sell his television film, 'Wait for the Laugh.'"

On the same day, the *Long Island Star-Journal* spilled that Sammy was going to announce his new singing partner onstage that night at the Club Safari in College Point, Queens, a remote, northwestern section of the borough that jutted out into Flushing Bay. Under the headline "Broadway Rushes Safari Comic," the plan was laid out:

> Sammy isn't talking and neither is the club. But from the rush by Broadway booking agents to ringside seats at the Safari, there appears to be big things in store for the comic who looks and acts more like Jerry Lewis than Lewis does.
>
> Could it be that since the Lewis and Dean Martin split, the Broadway eager scouts are eyeing Sammy and his secret pal as possible successors to the L and M crown[?]
>
> "My new partner and I were clowning around at the club last week," Sammy said. "The management liked us so we decided to try it out this weekend. If we click this weekend, who knows?
>
> "Show business is funny. I've been kicking around since I was 12. At 24 I'm considered a veteran. I've good material, but they tell me I look too much like Jerry Lewis. Who knows, this may be a blessing in disguise. I'll know this weekend," Petrillo declared.

Also advertised on the bill were the Wong Sisters and the "star of 'Phenix City Story,'" "Chesty" Meg Myles. Oddly enough, Meg had previously teamed up with Duke, post–*Brooklyn Gorilla,* in the "vaude team" of Mitchell and Myles.

Sammy's new singing partner was revealed that night at the Club Safari to be Tony Landi, briefly spawning the comedy team Petrillo and Landi. It was reported by the *Long Island Star-Journal* that Petrillo and Landi had "taken Queens by storm," yet precious little is known about Tony Landi. Fortunately, he cut a single that year for Safari Records, so his talents as a singer can be assessed. The A side of the record was "Bubbily Bubbly," a cute romp of a song, spotlighting exaggerated Elvis intonations amid the moronic lyrics:

> Bubbily bubbly
> I'm bubblin' all over
> Every time you pass by
> Bubbily bubbly
> Come on over
> My heart is gonna fry

The B side is the unremarkable "Angels Cried," a sluggish ballad that presents Tony doing battle with syrupy background singers and a clanging bell. He sings of a lost love affair using a June–moon rhyme scheme:

Angels cried
While stars in the sky hid from sight
And I was alone in the night

How I yearn now that you are far away
Please return and turn this night into day

Tony meets the bland lyrics halfway, with a teenage voice too thin to carry out the operatic gymnastics needed to elevate this stinker even by one notch. A review in the *Capital Times* of Madison, Wisconsin, described Tony as "A new Italian voice, replete with solid feeling."

"Angels Cried" was penned by Don Canton and Ira Kosloff, who each had multiple songwriting credits to his name. Canton had co-written "(I Know My Baby Loves Me) In Her Own Peculiar Way" for Chet Atkins and His Colorado Mountain Boys in 1947, and later, in 1963, "Dear Santa Claus" for Buddy Hackett. Elvis Presley's 1956 A side "I Want You, I Need You, I Love You" is Ira Kosloff's most famous co-composition and it's one of the King's better ballads from the time. That same year, Canton and Kosloff composed a novelty B side for Frank Sinatra, "Five Hundred Guys." ("Five hundred guys have 1000 eyes.") What makes "Angels Cried" uniquely baffling is that Sammy Petrillo is listed as the third writer of the song—or, rather, the writing credits read, "Petrillo-Canton-Kosloff."

There are several reasons why someone's name might end up on a record label, especially back in the mobbed-up '50s. Sometimes a label owner might want a piece of the publishing action, so he becomes a co-author. Morris "Moe" Levy would make a career out of attaching his name to songs and subsequently the publishing credits on his Roulette Records label. In 1955, the WINS disc jockey Alan Freed was listed as a co-author on Chuck Berry's "Maybellene," along with Russ Fratto, a Chicago businessman who was leaning on the Chess record label for unpaid loans. Assigning writing credit was used as a poker chip, a form of legit currency among wiseguys in the business.

The fact that "Angels Cried" was the first release from Safari Records points to a tie-in with the Club Safari, where Tony Landi was first paired up with Sammy. Perhaps it was a way for Safari's owner, Andy Leonetti, to pay Sammy dues owed from the club that didn't involve cash, check, or money order. The 45 was also a great souvenir for tipsy patrons as they maneuvered their way past the Club Safari coat check to the exit.

Maybe Sammy really did co-write "Angels Cried." He told people that he did. However, Sammy never mentioned Tony Landi; he would only refer to the singing group that covered the record later that year: the Isley Brothers. Coincidentally, Sammy's cousin was Irwin Levine, who co-wrote "Tie a Yellow Ribbon Round the Ole Oak Tree" for Tony Orlando and Dawn and "This Diamond Ring" for Gary Lewis (Jerry's son) and the Playboys, among other hits.

Released on Teenage Records and produced by the musically-inclined gangster George Goldner, the Isley Brothers' first record, "The Cow Jumped over the Moon," was an uptempo curiosity in the style of Frankie Lymon and the Teenagers. "Angels Cried" on the flip, now credited to "Canton-Kosloff-Petrillo," is an improvement on the Landi original. With Ronald Isley taking the falsetto lead, the dirge is more palatable, with a pseudo–Ink Spots feel to it. Still, a clunker is a clunker, and the single became a forgotten blip in a sixty-plus-year career fueled by blockbusters like "Shout," "Twist and Shout," and "It's Your Thing."

Petrillo and Landi continued at the Club Safari through August before headlining a stint at the Van Horn Show Bar in West Springfield, Massachusetts. Touting "Continuous Entertainment" and "2 Floor Shows Nightly," the self-proclaimed "Only Bar of its Kind in Western Mass." boasted that the pair were "Terrific!" In the ads, under a banner reading "The Greatest Impersonation of Dean Martin and Jerry Lewis That You Have Ever Seen," was a publicity shot of Sammy, hanging on to Tony's back like a demented monkey with a nice haircut. Sammy is cross-eyed, a gimmick he had lately utilized for photo shoots, distinguishing himself from Jerry Lewis, who rarely struck that pose.

Sammy's next significant venture involved traveling to the subtropical clime of Ocala, Florida, for a television pilot starring his old buddy, Lawrence Tierney. *Wings for Hire* (a.k.a *Civil Air Patrol*) was pitched as the adventures of two charter-plane pilots, Larry Quinn (Tierney) and his hapless sidekick Flaps (Sammy). Filmed with the full cooperation of the Tactical Command of the U.S. Air Force, *Wings for Hire* required both Sammy and Tierney to take rudimentary flight lessons at Silver Springs Airport for at least the takeoff and landing shots. Sammy's brother Marvin came down for the shoot and said that "Sammy and the instructor had taken me up in a little private plane and they stalled the engines trying to scare me." Tierney, in between bouts of binge drinking and public brawls,

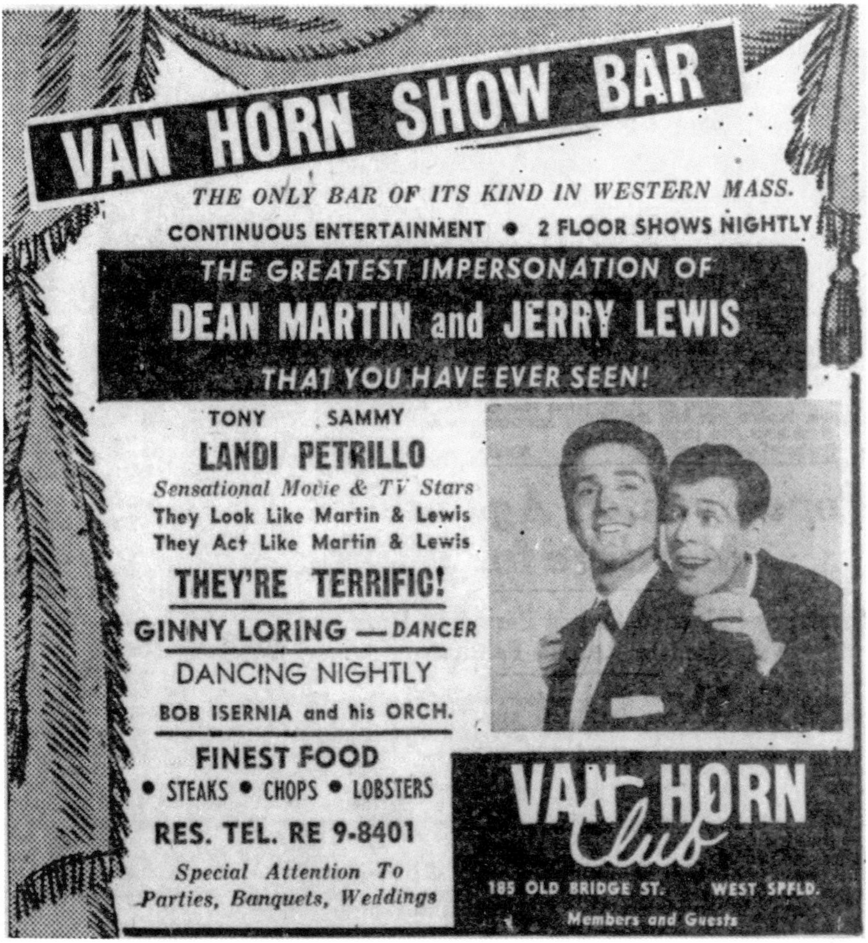

Another partner. *The Republican*, September 17, 1957.

was looking to get his acting career back on track, a feat which required round-the-clock babysitting from Sammy. Entrusted with distracting Tierney from the bottle, Sammy kept the itinerant drunk preoccupied any way he knew how. "I'd be exhausted running track with him, before we'd shoot, after we'd shoot," Sammy told *Psychotronic Video* in 1991. "Then we started playing cards but he wanted to bet money. It cost me 800 bucks to keep the guy sober."

The pilot episode sees Sammy as Flaps getting bitten by an escaped rattlesnake mid-flight, landing his plane in a swamp, and getting rescued by Larry. The show was not picked up. However, both Sammy and Tierney made the best of their time in Ocala by cutting the ribbon and performing schtick at the opening of a remodeled movie theater. On the bill was a second run of Jerry Lewis's sophomore solo movie, *The Sad Sack*.

Sammy also showed up at Ocala High School, where the *Orlando Sentinel* reported that "Petrillo outlined schools for interested students to attend to launch a movie or TV career and gave advice on how to break the ice."

Wings for Hire's producer, Dick Randall, wasn't done with Sammy—not by a long shot. Randall, an eccentric former television quiz show and gag writer, saw potential in the twenty-four-year-old comic, and a friendship was cultivated. Randall's next project was a quasi-documentary about the 1958 Brussels World's Fair (Expo '58) for the TV market. Sammy is credited with producing and co-writing the show for Randall's Network Film Corporation. The special mixed stray footage of Expo '58 along with scenes of Sammy shot locally, with New York City's Central Park standing in for Brussels. It featured a jazz score by Steve Allen, narration by Georgie Jessel, and a Chaplin-esque pantomime appearance by the photojournalist Weegee. Due to the Steve Allen connection, *Holiday in Brussels* was actually shown on NBC-TV, the home to the Sunday-night *Steve Allen Show*.

Sammy was back headlining at the Club Safari on Labor Day weekend, where it was advertised that he had "Just Completed A Tour Thru The Midtown Tunnel." The *Long Island City Star-Journal* noted that, due to his resemblance to Jerry Lewis, Sammy "was never able to get off the ground with his own act. But the story is different now. He has new material, and Dean and Jerry aren't a team anymore, so Sammy is hoping to strike it rich."

In an unlikely and unexplained twist, Sammy was briefly back with his most famous ex-partner, Duke Mitchell. The event was a return to the Spade Cooley TV show out on the coast, site of one of their most chaotic performances five years earlier. No other information is available regarding this tantalizing bit of reunion magic, their first since the Martin and Lewis breakup.

The next event in Sammy Petrillo's story might not have even involved Sammy Petrillo at all. Here's the tale: in December 1958, Jerry Lewis, in a moment of vindictive hubris, decided to roast the talk-show host Jack Paar on the second episode of his "full-hour colorcast" variety show. Jack Paar was an offbeat yet popular entertainer who, despite an abundance of charisma, was plagued by self-doubt and was, in turn, notoriously sensitive. Jerry's impersonation tore into Paar with a quiet subtlety that the columnist William Ewald described as "unhurried, penetrating and painfully accurate . . . very funny in its almost deliberate lack of real wit." The *Kansas City Star* found that the skit "effectively pinpointed Paar's weaknesses, but it wasn't very funny." Paar retaliated. According to Ewald, "Jack Paar opened his NBC-TV show Wednesday night by trotting out a gentleman who, complete with weird-o haircut and short pants, spoofed Jerry Lewis."

Years later, there was a newspaper ad for Sammy that mentioned *The Jack Paar Show* as one of his recent appearances. However, they also have him showing up on *The Ed Sullivan Show,* which definitely never happened. In interviews, Sammy never mentioned appearing on *The Jack Paar Show,* so it's possible that the Paar producers procured a knockoff version of Sammy. In the end, Jerry was on the butt end of the joke and he didn't like it.

This bit of business paled in comparison to the whirlpool Sammy jumped into (or was thrown into) next. In April 1959, Jerry hosted the Academy Awards for the third and final time. The ceremony unexpectedly ended twenty minutes early, leaving the funny man on live TV, standing in front of scores of movie stars, adrift in a sea of flop sweat. He got off one successful ad-lib.

"And they said Dean and I wouldn't be on the stage together again," Jerry said to the last smattering of applause he would receive that evening. Clearly caught off-guard, he rattled off jokes about Danny Thomas and the Three Stooges that were met with silence. In desperation, Jerry grabbed the baton from the orchestra leader, Lionel Newman, and asked the band to play "Three hundred choruses of 'There's No Business Like Show Business!'" The ninety or so celebrities on the stage paired off and danced with each other while an unseen announcer slowly recapped the night's winners of awards that night. Off camera, Jerry grabbed a trumpet and blew into it maniacally. After a few minutes, NBC cut away to a rerun of a sports show about firing pistols.

It was a classic live-TV trainwreck with accusatory fingers pointed in all directions amid the smoking debris. Some say that the producer, Jerry Wald, had cut too many musical numbers in an effort to keep the show running on time; others implicate Jerry Lewis, who unofficially stage-managed and noodged and cajoled everyone into picking up the pace. After the pinnacle of *The Colgate Comedy Hour*, Jerry would never again reach any level of success on television. The 1959 Oscars were just another banana-peel slip on the way down, and Steve Allen was standing by with an armful of bananas.

Representing two distinct schools of comedy in their crowded and highly competitive world, Steve Allen and Jerry Lewis were not buds. Steve was a new breed of thinking man's comic—the intellectual observer commenting on society and standing up for civil rights at a time when it wasn't popular to do so. Showcasing his offbeat sensibilities, Steve dipped his toe into the jazz and beatnik scene, cutting a record with Jack Kerouac, as well as bringing the writer on his show to read from *On the Road* to piano accompaniment. Steve considered Jerry Lewis to be old hat, a relic chained to creaky slapstick tropes. Like the rest of America on Oscar night, Steve saw Jerry fumble spectacularly. Unlike the rest of America, Steve seized the moment and served it back in Jerry's face.

The following Sunday, *The Steve Allen Show* opened on Sammy with his back to the camera conducting a standing studio audience while the orchestra belted out "There's No Business Like Show Business." Sammy turns around and does a quick succession of comic takes—pulling his mouth apart with his pinkies and crossing his eyes, patting the top of his head and waving his arms around. Dressed in a suit and tie, Sammy looks more like Jerry Lewis than ever. However, he brings a manic, sped-up energy that even Jerry Lewis couldn't tap into. Sammy stops the intro music.

"Hold it, hold it, will ya? All right already! How much time do we have left here?" he asks an off-camera stagehand.

"One hour? One hour." He looks at his watch.

"Okay, thank you. We're ad-libbing. One hour. Okay, uh, do we have any more awards to give out? No more awards to give out?" Sammy wipes his brow.

"Okay, looks like we'll have to do thirty more choruses of this," referring to "There's No Business Like Show Business." Then things get nasty. Sammy, in a mocking tone says, "And they said Dean and I would never be on the stage together again!"

"Okay, I'll tell ya what we'll do," Sammy continues. "Ladies and gentlemen, we have some time to kill, so for the rest of our time, here is *The Steve Allen Show*!" Sammy turns back to the audience, swinging his arms, occasionally looking back at the camera, cross-eyed with his mouth agape.

His previous television appearances, as well as *Brooklyn Gorilla,* might charitably be called a tribute. This time there was no doubt. Sammy had been fully weaponized to torpedo the massive Lewis ego. If Jerry hadn't actively sought a blacklist against Sammy in the industry before, he certainly did now.

In the syndicated column "It Happened Last Night," Earl Wilson reported that "Sammy Petrillo, who impersonated Jerry Lewis on Steve Allen TV'er, says that was the last time—he'll let his hair grow and try to make good on his own."

Sammy was back at the Club Safari in May on a bill with Sam Cooke, who was promoting his latest single, "Everybody Loves to Cha Cha Cha." In June he returned to the Talkie Temple in West View Park with a trapeze act, the Flying La Vals, and the "rock and roll singer" Dave "Diddle" Day.

At Bruno's in East Liberty, Pennsylvania, Sammy shared a bill with the Nairobi Trio knockoff the Nirobi (*sic*) Trio. One of Ernie Kovacs's most popular routines on his TV show featured the Nairobi Trio—three gorillas in hats and overcoats playing along to a syncopated version of Robert Maxwell's "Solfeggio," while bopping each other on the head with mallets. Hollywood's biggest in-joke had Ernie's buddies Jack Lemmon, Milton Berle, and Frank Sinatra appearing, at one time or another, anonymously inside the gorilla suits. Sammy, who was promoted at Bruno's as being "recently seen on *The Steve Allen Show,*" stayed on with the Nirobi Trio for several weeks.

The late '50s and early '60s were a pivotal time for Dean and Jerry and Duke and Sammy. Fresh opportunities brought varying levels of success, and their respective careers would spiral in distinct directions. Though these ex-partners were now estranged, they all shared a unique experience that would bond them forever. Like the Beatles or like astronauts on the same mission, whatever ill feelings they might have had for each other were outweighed by the circumstances of time and proximity. Call it the "astronaut syndrome." A better example would be the punk legends the Ramones, who famously hated each other but considered themselves "brothers," a united front against the rest of the world. You can't spell "ex-partner" without "partner."

Duke distanced himself from *Brooklyn Gorilla* and continued as if nothing had happened. According to Duke's son Jeff, there wasn't any love lost between him and Sammy. "My dad didn't want him in his life," Jeff says. "He was done with him after that movie. When anyone would ask my dad what Sammy Petrillo was doing, he'd say, 'I dunno, he's probably guessing weights on Coney Island.'"

Impersonations gave Duke's stage act an extra zing, and he swung with it. He'd offer his takes on Billy Eckstine, Frankie Laine, Vaughn Monroe, and, most notably, the comically melodramatic Johnnie Ray, his ex-partner's second-best impression. *Variety* noted that his "brief act could easily be expanded. Mitchell's selling of 'Rags to Riches' and 'Got You Under My Skin' reveal savvy as a crowd pleaser, with reliance more on entertainment than on showcasing of voice."

"My dad never quit for lack of work," Jeff Mitchell says. "He quit because he hated [Sammy]. He also did a short stint with the Happy Jesters, a successful Vegas lounge act, so he had money pouring in."

In 1956, Duke signed to Liberty Records, home to Alvin and the Chipmunks and Julie London. A handful of singles sold modestly, mostly at club engagements. His single "The Careless Years" b/w "Crazy Heart" mostly flew under the radar. The *Kings County Chronicle* wrote that "Duke always endeavored to sing like a combination of top crooners, which is his trouble. Next time we see him, we would suggest he try singing like himself for a change and stop imitating those who have already made the grade."

Dabbling in acting netted Duke a couple of small roles as thugs in *Crime in the Streets* and *Baby Face Nelson,* but he continued to hold down the fort for most of the '50s at Tabletoppers, his old Bob Romeo and James Dean beatnik hang down on Sunset. James Dean was gone, but Bob Romeo kept the hipster vibe alive with his bongos, flute, and poetry and his new pal eden ahbez. A wigged-out *Los Angeles Mirror* proclaimed it to be "the weirdest, wildest music you'll hear this side of Damascus."

Duke put together an act with "Chesty" Meg Myles (see above), the actress, singer, and pin-up model whose 42-24-36 measurements were purported to "make Jane Russell feel like a boy." *Variety* enjoyed "their songs and happy patter," but the team of Mitchell and Myles was short-lived, with Meg appearing with Sammy at the Club Safari in Queens only a few months later.

While still headlining at Tabletoppers, Duke was spending his weekends in Palm Springs, where he performed with his Duke Mitchell Trio to the delight of celebrity club-goers, which on any given evening might include Jimmy Durante, Lucy and Desi, and Jack Benny. Sometimes Duke would bring his children Susan and Jeff onstage with him. A photo taken at the Ranch Club shows Duke and his kids in full blackface at a *Showboat* party where the *Desert Sun* reported that they "were the hit of the minstrel show . . . Many in the audience jumped to their feet and clapped enthusiastically at this performance."

In September 1959, Duke premiered *Table Hopper*—a half-hour "live-tape" weekly show that was broadcast on the local station KTLA. Featuring "the little lady with the big voice," Betsy Duncan, and a nine-piece orchestra, *Table Hopper* was sold as a casual night on the town with Duke and his celebrity pals—a proto–*Playboy after Dark,* which *Variety* summarized as "ersatz impromptu banter [that] looked phoney." Among Duke's guests were Jerry Lewis's father Danny and Joe E. Ross with his James Cagney impersonation. *Variety* added that Duke "was interesting but good for only two or three songs. Also, he bounces up and down for no apparent reason." *Table Hopper* ran for twelve weeks before being canceled.

Table hopping with Duke Mitchell and gang. *Valley Times,* September 18, 1959.

Duke landed a job at Hanna-Barbera, scat-singing as Fred Flintstone in a couple of early episodes, as well as voicing the beatnik Boppy Barrin in "Yogi's Birthday Party." *Variety* reported that Duke was tapped to "double as a hepcat" in the pilot *Five Cats,* a cartoon that would ultimately air as *Top Cat,* without Duke's involvement.

Crowned the "King of Palm Springs," a title that stuck for a few decades, Duke happily shuttled between Palm Springs and L.A., with his eyes set on getting back in the movies with a gangster picture, *Contract Killer,* that he wanted to write, direct, and star in. Duke would eventually film his *Godfather*-inspired epics *Massacre Mafia Style* in 1974 and *Gone with the Pope,* released posthumously in 2010.

After the breakup with Jerry Lewis, Dean Martin was written off as a has-been by soothsaying critics. He almost proved them right with 1957's *Ten Thousand Bedrooms,* an MGM stinker of a musical that nearly sank his movie career. Dean came firing back in short order with three solid dramatic performances in a row: *The Young Lions* with Montgomery Clift, *Some Came Running* with Frank Sinatra, and *Rio Bravo* with John Wayne. These were all prestige pictures directed by established pros: Edward Dmytryk, Vincent Minnelli, and Howard Hawks, respectively.

Dean was selling records again—"Return to Me," "Volare," "Ain't That a Kick in the Head"—those and other monster hits kept the Capitol Records pressing plants working overnight shifts for years. Updating his image, Dean slyly cultivated a drunk persona onstage, even though he was mostly sipping iced tea, at least early on. Pretending to be tipsy gave him the leeway to ad-lib, forget punchlines, or even get punchlines wrong. It was a smart move, and audiences ate it up.

Securing a lucrative five-year deal at the Sands put Dean on Sinatra's level of success, except he went a step further by conquering the boob tube as well. Starting with a series of triumphant NBC specials in 1957, Dean was a fixture on prime time TV for the next twenty-five-odd years. Dino, as he was affectionately known, was a cultural phenomenon, a natural talent with superior comic and singing chops who made everything he did look easy. Add some Matt Helm movies to the mix, James Bond parodies tailor-made for Dean's breezy personality, and the 1960s were looking good for the former Dino Paul Crocetti.

Terrified to continue as a solo act, Jerry was thrust back onstage only two weeks after his last show with Dean. Judy Garland was set to perform at the New Frontier in Las Vegas but had come down with laryngitis at the last minute. Judy's husband Sid Luft called Jerry and begged him to fill in for her. Jerry agreed, but only on the condition that Judy sit next to him onstage during the entire performance, which she ended up doing, much to the audience's delight. It was the first time that Jerry had worked solo in ten years, and he won over the audience with a collection of well-worn razzamatazz from his pre-Dean days. He ended the show with Judy's usual closing number: Al Jolson's number-one hit from 1918, "Rock-a-Bye Your Baby with a Dixie Melody." Jerry crawled inside the song and emerged as a different person. He gave the full Jolson that night—teary-eyed, clasping his hands and dropping to one knee for the finale. The crowd went nuts and Jerry was terrified no more.

Inspired by the reaction to the Jolson song, Jerry approached Capitol Records about releasing a set of straight, non-goofy numbers, including "Rock-a-Bye Your Baby." After recording a handful of tunes, Capitol passed, and Jerry took the tapes to Decca, where he added a few more songs, including another Jolson hit, "I'm Sitting on Top of the World." In August,

"Rock-a-Bye Your Baby" went to number ten on the *Billboard* charts and the LP *Jerry Lewis Just Sings* went to number three and promptly sold a quarter of a million copies.

Al Jolson's legacy endured, even though Al didn't. Jolson had keeled over from a massive heart attack during a hand of gin rummy six years earlier. That didn't stop Jerry from canonizing the old Broadway belter whenever he got a chance. On the second episode of *The Jerry Lewis Show* in 1957, Jerry's father Danny sang the old Jolson weeper "Sonny Boy" to an interrupting and wisecracking Jerry. This was followed by Jerry singing "Sonny Boy" to his eight-year-old son Gary, perched on his lap and armed with similar retorts.

Jerry's mother Rae kept herself busy by fending off any supposed heirs to her little *bubbeleh's* throne, even when it came to rock-'n'-rollers. Jerry Lee Lewis was encroaching on Elvis Presley's popularity in the late '50s when he received a frantic phone call from Rae begging him to change his name. Request denied. For the next fifty years Jerry Lee Lewis would refer to himself by name on more records than any other recording artist in history.

After six years on *The Colgate Comedy Hour,* Jerry never really clicked as a solo act on television, but not for lack of trying. He did get to star in his dream television project, yet another version of *The Jazz Singer,* this time for the *Ford Startime* anthology series on NBC. It's a tedious hour of hokum, which even hardcore Jerry Lewis fans might have trouble enduring. Thankfully, Jerry chose to go with clownface over blackface for the climactic scene in which he sings the Kol Nidre at the synagogue, subbing for his dying father. Oddly enough, according to the *Los Angeles Mirror,* in 1950 Dean Martin was rumoured to be cast in a *Jazz Singer* remake for Warner Bros. after Frank Sinatra had already passed or had been dismissed from the role.

Jerry's next movies, *The Delicate Delinquent* and *The Sad Sack,* both did well at the box office. The welcome return of the screwball director Frank Tashlin fueled *Rock-a-Bye Baby* and *The Geisha Boy,* two films which the paternal Tash allowed Jerry to unofficially co-direct. In early 1960, when Paramount insisted on releasing the already-finished Tashlin-directed *Cinderfella* that summer, Jerry pleaded with them to hold it for a Christmas release. He struck a deal whereby he would deliver a summer movie for them from scratch, even though he only had a few months to do it in.

Under the gun and working around the clock, Jerry filmed *The Bellboy* on location at the Fontainebleau Hotel in Miami during the day at the same time that he was performing two shows there every night. A collection of silly blackout gags, peppered with cameos from Jerry's showbiz buddies, *The Bellboy* is almost a documentary, a glimpse into what it's like to live inside Jerry's fevered brainpan for a few weeks.

Such a schedule could not have been maintained were it not for his wise investment in a new type of technology that would one day be standard in the film industry and what was known on the set as "Jerry's noisy toy." In the latter half of Jerry's life, an interviewer's best way to immediately get into his good graces was to compliment him on his pioneering work on the innovation that would one day be known as Video Assist. It was a quick, insiders' way of showing Jerry that you had done your homework before speaking to him. Always intrigued by gadgets since he was a kid, the prototype Jerry used was groundbreaking in that it allowed directors to immediately view a shot that was captured by a synced-up video recorder. Video Assist eliminated second-guessing whether a take had worked out or not and then having to wait twenty-four hours to look at the dailies. For comics directing themselves, it was a game-changer. Keaton or Chaplin would have given their left nuts for one of these back in the day. For a director/actor, to be able to access their own performance immediately was a perspective that no filmmaker had ever experienced.

After two weeks of shooting, Jerry took the footage to the Sands in Vegas and edited *The Bellboy* into cohesion. It was the first movie that Jerry had written, directed, and starred in, and it felt good. With the assistance of liberating technology and a handful of pep pills, Jerry was working at the apex of his creative powers. It was the beginning of an inspired journey, bursting with ideas, that would take him to the career heights of *The Ladies Man*, *The Nutty Professor,* and beyond.

Sammy Petrillo was keeping busy as well. He was about to star in his first nudie movie.

CHAPTER 14

SHANGRI-LA AND OTHER PLACES

Carme Daniel Pitrello started entertaining in high school in upstate New York in the early 1950s. He enlisted in the army at age eighteen and represented his company as a boxer, if only to get out of KP. Seeing action in Korea, his platoon was separated from support forces after a designated drop zone was bungled. He survived freezing temperatures for two weeks in the Taebaek Mountains, where he "killed a pursuing enemy squad" and buried his best friend. Carme was the only survivor in his unit. Returning to the States, he was reassigned to Operation Desert Rock in Nevada, performing tactical maneuvers during the detonation of thirteen atomic bombs. In 1959, he changed the spelling of his name to "Petrillo" to match that of his new partner, Sammy Petrillo.

Sammy was Carme's first partner. "He taught me how to be a good straight man," Carme would say. Tweaking the act to follow the lead of Dean and Jerry's maturation into pathos, their press materials claimed, "A touch of seriousness in the right places makes this act sensational." In an accompanying publicity photo, Sammy and Carme sport white dinner jackets and black bow ties. Carme has a high pompadour and pronounced, black eyebrows. His left arm is draped over Sammy's shoulder while his right hand is holding Sammy's jaw open as if he's inspecting a dog for cavities. More promises from the press kit: "Good Clean Comedy" and "Impersonations—You name 'em they'll do 'em." Petrillo & Petrillo secured a radio show on 1,000-watt WMCK in McKeesport, home of Pittsburgh Pirates live broadcasts. Carme would also be the second and last of Sammy's partners to appear with him, albeit briefly, in a motion picture.

The director Russ Meyer had just launched his long and smutty career with the unlikely success of his skin flick *The Immoral Mr. Teas*. A colorful nudie-comedy, it featured the titular character spying and drooling over naked women accompanied by moronic observations from an unseen narrator. Seizing the moment, Sammy's next movie would be one of the hundreds of *Mr. Teas* knockoffs that attempted to capture that same cinematic magic.

Shangri-La was the brainchild of Sammy's new producer pal, Dick Randall. Throughout Sammy's career, he would gravitate towards boisterous showmen, whose broad gestures and grandiose plans evinced a P. T. Barnum sensibility. Dick Randall was a huckster cut from that cloth. Born Irving Reuben in the Catskill Mountains, Randall started in the business as a writer, supplying gags to Milton Berle and TV quiz shows. He ingrained himself in the sketchy world of low-budget exploitation movies, often making deals out of his huge apartment above the Stage Deli on Seventh Avenue, two blocks south of Carnegie Hall. Will Jordan, whose short-lived TV quiz show Randall produced, remembered that "Everyone loved him. He was a big, fat, kind of a Jewish Buddha who would do favors. His whole apartment was filled with refrigerators and washers, things that he would get instead of payment." His apartment was also an "open house for bookies, loan sharks, the racket boys and girls that were 'in the business,'" the photographer Arthur Fellig, a.k.a. Weegee, wrote in his autobiography. "I liked the informal atmosphere and I spent a lot of time there," he added. Working around the periphery of the film business, Randall sought seed money for his projects from small-time sources: cabbies, dentists, waiters, and grocery-store clerks, as well as "the racket boys." After raising $50,000 for *Shangri-La,* Randall hired half a dozen showgirls, rented a few station wagons, leased a gorilla suit, and grabbed Sammy Petrillo. It was late summer 1959, and their first stop would be a nudist colony in New Jersey.

Double trouble. Promotional photo, circa 1960.

Newspaper advertisement, circa 1961.

Weegee also jumped into one of the station wagons. Born in what is now Ukraine, Weegee became a fixture on the New York City tabloid scene in the late 1930s and 1940s. Sleeping with a blaring police-band radio near his head, Weegee would race the cops to fresh crime scenes, often beating them by several minutes. Armed with a 4x5 Speed Graphic camera and a bag of flash bulbs, his beautifully sordid photographs were a lowbrow and highbrow sensation, capturing Fun City in all of its histrionic detail. For added oomph, he carried a battered toy doll with him, which he would toss into the tragic tableaus to amp up the drama. *Naked City,* a 1945 collection of his photographs, was a bestseller, making Weegee an instant celebrity. His work, originally created for smudged newsprint, now hangs in museums and galleries, a validation of his effortless style. In the 1950s and '60s, Weegee began to experiment with prisms, kaleidoscopes, and other trick lenses, even producing an infamous distorted close-up of Marilyn Monroe.

After shooting footage in a New Jersey nudist camp, the convoy rolled down to Silver Springs, Florida, for an airplane scene and more raw footage. Real nudists appear as extras; in fact, due to camp rules, everyone on the crew, from the director down to the script girl, had to work naked. Weegee, being a nudist himself, was fine with that. Listed in the credits as providing "Trick Photography," Weegee also held down the job of technical director, meaning that he had to make sure that no crotch shots made it into the movie.

The *Shangri-La* opening credits state, "We regret that this film has NO Director. We couldn't find one to keep his mind on the job!" But it turns out that a naked Sammy Petrillo co-directed with a similarly unclad Arthur Cohen. Cohen, a veteran filmmaker, had several one-reelers under his belt, including a series for Universal-International that he wrote and directed, starring Phil Foster as a lovable lug named Brooklyn. Cohen's history of hoary schtick would make him an apt fit for Sammy's directorial debut. Sammy was also allegedly responsible for writing *Shangri-La,* even though official credit goes to the mysterious E. S. Seeley, Jr., whose only other credit is co-writing 1958's *The Hideous Sun Demon*. According to Weegee, "We ad-libbed the story as we went along," and, for a man who was known for stretching the truth, this is a good time to take him at his word.

Shangri-La opens with Sammy, as a zookeeper about to go on vacation for two weeks, standing in a gorilla cage, tearfully saying goodbye to his pal, Pinky the Gorilla. Once again playing a character named Sammy, he agrees to a last-minute game of poker in which bananas and other fruit

Sammy in *Shangri-La*. Courtesy of Something Weird Video.

are wagered, as well as a gold tooth that Sammy plucks from his mouth (and promptly loses to Pinky). Sammy's traveling companion, Jim, a pipe-smoking, academic nerd, enters through a hole in the wall and asks where they are going on the vacation. The remaining sixty-three minutes of the movie are Sammy telling Jim about his adventures on his previous trip to the beatific Camp Shangri-La. "Where we're going," he tells Jim, "all you'll have to wear is that big grin of yours."

There are flashbacks, mostly shot silent, that, combined with Sammy's voice-over narration, describe the bare bones of the plot amid an avalanche of double entendres. Sammy recounts running into "two cute dames" and then following them by car to their destination, a nudist camp called the Pines Forest Club. He is seen gawkishly ogling the now-naked girls frolicking with other nudists from behind various foliage and trees. Garishly dressed in a bow tie and wide-brimmed hat, with his eyes bugging out of their sockets, Sammy resembles a deranged version of the film-noir creep Dan Duryea. One-liners are flying: "They were undressed, and that's the naked truth," "The sight I had seen left me petrified in the forest," "I decided to stand firm until I could solve this riddle." The "script" has Sammy written all over it.

After more leering eye-candy footage, a now-disheveled-looking Sammy follows the girls to Washington, D.C.—first to the Washington Monument and then to the National Historical Wax Museum. Shot on sound film, the film next features Sammy riffing through a series of corny jokes. "I'm here for the Boston Tea Party," he says to a wax patriot. "I married one of the bags that they threw overboard." He approaches a Patrick Henry dummy standing next to a hanging noose. Sammy grabs the bottom of the noose and, bouncing up and down, says, "Pardon me, does this train stop at Canal Street?" He places a copy of *Playboy* in General Grant's hands instead of a map and stands between Abraham and Mary Todd Lincoln at Ford's Theatre. He turns on the figure holding a pistol behind them: "John Wilkes Booth! How are ya? How's your brother, Telephone?"

Dick Randall was a small-aircraft enthusiast, so naturally there would be a sequence with Sammy piloting a plane or, since the wheels never leave the ground, driving a plane like a car. Subsequent scenes involve naked swimmers, alligator-wrestling, and the Cypress Gardens water clowns, a genre of buffoonery that is as endemic to water parks as rodeo clowns are to bullfighting arenas—a clown for every occupation. In a trick-camera shot, Sammy, wearing an 1890s-style bathing suit, appears to be waterskiing as he screeches and crosses his eyes.

Sammy then follows the girls to Camp Shangri-La—an outdoor hobbyist paradise populated with happy nudists playing topless tennis, topless darts, and topless shuffleboard. Everybody's smoking cigarettes as they squint into the sun. Getting accustomed to the nudist way of life, Sammy decides to doff his threads as well. He checks into the camp and encounters the gruff, half-naked Harold Gary as the chief registrar, Mr. Van Bottom. Harold Gray began his acting career as one of Eugene O'Neill's original Provincetown Players and appeared in hundreds of TV shows, as well as starring in the award-winning Broadway production of Arthur Miller's *The Price* in 1967. He brings a surprising gravitas to his scenes as the Big-Brother-like supervisor. In a barrage of legal jabberwocky, Mr. Van Bottom warns Sammy not to break any rules, else he risk expulsion.

In an effort to squeeze Sammy's new partner Carme into the movie, a brief nightclub scene at the Shangri-La Casino is cagily inserted. Standing close to each other in a spotlight, a fully clothed Petrillo & Petrillo run

A night at Ford's Theatre—Sammy Petrillo style. *Shangri-La.*
Courtesy of Something Weird Video.

through their schtick at lightning speed. Carme makes a non-joke about nudists taking their clothes off outside and putting them on inside. Sammy, not imitating Jerry Lewis but in his own naturally raspy voice, says, "Hey, Carmie. You know, I was thinking before . . . I don't appeal very much to women, so I was figuring if I became something that women would go for, sort of like an actor, because I like this show business thing, maybe they would go for me. But I can't think of the right role."

"You look like a Jimmy Stewart type," Carme says. "A clean-cut American. Can you do Jimmy Stewart?"

Sammy does Jimmy Stewart. Now the act shifts into high gear.

CARME: Sammy, you're a natural.
SAMMY: I'm a natural comedian.
CARME: I'm a natural singer.
SAMMY: That's right.
CARME: Don't it seem natural we . . .
SAMMY: . . . team up together and then women will go for me like they

go for you as a handsome singer. That's wonderful. Yes, maybe we can do an impression of a comedy team.

CARME: Dean Martin!

SAMMY: And Jerry Lewis!

Sammy combs his hair down over his face and runs through a five-second sizzle reel of Jerry Lewis facial tics. With pursed lips and crossed eyes, Sammy shrieks, "Hey sir! I wanna sing a song with you! I wanna sing that song, 'I Dream of Brownie with the Light Blue Jeans!'"

"'I Dream of Jeanie with the Light Brown Hair.'"

"You dream about who you want, and I'll dream about who I want!"

There's no time or budget for a song. After seventy-five seconds, the only known footage of Petrillo & Petrillo has run out the clock, and *Shangri-La* is ready to serve up some more cheesecake.

For the climactic beauty-contest sequence, Weegee rigged up a kaleidoscope lens which creates shimmering reflections of light across a parade of naked women as they walk alongside a swimming pool. Weegee referred to it in his autobiography as "a beautiful underwater nude ballet." The contest is officiated by three shirtless judges—possibly someone named Bernard L. Goldenberg, probably the schlock movie producer George Weiss of *Glen or Glenda* fame, and most definitely Sammy Petrillo's partner, Carme Petrillo. They sit solemnly at a card table making notes on the array of female pulchritude on display before them. Sammy, as the emcee, gets unfairly blamed for fixing the contest, and, in a Kafkaesque plot twist, is booted from the camp for an unexplained infraction by Mr. Van Bottom.

Sammy is inconsolable. "The whole world looked different to me," he says over Weegee's blurry, Coke-bottle images of nudists playing shuffleboard. Back in the gorilla cage, Sammy has an epiphany: "I began to see things in a new light. There was still hope for me. I figured I could always return next year and make amends and start anew."

In the final moments, the two girls he was stalking earlier show up outside the gorilla cage, and the gag is that Sammy doesn't recognize them with their clothes on. Pinky the Gorilla makes noises at the camera and *Shangri-La* concludes with a smooth right-to-left pan of five bare asses. The End.

In order to appease the censors, *Shangri-La* presents itself as an educational film, a meditative look at the physical and mental benefits of a nudist lifestyle, as opposed to what one might consider to be cheap smut for the sticky-floored popeye crowd. Occasionally, Sammy peppers his jokey running monologue with a sincere plea for understanding. "Nudism was nothing to joke about," Sammy thoughtfully considers. "It's a wonderful and natural way to live happier and healthier and longer."

Even though *Shangri-La* was promoted as being "Filmed in Beautiful Eastman Color," all known prints are in black and white. Ironically, Weegee recalls in his autobiography that he suggested to Dick Randall that *Shangri-La* be shot in color. Randall apparently laughed and told Weegee that "people who came to watch nudist films were not interested in color or in beautiful sunsets. They just wanted flesh . . . black-and-white was good enough."

Weegee was proud of his involvement with *Shangri-La,* citing it as "a real work of art, if I say so myself. The picture turned out to be a great financial success, and everyone was happy." *Shangri-La* was held from release for two years, after first getting banned by the New York State Censor Board, the Maryland State Board of Motion Picture Censors, and other local authorities. It eventually opened in September 1961 at the Paris Theatre in Los Angeles, on a bill with a return showing of 1958's *God's Little Acre* starring Robert Ryan, Buddy Hackett, and Jack Lord. The ad copy for *Shangri-La* read, "It's Frenchy, it's saucy, and it's definitely for ADULTS. You'll have to see it to believe it, and it will never be on TV."

That same year, Sammy had an unbilled cameo in the horror movie *The Brain That Wouldn't Die*, written and directed by his friend Joseph Green. It's a feel-bad B movie about a mad doctor who keeps his girlfriend's head alive after a fatal car crash and his subsequent search through seamy strip joints in search of a replacement for her body. Sammy appears in a scene with a gaggle of photographers, snapping cheesecake shots of the model Adele Lamont. He jumps around in front of the other shutterbugs, holding and tilting the camera in various positions in a sequence that would be filmed twice—once with Adele's clothes on for the domestic release, and once with her clothes off for the less-puritanical European market. *The Brain That Wouldn't Die* sat in the can for three years until AIP picked it up for distribution, coupling it on a bill with *Invasion of the Star Creatures*.

The movie work continued. Dick Randall took another stab at pairing Sammy with Lawrence Tierney in *Unholy Alliance,* a gangster story that went unreleased and was possibly never completed. Years later, Sammy could only recall filming a scene with Tierney in which they were picked up hitchhiking by "a guy that was gonna kill us."

Sammy rang in the 1960s performing solo for a few nights in January at the Show Boat in Rochester, New York, on a bill with Four Lucky Girls ("Direct from Las Vegas") and Flame Fury ("Attractive Dancer"). Sammy cultivated a reserve of impersonations that he could draw upon besides his Jerry Lewis showstopper. He could easily pull off a Dean Martin as well, along with Wallace Beery, Humphrey Bogart, Elvis Presley, and Robert Kennedy. "I had a great resemblance to the Kennedys," Sammy said. "Just like people used to think I looked like Jerry, people thought I looked so much like Robert Kennedy that it was unbelievable."

In mid-April 1960, Petrillo & Petrillo were back, held over for a second week at the Showcase in Pittsburgh, sharing a bill with a "rock 'n' roll unit" called Bert Dantow and His New Night Owls. There was nothing noteworthy about this engagement, except that it led to Sammy meeting a new comedy partner and siring four children with her.

Elaine Freycent lived in Monongahela, colloquially known as Mon City, a small town forty-five minutes south of Pittsburgh. Elaine and her friends sneaked away to nightclubs in Pittsburgh whenever possible. Looking for laughs, they ended up at the Showcase, in the East Liberty section of town, where Elaine took part in an audience-participation bit. That was the story that Sammy and Elaine's eldest son Shawn was told. "My mom was extremely funny," Shawn says, "and at some point in the show she went up there and carried Sammy offstage. That's how they met."

Sammy and Elaine formed an on-again, off-again act called Sammy and Elaine. Whether they ever actually got married is a question that even Shawn can't answer. (And the public records are less public and less complete than one would think.) It would appear that Sammy led a freewheeling and probably complicated love life. Divorced or separated from his first wife or common-law wife, Lucy Beell, in 1955, Sammy may have left two other marriages in his wake—one in Los Angeles to Marta Malott in 1956 and another to Evelyn Keller of the Bronx in 1958. The comedian Jack Carter told Kliph Nesteroff, a writer, in 2011 that Sammy had married Clair Fitzpatrick ("giant body, giant girl"), a showgirl and waitress in Las Vegas. Years later, to add to the mystery, Sammy said that he was married "only once in my life" and that it wasn't to Elaine.

And this is where the story gets vague.

According to Sammy's cousin Martin, "Sammy worked for the USO in Europe in the early '60s. Could be 1960. And also, for whatever reason, Sammy wound up in Hong Kong." Another partner popped up around this time—Art Riley, an actor turned newsman in the Dallas–Fort Worth area who said that he traveled in the USO for two years as half of the comedy team Petrillo and Riley. Possibly it felt like two years for Art Riley, but Sammy's engagements in the States during that period make a two-year

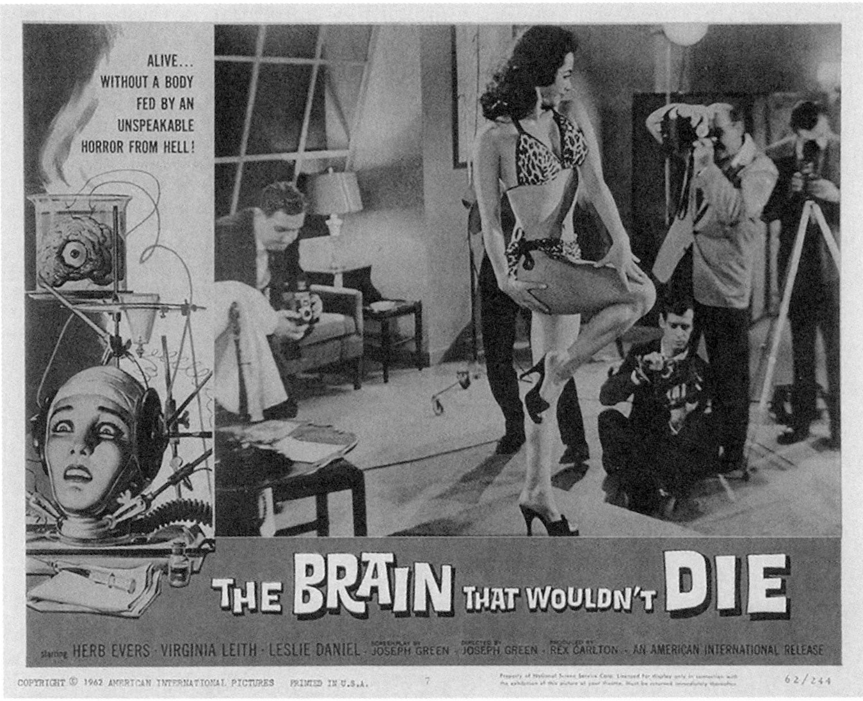

Lobby card for the clothed sequence featuring Adele Lamont.
The Brain That Wouldn't Die, 1959 (released 1962).

Sammy and Elaine. Circa 1963. Courtesy of Shawn Patrello.

stint in the USO unlikely. Ten years later, Riley would partner with Sammy again at the Rex Theatre and at its sister venue, the Lido in Dallas, Texas. (Ten years after that, as a radio announcer, Riley reported at the scene of the exhumation of Lee Harvey Oswald, who was dug up to see if it was true that a look-alike Russian agent had been buried in his place. It wasn't.)

In October, Petrillo & Petrillo were held over for a second week at the Bon Ange nightclub in Pittsburgh. By the end of the year, the act had dissolved. Carme found a new partner, Paul Salos, with whom he would stick until 1970. Carme and Paul, as they were known, had a unique chemistry by which they could easily switch back and forth with their Martin and Lewis impersonations, even though Paul was the main Jerry Lewis guy. "We were so much more than Martin and Lewis were," Paul said later, "but we never got the big break that Martin and Lewis got." Carme and Paul palled around with Jack Ruby and performed at Ruby's Carousel Club, earning them the distinction of becoming the second and third Sammy Petrillo affiliates (after *Brooklyn Gorilla*'s screenwriter, Ukie Sherin) mentioned as persons of interest in the Warren Commission Report.

Dick Randall snagged a contract with the Flushing Meadow Amphitheatre in Queens to present a summertime water variety show he called *Aquarama 1960*. Site of the former and future New York World's Fair, this "Musical Variety Water Spectacular" featured, at various times during the summer, the Mystics (a rock 'n' roll act), the WNTA-TV personality Clay Cole, the former *Flash Gordon* star Buster Crabbe, Vincent Lopez and His Orchestra, and the Dancing Water Aquamaniacs, who were an assortment of diving clowns, belly flopping and skipping ropes off of high diving boards. Sammy, now head of production for Dick Randall's Network Film Corporation, was added to the bill as an emcee for the last week of the summer season. It was a moderate success, with the *New York Times* saying the "amiable" show "manages, in spite of the planes from LaGuardia Airport and the helicopters, to hold attention through most of a long program."

The beginning of 1961 found Sammy back in Pittsburgh at the Apache Lounge, appearing twice nightly with a stripper named Lillian Angel and, at the top of the bill, a singer named Jimmy Massey. Billed as "Movieland's Newest Comedy Star," Sammy made an impression on one Apache Lounge patron, Jack Blanchard. "The crowd and even the club owner had their doubts that Sammy had ever made a movie," Jack said. "When Sammy found out that we'd seen one of his pictures, he took us around to the boss and the customers. We were his 'proof' to the bunch of dummies who didn't know who he was." After the show, Sammy and Elaine brought Jack up to their room where they sat up all night and talked. "He didn't do much Jerry Lewis in his show that night," Jack recalled, "but he did a lot of other good stuff. He seemed as though he could look like anybody he wanted!" The Apache Lounge added another week of Sammy, with the ads screaming, "Held over by popular demand—You've Never Lived, You've Never Laughed Until You See Fantastic Sammy Petrillo Clown Prince in Miami."

In July 1961, the *Pittsburgh Post-Gazette* reported that Sammy Petrillo had a new partner: Sabor the Robot. Bolted together in 1938 by August Huber, an inventor, in Zurich, Switzerland, Sabor, at over seven feet tall and nearly 600 pounds, was able to speak, walk, and light a cigarette. Presumably not invited to the 1939 New York's World's Fair to compete with Westinghouse's Elektro the Robot, Sabor's showbiz career stalled out prematurely in the 1940s. Turning up at Expo '58, where Dick Randall was shooting footage for his *Holiday in Brussels* special, Sabor, retrofitted to play harmonica and dance the samba, was ready for a comeback. Earning Huber $2,500 for an appearance on *The Ed Sullivan Show,* Sabor was creating a minor buzz in the variety industry. Sammy cracked to the *Post-Gazette* that, "If this act breaks up, at least something can be salvaged—my partner."

Disappointingly, this was the last mention of the proposed comedy team. However, the article intriguingly suggested that "Petrillo and two other Pittsburghers, Carme Petrillo and Harry Albacker, currently appearing in the movie *Shangri-La* at the Art Cinema, are planning another feature film venture dealing with *Nature's Mistakes*." This project never reached fruition, either.

Inspired by *The First Family,* Vaughn Meader's comedy LP that became the fastest-selling record in history, Dick Randall hatched a new plan. Fixated on busting into the recording industry, Randall set his sights on producing comedy albums, and he was taking Sammy Petrillo along with him.

CHAPTER 15

PANTIES INFERNO

"Do not be afraid; our fate
Cannot be taken from us; it is a gift."
—*Inferno* by Dante Alighieri

Wanda is a revelation. A 1970 feminist movie with a non-feminist main character threw a lot of the critics off at the time. The film opens with the titular Wanda leaving her husband and young children, only to randomly hook up with an abusive bank-robbing boyfriend. Set against the coal-mining bleakness of eastern Pennsylvania, *Wanda* was shot on location in grainy 16mm, evoking a documentary feel, as if we were eavesdropping on the characters. The cast of mostly non-actors shapes the movie into a realistic sullenness, which gives its writer, director, and lead actress, Barbara Loden, a chance to shine. Wanda is defeatist and passively takes abuse as if she actually deserves it, and Barbara lives inside that role. One critic, Amy Taubin, wrote that "Loden's performance spoke to Wanda's humanity and to that of the majority of women worldwide who can't envision a way to fight back."

After she worked on it for almost ten years, her debut film would also, infuriatingly, be her last. Born in the Depression, Barbara was raised by her grandparents in Marion, North Carolina. She allegedly joined a traveling circus as a teenage acrobat and moved to New York City, where she posed for detective and pin-up magazines under the name Candy Loden. After dancing in a chorus line at the Copacabana, she joined the Actors Studio, where her talent fully flowered. By 1960, she had appeared in a handful of stage hits: the Broadway production of *Compulsion, The Highest Tree* with Robert Redford off Broadway, and *Night Circus* with Ben Gazzara. She honed her comedy chops as a stock player on *The Ernie Kovacs Show,* dressing up in a gorilla suit as one third of the Nairobi Trio and dressing down as Ernie's usually scantily-clad sidekick. She appeared in *Wild River,* directed by Elia Kazan, beginning a long creative and, at times, contentious romantic partnership with Kazan, whom she eventually married in 1967. Even with her stage and screen successes, Barbara still felt as though she were drifting aimlessly through life. "I had no identity of my own," Barbara said. "I just became whatever I thought people wanted me to become."

A chance browsing through the March 27, 1960, issue of the Sunday *Daily News* was an epiphany for Barbara. A random article about a "Go-For-Broke Bank Robber" resonated deeply, not so much for the inept crook killed by the police but because of his wayward girlfriend, Alma. Aimless and sleepwalking through life, Alma had run off with this heartless drifter because there appeared to be nothing better to do. When brought before the judge and sentenced to twenty years in prison, Alma, relieved that it was all over, thanked the judge, an act that sent Barbara's mind reeling. Alma was a lowbrow version of what Barbara might have been, and she needed to tell that story, even down to outfitting the actor who played the bank robber in Kazan's old clothing.

"I used to be a lot like [Alma]," Barbara said later. "I was worth nothing. I didn't know who I was." Alma's story sent Barbara down the path of self-discovery that would result in a genre-busting movie. Unfortunately, the Hollywood PR machine didn't know how to spin such a despairing film created by a beautiful actress. Despite winning for best foreign film at the Venice Film Festival, *Wanda* didn't catch on with the public and disappeared quickly. Promoting the movie, Dick Cavett patronizingly introduced Barbara on his talk show as "the attractive and very determined Barbara Loden." Her reception on *The Mike Douglas Show,* during the week John Lennon and Yoko Ono co-hosted and chose the guests, was less condescending, yet equally awkward. No one was comfortable discussing such a downbeat movie.

Decades later, after Barbara's tragic, early death from breast cancer, *Wanda* was rereleased and reassessed as the unique and subtle masterpiece that it is. An inspiration for indie filmmakers, its improvisational shagginess evokes the best of John Cassavetes's work, with the filmmaker John Waters going so far as saying that, "If you don't like *Wanda,* you're an asshole."

Barbara's ability to tell her story through the actions of someone else was a breakthrough, creatively and otherwise. Putting down the newspaper that Sunday afternoon in 1960, Barbara knew that she had found a clear direction, one that would bring peace of mind and renewed purpose. She was inspired and happy, maybe for the first time in her life. Living in New York during this period, Barbara also got to know her husband's good friend, Sammy Petrillo.

In 1954, Barbara had married the film producer and distributor Larry Joachim and stuck with him even through her fractious relationship with Elia Kazan. Barbara and Larry's son, Marco Joachim, remembered that his parents "somehow were friends with Sammy Petrillo, Will Jordan, Sid Caesar, Ernie Kovacs, and all those people."

Born in Brooklyn, Larry Joachim entered showbiz writing gags for fun and then eventually selling his material to Bob Hope, Milton Berle, and Frank Sinatra. He also wrote for CBS radio's Bob Hawk, a pioneering broadcaster who, in 1927, at KSCJ in Chicago, had been the first modern disc jockey, making jokes in between records and interviewing performers. At sixteen, Larry hosted his own radio show, *Comedy Convention,* followed by *College Daze with Larry Haze* on WNEW in New York City. Larry's real innovation was, if not creating, then at least perfecting the "plug business"—determining which products would be talked up and given away as prizes on game shows. In 1961, Larry produced *Murder, Inc.,* which led to a best-supporting-actor Oscar nomination for Peter Falk, in his first major role. By the end of the decade, Larry would move into film distribution, securing the rights to G-rated kiddie movies, grindhouse slasher flicks, and kung fu movies. Larry would later be instrumental in exposing Jackie Chan to a worldwide audience in a dozen movies in the late '80s and early '90s.

"Sammy was pretty good friends with my father," Marco says. "My father always liked Sammy's ideas for movies and things, his treatments." Sammy wrote several scripts and shared them with Larry and Barbara and would one day claim to have created the pitch for a TV show that would eventually be known as the beloved sitcom *The Munsters*. The truth is more complicated.

Not unlike *Wanda*, the concept for what would become *The Munsters* was long in gestation. Barbara was working on a comedy about a family of monsters that at times was variously called *My Daddy Was a Monster, Love Thy Monster,* and *Monster, Go Home*. On July 22, 1958, copyright was filed for a screenplay titled *My Daddy Was a Monster,* attributed to Barbara Coden—a play on her former dancing name, Candy Loden.

"I'm sure that she didn't want her name on this thing," Marco says. "My father may have propagated the story that it became *The Munsters*. It was a small world back then. Maybe they sold the script and somebody bought it and then came up with the Munsters' name. It's also possible that my dad and mom gave Sammy the script to rewrite or add to it."

On August 8, 1961, an article in the *Warren Times Mirror* of Warren, Pennsylvania, mentioned that "[Sammy] Petrillo leaves for Europe to make an independently-produced film, *My Daddy Was a Monster*."

Officially, Norm Liebmann and Ed Haas are credited with developing *The Munsters*, with the Jay Ward cartoon-writing team of Allan Burns and Chris Hayward receiving credit for creating the show for the television division of Universal. "We sort of stole the idea from Charles Addams and his *New Yorker* cartoons," Allan admitted. The concept for a monster family was allegedly first suggested to Universal in the 1940s by the animator Bob Clampett as a new cartoon series. Since Universal owned the rights to the classic movie monsters, it was a no-brainer refitting the iconic characters for a TV sitcom.

Suzie Perkovic, Sammy's longtime partner and one-time girlfriend, remembered *The Munsters* situation this way: "Larry Joachim was in L.A. He did a lot of things for Sammy. Sammy wrote a treatment for *The Munsters*. It was an idea for a show called *My Daddy Was a Monster*, and he sold that treatment for $250. Larry Joachim may have sold that to somebody, and they changed the title to *The Munsters*. Sammy wasn't happy about that, but Larry told Sammy that once the idea's out there it's out there." According to Larry's son Marco, "My dad never said that he sold the treatment or the script. He said that they stole it from them. Or that they stole the idea."

Sammy soldiered on, working an erratic nightclub schedule while trying to secure a regular paycheck. He placed a classified ad in the *Pittsburgh Press*:

> I am starting a new toy and appliance company, called Toys N' Stuff, and need salesmen to contact people for home demonstrations. Comm. Write P 578, Press, Sammy Petrillo.

Nineteen sixty-two started out rough for Sammy. The *Pittsburgh Post-Gazette* reported that he was under a doctor's care for head and neck injuries he received after getting whacked by a suitcase in a bus while returning from an engagement in Johnstown, Pennsylvania. At the time, Sammy's wife Elaine was checked into Allegheny General in Pittsburgh for a kidney ailment, so life was a little difficult.

Gigs were still available back in the New York metropolitan area. In March, Sammy showed up at the Lowerre Post in Yonkers on a bill with his cousin, Dr. Marshall King, whose real name was Marvin Hersh. At one point, Hersh worked with Sammy's brother Marvin in a family business.

"They were 'Marvin and Marvin,' but they called my dad 'Larry' so no one got confused," Marshall's son Stuart said. Marshall was a stage hypnotist (who decades later was still popping up occasionally on Howard Stern's radio and TV shows). In April, Sammy was back with "the Dynamic Mr. Mickey Marlowe" at the Full Moon in Long Island and Hackensack, New Jersey, with "TV and Recording Star Sunny Dale." Also in April, Elaine gave birth to Shawn, the first of her four sons with Sammy.

Comedy had changed a great deal since Sammy popped his head out of the crib on *The Colgate Comedy Hour* back in 1950. Long-playing records proved to be a lucrative delivery system for aspiring comics. Not wanting to give away his best material, Redd Foxx initially rebuffed an offer from Dooto Records to record a comedy album for them. Down on his luck, Foxx eventually relented, and his LP *Laff of the Party, Volume 1,* sold over a million copies, ushering in a new era of home entertainment. Others followed: Stan Freberg, Lenny Bruce, Shelley Berman, Bob Newhart, Vaughn Meader, Nichols and May—with several picking up multiple Grammy awards along the way. Dick Randall wanted a piece of that action. He made a deal with New York's Surprise Records, home to Nipsey Russell, B. S. Pully, and Bobby Dell, to record a Sammy Petrillo prank-phone-call record.

While prank calls were probably born within minutes of Alexander Graham Bell's invention of the telephone, it took almost a hundred years for the first prank-phone-call record to be recorded. Steve Allen released *Funny Fone-Calls* in 1963, but one of the first was Harold Flender's *Candid Telefun* in 1961. Flender, a former writer for Sid Caesar and Bob and Ray, called up various businesses—a pet shop, a beauty shop, a record store, and a fortune-cookie manufacturer, among others—and gave them the business. Flender's delivery sounds so similar to Sammy's that years later his recordings would be misidentified as Sammy Petrillo's on a *Celebrities at Their Worst* CD.

Randall booked time in a Manhattan studio and huddled with Sammy over a phone book while Elaine and baby Shawn waited in an adjoining room. "They were real prank calls," Sammy said, "[Dick Randall] gave me ideas. He said, 'Hey, try this, maybe this line will work.' It was like *Candid Camera* on record, on the telephone. I called people and got them into bizarre situations and would ad-lib with mostly straight-line ad-libs, getting them into situations that were funny, off-the-wall, strange, hard for them to get out of, and hard for me to get out of, sometimes."

My Son, the Phone Caller, a riff on Allan Sherman's top-selling *My Son, the Folk Singer* LP, features thirty-three squirm-inducing minutes of Sammy pestering local businesses with risqué questions on a variety of perverted topics. There isn't a Jerry Lewis moment on there. It's pure Sammy, uttering ridiculous things, playing it straight, and beautifully pulling it off. After years of telling off hecklers in nightclubs across the country, Sammy was in his element. His off-the-cuff patter is painfully sharp, as he amuses and torments the poor jerks at the other end of the line.

In a call to a horse supply company, Sammy peppers the salesman with questions about the size and strength of their whips. "Which is the one that hurts the most? Do you have one that stings the most?" Sammy asks, before confessing that "Someone is going to use it on me . . . and I just wanted to know how it would feel." After asking for the "ass department" at a pet cemetery, Sammy inquires if they would be able to bury his "dead ass," which died "because he sat on it." He calls a company that supplies one-way mirrors to see if he can get a large, wall-sized one installed in his bathroom, so he can spy on his "lady friends." Calling a lingerie store, Sammy inquires after the availability of sheer, fur-lined panties with jock straps built in, especially for men. He dials up an animal hospital and gets step-by-step instructions on mid-wifing a gorilla that's about to give birth in his apartment. A series of frantic veterinarians tell Sammy how to cut the umbilical cord: "Tie it on both sides and tie it tight!" Sammy asks, "When the gorilla comes out, do I hold it upside-down by its feet and spank it?" (The answer is yes.)

The cover of *My Son, the Phone Caller* is a snapshot of Sammy in a phone booth on an unidentified midtown sidewalk. He's holding the receiver of the payphone in his mouth and staring at a naked woman on the sidewalk who is turned away from the camera. Wearing only high heels, elbow-length black gloves, and a hat, the model is clumsily pasted onto the street scene with Sammy. She also appears six more times in different poses running down either side of the front cover, earning this comedy record under-the-counter, brown-paper-bag status. *My Son, the Phone Caller* is stupidly entertaining, and Sammy is engaging and droll throughout the thirteen prank calls and one busy signal that make up the record.

Sammy continued hitting the club circuit, surfacing at the Chez Joey Supper Club and the Palma Room, both in North Bergen, New Jersey, and Nick Beni's Anchor Inn in Poughkeepsie, New York. At the Elms in White Plains, Sammy was paired with "Beautiful European Exotic Dancer," Nai Bonet, and he shared the bill at the Gold Key Supper Club in West Babylon, Long Island, with "Exotic, Big, Bold and Beautiful" Lia Camay. There was a quick trip down to Austin, Texas, to headline at the Jade Room on a bill with "Gals—Gals—Gals."

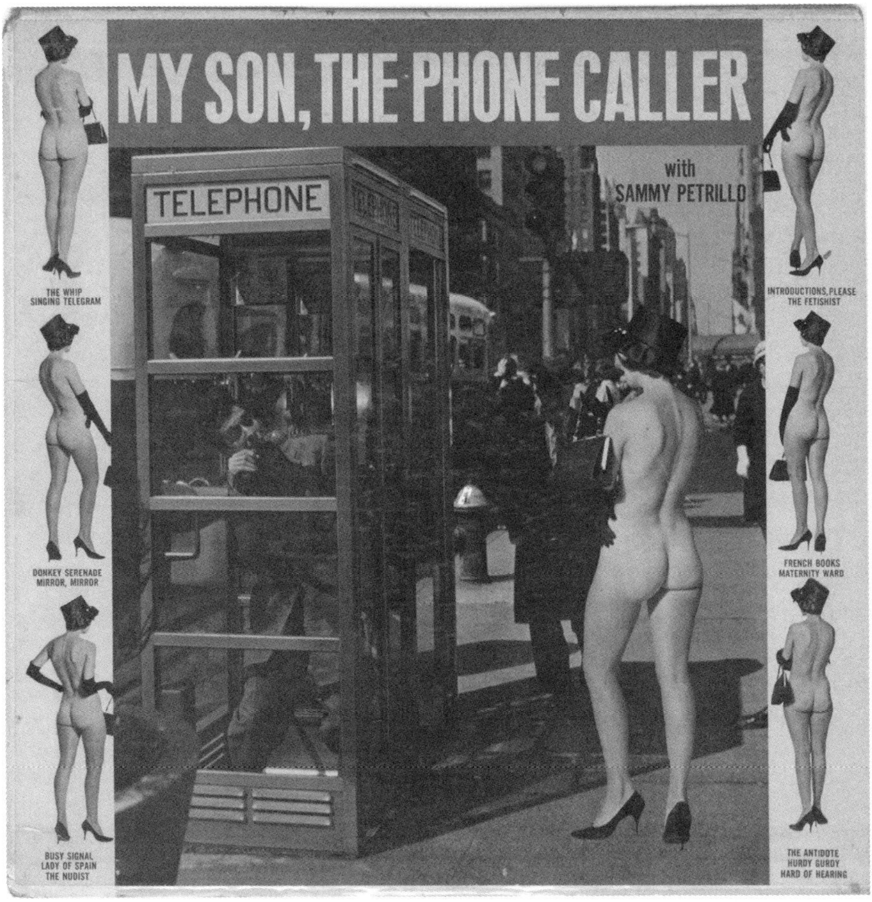

Cashing in on the *My Son, the Folk Singer* craze.
My Son, the Phone Caller, Surprise Records,1963.

Dick Randall was also keeping busy in 1963. Aside from producing the soft-core sizzlers *Paris Ooh-La-La!*, *Around the World with Nothing On,* and *My Bare Lady,* he was ready to tackle the Cleopatra craze that was sweeping the nation. This would take the form of a topical comedy album that was expected to give Vaughn Meader's million-selling *First Family* LP a run for the money.

America, looking for any diversion from Cold War realities, relished and gobbled up any gossip about the 20th Century Fox production of *Cleopatra*. Nearly bankrupting the studio with its long shooting schedule, many of the problems for *Cleopatra* were blamed on Elizabeth Taylor's health issues. What really piqued the public's interest, and set it aflame, was Liz's on-set romance with her co-star, Richard Burton, right in front of her husband, the singer Eddie Fisher. The flaunting of the extramarital affair was even more scandalous due to Eddie having left his wife, the beloved actress Debbie Reynolds, for Liz only several months earlier. Running off with Liz was show-business poison for Eddie, and his career never fully recovered, making the once-popular teen idol a cottage industry for stand-up comics and movie magazines. Dick Randall saw comedy gold.

All about Cleopatra, "Starring Will Jordan, Sammy Petrillo, Dave Starr and the First Family of Egypt," was timed to be released just as *Cleopatra* was set to premiere at the Rivoli Theatre in New York. The LP is a series of sketches almost solely focused on lampooning Eddie Fisher's cuckold status and Liz Taylor's promiscuity. Dick Randall "Produced & Directed" *All about Cleopatra,* in addition to co-writing it with Art Paul, the seasoned gag-writer who famously created the bunny logo for *Playboy* magazine, as well as becoming its founding art director. "Art Paul would write these little jokes in tiny little handwriting on tiny pieces of paper and they were often very good," recalled Will Jordan. "He would say something like, 'Are you European? Cause when you go to the bathroom, you're a-peein'.' Bad stuff like that, but still, Art was not without talent."

Another comic involved in the record was Dave Starr, a one-time comedy partner of Joe E. Ross who "had the reputation of being one of the dirtiest comedians in the business," according to Hank Garrett, one of Ross's co-stars on *Car 54, Where Are You?* Another voice on the album belonged to Joel Holt, who had recently directed and starred in *Karate: The Hand of Death,* the first American-made martial-arts movie. Holt would go on to narrate *It's a Sick, Sick, Sick World, Chained Girls,* and *Way Out Topless,* in addition to directing *The Wild, Wild World of Jayne Mansfield.*

Dick Randall's business partner Larry Joachim provided the budget for the recording at Gotham Recording Studios in midtown Manhattan, with Larry's wife Barbara Loden performing on the album just for fun, using the pseudonym Roxanne Lacerne. Barbara sounds like she's having a ball, doing various impressions, including Zsa Zsa Gabor and Marilyn Monroe, predating her fictionalized version of Monroe in Arthur Miller's critically acclaimed play *After the Fall.*

Sammy does various voices, including President Kennedy, Jimmy Stewart, and a character named "Jerry" in a Jerry Lewis voice. Other arbitrary impressions include José Jiménez, Peter Lorre, and Señor

Ed Sullivan impersonator Will Jordan and cover girl Carol Tiger feed grapes to Sammy. Topical Records, *All about Cleopatra*, 1963.

Wences, but, decades later, Will Jordan wasn't able to identify who did what voice: "I just remember that everybody loved [Sammy] and they told him, 'Go do anything you want.'"

Recording *All about Cleopatra* was not a happy experience for Will Jordan, though: "[Dick Randall] wanted to do an album satirizing Richard Burton, and I said, 'I can't do Burton,' and I thought he'd go get a hundred mimics who could do Burton, but no, they had me do James Mason as Richard Burton, and I said 'This makes absolutely no sense.'"

"The whole thing was a disaster," Will Jordan told the comedy historian Kliph Nesteroff in 2011. "Well-intentioned, but completely miscast and completely wrong."

Another silent partner on *All about Cleopatra* was a hustler from Texas who would become another one of Sammy's best friends: J. G. Tiger. With a southern drawl and a handlebar mustache, the brash and heavyset Tiger would soon become a trusted confidant within the expanding Patrello family. "He said he was a big movie producer," Shawn says. "He would pull a quarter from your ear, so he was like the fun uncle." Years later, Shawn thought that perhaps J. G. Tiger's real name might have been Jack Goldman, but he wasn't certain.

By any name, Tiger was at heart a promotions man, escaping unfazed from one situation to another. In 1953, he popularized weekly wrestling bouts in Paris, Texas, featuring the likes of Chief Golden Eagle, Dirty Johnny Dobbs, and 265-pound Blakesnake, who would take an eight-foot snake into the ring with him. Working as an "advance man" for a police association benefit in Abilene in 1957, Tiger devised an elaborate evening featuring Brandon the Magician, along with sixteen assistants, "mostly girls."

The *Abilene Reporter News* reported that, on the afternoon of the show, Tiger had Brandon "demonstrate his 'blindfold driving' trick," which involved the magician, accompanied by officers, driving through the town. Brandon had a blindfold over his eyes and a hood over his head." Two months later Tiger had bounced checks all over town, requiring an embarrassed police association to make good on the bad paper. J. G. Tiger was long gone, with some believing that he had hightailed it down to San Antonio.

Five years later, in Cherry Hill, New Jersey, a similar driving-blindfolded stunt was sponsored by the Patrolmen's Benevolent Association. A photo in Camden's *Courier-Post* identifies the "magician" J. G. Tiger at the wheel of a convertible with a black hood over his head. Seated behind Tiger is "his assistant," Miss Carol Angel, who also appeared on the front cover of *All about Cleopatra* as Cleopatra, disinterestedly feeding grapes to a cross-eyed and reclining Sammy Petrillo. Accompanying Miss Angel is Val Vasilieff, Mr. New Jersey of 1961. A police lieutenant sits in the front seat "keeping an eye on things."

J. G. Tiger held fast to the Cleopatra concept. Timed to coincide with the *All about Cleopatra* LP, he brought a live-action burlesque equivalent to the New Frontier Hotel in Las Vegas. Originally known as the Last Frontier when it opened in 1942, the casino was given a space-age makeover in 1955 and rebranded the New Frontier, complete with a futuristic design and the slogan "Out of this World." Elvis Presley, at the peak of his popularity in 1956, bombed at the New Frontier when the median age of the audience was at least ten years too old for him. Tiger had big plans to present a tasteful "girlie" show, with enough variety to keep it all sizzling along for what *Variety* termed "an indefinite run."

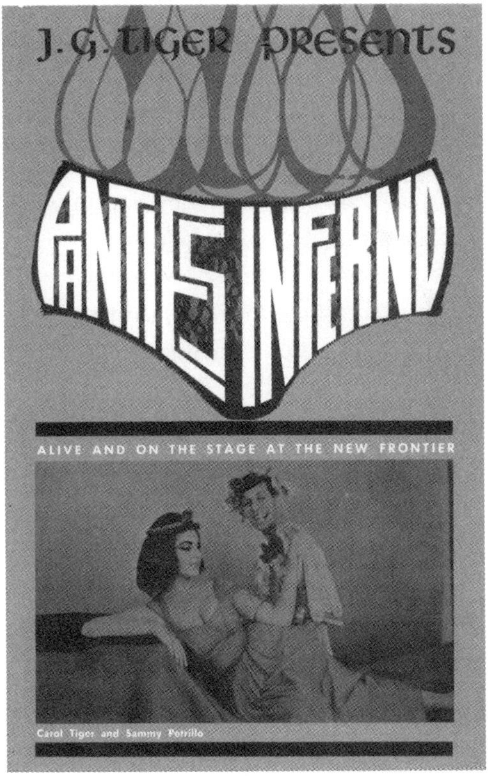

A hot time in Vegas, June, 1963.

Originally titled *Cleo's Asp,* the cover for the *Panties Inferno* program features Sammy and Carol Tiger (formerly Carol Angel) in Roman garb, loosely mimicking the *All about Cleopatra* record cover. "Created, Produced and Directed by J. G. Tiger," *Panties Inferno* was predicted by *Variety* to "be the season's sleeper." The revue featured four "Technicolor Nudes," each in different, full-color body makeup—one red, one green, one blue, and one brown. They were introduced as Marla Brando, Fran Sinatra, Rickie Burton, and Rocky Hudson.

Also on the bill were the Greenwich Village comedy team Greco and Willard. Vic Greco and Fred Willard were described as writing their "own material, consisting of dialogue and pantomime blackouts which are hilarious, especially to hip audiences." Greco and Willard soon became favorites at various Playboy clubs and on *The Tonight Show, The Ed Sullivan Show,* and *The Smothers Brothers Show* before splitting up. Known as a "comedian's comedian," Greco remained relatively obscure, while Willard achieved fame co-hosting *Fernwood 2 Night* and *America 2-Night* for Norman Lear before joining the writer and director Christopher Guest's troupe of mockumentary regulars. Fred Willard and Sammy were friendly during this period and, according to Sammy's second son, Kurt, Fred used to occasionally babysit Shawn.

Other acts on the bill included the percussionist Chaino (now working as Prince Chaino), the Yul Brynner impersonator Danny Davis, the 37-inch tall Venus Ford ("who moves like a miniature Gypsy Rose Lee"), the Bhaskar Dancers, and Carol Tiger, described in promotional material as "the most beautiful woman in America." There was a Cleopatra sketch written by Sammy and Danny Davis which featured Carol as the vixen of the Nile.

In a preview of the show in *Variety,* Sammy was cited as "neatly" weaving the show together, though some of his jokes were "worn out by dozens of other comedians on the Strip. . . . Sammy would be more effective without them."

Panties Inferno was scheduled to debut Friday, June 21st, but was postponed for a week for some last-minute "doctoring." Three days after opening on Saturday, June 29th, there was a major overhaul, and the title of the revue was changed from *Panties Inferno* to *Oriental Inferno* and Sammy was out. Whether he quit or was fired is unknown. By Sammy's account, he went back to Dallas, where Elaine and Shawn were living. After purchasing a .22 caliber pistol, he accidentally shot himself in the left leg.

APTER 16

HAT 'N' CANE

I was comfortable being a single or part of a two man act. . . . As a single, I had an agent named Don D'Carlo, who was a terrific guy. . . . Don kept booking me at the same nightclub over and over again. The owner told him, 'We see Sammy Petrillo every week! This [is] a small town—we need *new* faces!' So Don would say, "No, no . . . this isn't Sammy *Petrillo*, this is Sammy *Petrilla*." And the owner said, "Oh . . . that's okay then." [laughs] When I found out, I said to Don, "What are you doing? When I walk in, that guy's gonna throw me out the window." But he said, "Don't worry, it'll be fine. Just go." I went and I got paid, so Don was right.

—Sammy Petrillo, *Filmfax* #53, 1995

The story regarding what really happened when Sammy shot himself in the leg is a contentious one. One version has Sammy protecting Elaine and Shawn from a burglar, with the gun discharging accidentally. In 2008, Sammy vaguely blamed the gunshot on a "consequence of one of [Elaine's] schemes and lies." Sammy's nephew Stuart Hersh says, "It was one of those cleaning-the-gun things. It wasn't deliberate." The bullet remained in Sammy's leg for the rest of his life.

Years later, Sammy's cousin Martin and nephew Stuart would describe Sammy's act during this period. "Sammy was the emcee and the comedian," Martin says. "Sometimes he would do a very dramatic bit about a kid—about 'my boy'—about his son."

"Sammy would write things that were very poetic and very deep," Stuart adds. "In those days—in the '60s—when you had people like Shecky Greene, they always ended with a serious number and they would like to bring it on home and show you that they had some depth."

Like Jerry Lewis and countless other in-your-face funnymen before him, Sammy insulted the wrong guy on occasion. An occupational hazard, it was a good way to end up with a mouthful of fist. Insult comedy can be dangerous, and only the brilliance and charm of "Mr. Warmth," Don Rickles, kept him alive and healthy for ninety years.

"We were up on the Berlin strip in Connecticut," Martin says, "and he started to do his raincoat routine—'If you need a raincoat you get it from this guy over here . . .'—and I realized that he was in trouble because this guy was getting annoyed, and that's when Sammy realized that this guy was a gangster."

Health issues took a low priority in Sammy's life. "He had his teeth capped in the mid-'60s, and of course he never went for a follow-up," Martin says. "He would actually be sleeping, I'd come to his door, be ready to drive him to a club, and the tooth would fall out, and he'd look over on the bed and find it and he would snap it back in. When he performed on a couple of occasions, it would fall out."

Sammy signed with yet another new manager—Don D'Carlo, who would loyally work with Sammy until the 1980s. D'Carlo, who could be depended on to break into a tap dance at the drop of a hat, was known as the King of the One-Nighters in the Pennsylvania–Ohio–West Virginia tri-state area. With an office in Pittsburgh's historic Fulton Building, D'Carlo preferred making deals in all-night restaurants—the Purple Cow, the White Tower, and Thompson's—where talent he met on the street could be sized up over a cup of coffee. Before becoming a theatrical agent, D'Carlo started as a bit player in silent movies, worked as a short-order cook in New York City, and traveled as a carnival promoter. In the early 1930s he managed amateur dance contests at theaters in Pittsburgh where he would bring in his "ringer," a teenaged Gene Kelly, who would nail the prize every time. At the height of his career, D'Carlo was booking talent at almost 100 nightclubs, with acts ranging from singers and comedians to magicians and mind-readers, with some dog acts and ventriloquists thrown in the mix. Marty Allen got his first break in the business from D'Carlo, and the early careers of Don Rickles, Frank Gorshin, Bobby Vinton, Lenny Bruce, and Gypsy Rose Lee owed a debt to D'Carlo's managerial skills. Cultivating a taste for women embroiled in sex scandals with celebrities, D'Carlo found nightclub work for everyone from Joan Barry, who brought a paternity suit against Charlie Chaplin, to Elizabeth Ray, the congressional sex-worker who famously confessed, "I can't type. I can't file. I can't even answer a phone." He also handled the conjoined twins Daisy and Violet Hilton, as well as Dorothy Lawler, a woman who would marry any man that would give her $10,000. Sammy was friendly with D'Carlo, and they would frequently converse solely in carny talk, a language not unlike Pig Latin, which would render their repartee incomprehensible to an outsider.

Sometimes D'Carlo would send Sammy out solo; sometimes he'd pair him with another comic. Sammy toured for a couple of months on the outskirts of Pittsburgh with one of D'Carlo's clients, the legendary Black comedian Stepin Fetchit. In the 1930s there was no one bigger than Fetchit when it came to embodying the stereotype of a "simple-minded, shiftless Negro." Billed as "the Laziest Man in the World," Fetchit appeared in dozens of movies and was the first Black actor to become a millionaire. In contrast to the character he portrayed, offscreen Fetchit wrote for the politically charged *Chicago Defender,* considered the most important African-American newspaper of its kind. Fetchit's act had a short shelf life, and by the late '40s he was seen as a painful throwback to more racist times. He filed for bankruptcy and went back on the road playing what was left of the vaudeville houses and burlesque shows.

"Step would come out and do imitations," Sammy said. "And he looked so young: he was in his sixties but looked like he was only thirty-five. . . . Step's biggest dream in life was to play Satchel Paige in a movie."

One time, according to Sammy, D'Carlo asked him to work a penniless and unknown Richard Pryor into Sammy's act. Years before becoming one of the most influential comics in the world, Pryor was having a rough go of it in Pittsburgh. He spent thirty-five days in jail on a domestic-abuse charge and was barely eking out a living doing stand-up at strip clubs. "We did a bit where I was onstage and Richard, dressed as a busboy, would heckle me," Sammy said. "Richard wound up staying with me and my wife at the time, making little flower centerpieces that we would wholesale to stores. So in addition to performing at the club, Richard would deliver these centerpieces and we'd pay him one dollar an hour."

The work was fairly steady. In August, Sammy emceed at the Flamingo in South Hackensack, New Jersey, with a "Young Singing Sensation" named Al Reno and a "Famous Exotic Dancer" named Little Star ("46″—22″—34″—Yes, We said 46!"). On Sammy's twenty-ninth birthday, the *Beacon Journal* touted his credentials: "Sammy is rated one of the top comedians in the country. Las Vegas paid him $750 a week in Nov. He stars in a movie with Jayne Mansfield. See him do J. F. K., Johnny Ray, Ed

Sullivan and other great stars." In November, Sammy was at the Adrilee Supper Club, also in Pittsburgh, and the day after Kennedy's assasination he performed for what was presumably a tough crowd at the Continental in Hempstead, Long Island. By the end of the summer of 1964, Sammy was back at a water park in Flushing Meadows, but this time as an official part of the New York World's Fair.

Spearheaded by the urban planner Robert Moses, the New York World's Fair in Queens was a financial sinkhole. A plethora of issues, including underselling, overcrowding, union strikes, and public apathy, led to its downfall. Eighty countries gamely took part in celebrating the fair's motto, "Peace Through Understanding," with the attractions divvied up into five sections—Industrial, Federal and State, International, Transportation, and the least successful, Lake Amusement.

The season at Lake Amusement opened at the 10,000-seat Marine Amphitheatre with a variety show called *Wonder World.* Situated on a stage in front of a massive swimming pool, it employed hundreds of performers, who at times outnumbered the patrons in the bleachers. The *New York Times* reported that the president of the fair, Robert Moses himself, "had inspected every costume to be worn in the amusement attractions to make certain that everything was in good taste." With its elaborate sets and moving platforms, *Wonder World* was an ambitious flop. It was quickly replaced by *Summer Time Revue,* a rock 'n' roll show hosted by the deejay Clay Cole that lasted all of three days before a disgusted Moses shut it down. Replacing Cole was a former Broadway sex farce, *Pajama Tops,* starring Sammy and the Danish actress Greta Thyssen. Specializing in suggestive humor, Greta doubled for Marilyn Monroe in *Bus Stop* and had the unique career trajectory of appearing in three Joe Besser–era Three Stooges shorts in addition to showing up in John Cassavetes's debut movie, *Shadows.* After a few shows, *Pajama Tops* was replaced by a new package, *Chips off the Old Blocks,* featuring "off-springs of movie greats."

Sammy returned to Brooklyn, this time to a club in the Flatlands called the Interlude. He shared the bill with the cornball rock 'n' roll singer Don Rondo, whose recorded output included "Blonde Bombshell" and "Cuckoo Girl." Then it was back to the 21 Bar and Lounge in Akron, this time featuring "America's Foremost Female Impersonators (9 Shows Nightly)."

Sammy took a stab at penning a column for *Backstage,* the entertainment industry magazine, in September 1964. Titling it "Hat n' Cane," accompanied by a pensive headshot of the author, smiling wistfully, head planted in his right palm, Sammy laid down his mission statement:

> When the average man can stay home and watch a television variety show with a hundred thousand dollar budget behind it, and see the biggest stars in the business for free, he's reluctant to go to a night club for a show consisting of 2 or 3 unknown variety acts especially when a few drinks and a meatball sandwich cost him eleven dollars. Nightclubbing, except for an anniversary, birthday or occasional Saturday night, is not what it used to be. Few night club owners have the showmanship to present something new to lure people away from that magical electric box and most night clubs throughout the country are down to one or two shows a week, using very few performers. Grim? Not completely. There is still a lot of work available, if you know where to look for it. This column is for those talented variety people who are not too lazy to go after what they want. Those that are not afraid to send pictures and resumes, make phone calls and meet people could cash in on the tips in this column. If you would like to work in Europe at a minimum of approximately ten thousand dollars a year, or make a living in New York; if you'd like to go out of town for a while, this column should be of benefit for you.

The rest of Sammy's debut column is peppered with summaries of his recent gigs ("We worked the bill with Don Rondo at the Interlude in Brooklyn last weekend. Rondo, who proves a few performers do sound as good in person as on wax . . .") and shoutouts to friends and family ("Caught one of the best hypnotists I've ever seen the other night—Marshall King. Chuck McCann will be a giant in this business"), as well as some self-ribbing: "Comedy albums aren't moving too well right now according to a top record producer. He didn't have to tell me since I had two floperoos this year myself!" There were plugs for a former and possibly future partner, the rock 'n' roll singer Larry Bene (an announced comedy LP on Kip Records with Petrillo and Bene never materialized), along with ink promoting his agents, King Broder and the recently hired Don D'Carlo. He would sign off his column with some jokes: "My wife told her hair dresser that she wanted to look like Barbra Streisand . . . So he broke her nose!" and "The cannibals have a new dish. It's called Baked Beings." Sammy's column lasted five issues.

Depending upon the workflow, Sammy would form bonds with various cities in his career. It was important to have a dependable place where

Kansas City Star, October 1, 1965.

he could leave behind more than a trunk full of clothes. The Bronx, Hollywood, and Pittsburgh had served this purpose in the past, and now Dallas would be Sammy Petrillo HQ. "When we came to Texas, I'm not sure what the original plan was," Shawn says. "I think it was for him to try to find work here. I think he had a bite on something. I don't know what kind of work would've been in Dallas for stage comics, but something brought us here."

Sammy's press kit at the time said he was handled "exclusively" by Marty Cavanaugh of Dallas. The material calls Sammy "Movieland's Newest Comedy Star" and "Star of *Las Vegas after Dark*," and there's a blurb about *Wings for Hire* being released in fall 1965. There are unattributed reviews of *Panties Inferno* ("His sharp mind and glib tongue make him a potential big time winner. . . . He scores most of his laughs from his handling of hecklers and his ad lib ability is unbelievable") and of Sammy's 1952 Copacabana appearance: "Scores heavily with stand-up comedy routines of fresh material and draws yochs. Fast with his lines to some finest squelching of loud-mouthed male ringsides."

In February 1966, one columnist, Earl Wilson, reported that Vincent Price would narrate a "shock documentary" titled *It's a Sick, Sick, Sick World*. Mondo movies such as this were a gift for budget-minded filmmakers in the early '60s. The Italian quickie *Mondo Cane* kicked off the trend in 1962 with its mix of bizarre and exploitative silent stock footage from around the world, edited together for shock value. Topless native ceremonies, geese force-fed food, bloodied penitents walking on shards of glass, Malaysian underwater cemeteries, drunk Japanese men getting massages—all staged for the urban grindhouse crowd, with genuine and sometimes horrifying actual footage randomly edited in. Upending the sleazeball aesthetic, the theme song for *Mondo Cane,* "More," won a Grammy and was covered by Bobby Darin, Frank Sinatra, Roy Orbison, Andy Williams, and over 400 others.

It's a Sick, Sick, Sick World was a worthy entry in the titillating subgenre of mondo movies. Stan Borden, whose previous credit was producing *Around the World with Nothing On* with Dick Randall, had purchased several reels of crude gold—German hookers soliciting johns, public fistfights in outdoor cafes, a heroin addict shooting up in a bathroom, concentration-camp ovens, and more. He asked Doris Wishman's cinematographer, C. Davis Smith, to make some sense of the random scenes. "I suggested we make it into a documentary and link it together with a voice-over narrator. I added all these fake foreign-sounding credits to make it seem more legit," Smith said, "but it was just me." Adding a continental-sounding Al Caiola guitar soundtrack and condescending narration from Joel Holt (Vincent Price had bailed), *It's a Sick, Sick, Sick World* just needed some new footage to sew it together. A sequence with nude strippers and Sammy Petrillo was concocted.

Sammy's uncredited appearance in *It's a Sick, Sick, Sick World* is similar to his also-silent role as a nudie photographer in *The Brain That Wouldn't Die*. Wearing a boxy, ill-fitting suit, Sammy is seen paying membership and camera-rental fees to an unctuous studio owner, as Joel Holt, in some Ed Wood–esque dialogue, intones, "To say that these studios are run on an honest basis would not be to tell the truth." Sammy comes across as sad but deadly serious as he empties his wallet and then joins four other hobbyists in the photo studio. A smiling brunette in a flimsy negligee sits in a chair and invites a similarly clad blonde to lie across her lap for a spanking with the heel of a shoe. The girls switch places and then the blonde is seen gagged with her hands tied above her head while the brunette gently whips her with a belt. Joel Holt patiently explains: "The whipping fetish

Sammy plays another smutty photographer. *It's a Sick, Sick, Sick World,* 1965. Courtesy of Something Weird Video.

is an art that has been with us since the beginning of time. The caveman was the first to practice this on his women." The blonde unhooks her top, slides her panties off, and poses with a small beach ball covering her nether region. Sammy photographs the models, rotating the camera into various positions, and gets impossibly close, seemingly snapping abstract sections of the half-clothed and naked bodies. "It had cost almost nothing to make," C. Davis Smith said, "and [Stan Borden] put together an outrageous sleazy ad campaign. It made him a lot of money."

That same year, J. G. Tiger's production assistant, Bill Gyorfy (pronounced "Gee-or-fee"), would become another long-term partner in Sammy's scattered film career. Gyorfy's first project was directing and producing a comedy movie starring Sammy called *Gas Is Best*. Gyorfy was involved with Eagle-Lion Films, a distribution company that handled reissues from the Producers Releasing Corporation (PRC), along with public-domain titles. *Gas Is Best* stars Sammy as a celery-juice-swigging, flatulence-propelled superhero in a role eerily similar to Howard Stern's Fartman character almost twenty years later. Depending on who's telling the story, *Gas Is Best* was either completed or, as Sammy told the journalist

Todd Rutt, was given to Doris Wishman to edit and remained a work in progress. Either way, *Gas Is Best* never saw release.

Back in Yonkers, Sammy was appointed as special-events director for the former mayor John E. Flynn's run for the New York State Senate. An "Old Palace Type Show" was held at the Strand Theater on the Saturday before the election, with Sammy providing the entertainment and emceeing. Billed as "Hollywood on Broadway," Sammy brought along his old partner, George DeWitt, and the singer Sunny Gale, whose biggest hit, in 1952, was "Wheel of Fortune." Also featured at the rally were the Classics (a "Famous Rock & Roll Group"), Basil Jovian, and the twenty-three-year-old former child star Frankie Lymon, who borrowed fifty dollars from Sammy but died of an overdose before he could repay him.

Variety reported on Sammy's return to Pittsburgh: "Miss Marshall, a local girl, was corralled by agent Don D'Carlo and is now swinging her tassels at Sneaky Pete's along with exotic named Pilar and comedian Sammy Petrillo. Latter is still getting lotsa laughs with his well-remembered jokes and his physical similarity to Jerry Lewis." At the end of November, Sammy emceed the first Miss Go-Go America contest at the famously seedy Peppermint Lounge. This would be one of Sammy's few gigs in Manhattan.

The following April, the Victory Club in Wampum, Pennsylvania, "by popular demand" announced "4-Big Nights with Mr. Comedy Himself, Sammy Petrillo." The show was billed as "Sammy Petrillo's Girls-a-Poppin' featuring Wild, Wild Girls . . . Tantalizing Temptresses In Their 20s!" The press material clarified that *Shangri-La,* suppressed for three years, was now a favorite with the "hep" crowd and that Sammy's past co-stars had included Bela Lugosi, Vincent Price, and Will Jordan.

Taking up temporary residence in the North Riverdale section of the Bronx, Sammy relied upon his cousin Martin to chauffeur him to gigs and meetings. "I remember dropping Sammy off at Lloyd Price's Turntable Club in Times Square," Martin says. After scoring massive hits on Specialty Records with "Lawdy Miss Clawdy" and "Personality," among others, Price had opened the Turntable Club in the same building that formerly housed jazz club Birdland. "Sammy would call me up and say, 'I need a ride!' and then he would tell me to 'pick me up at Lloyd's Club.'" Sammy also taught a fourteen-year-old neighbor, Harold Grabina, how to drive stick on a Chevy Biscayne so that once he got his license he would be able to drive Sammy anywhere he needed to be. "Sammy hated to drive. He was a nervous wreck," Harold said. Sammy preferred to be driven

Akron Beacon Journal, December 9, 1966.

to gigs, and frequently his nephew Stuart was enlisted with the task. "I would take my books with me, do my homework in the back of the club while he performed," Stuart says. "When he started to fade and I knew he needed a heckler, I would just yell something out, because I knew the whole act. When Sammy would ask for an impersonation—'Okay, *any* impersonation!'—and they weren't yelling out the right people, I'd yell out to him, 'Betty Crocker!' He loved that one. He'd go, 'Oh, a real crumb!' and that would get a laugh in the mid-'60s."

"One time Sammy was in my apartment in the Bronx and we're sitting around watching *The Joe Franklin Show*," cousin Martin remembered—"me and Sammy and my girlfriend—and all of a sudden Sammy goes, 'I haven't been on the show in a while.' He says, 'I think I'll go on there tomorrow.'"

A kindred spirit of the old showbiz school, Joe Franklin had peddled nostalgia on radio and TV since the late 1940s in the New York City area. Through his love of old Eddie Cantor and Al Jolson records, he created a cottage industry in a post-war America that hadn't given a thought to looking backwards yet. Inventing the talk-show format, which he received little credit for, Joe worked on the fringe of showbiz. Occasionally hosting Barbra Streisand or Woody Allen before they were famous, and Bing Crosby after he was, the majority of his time on the air was spent with third-rate cabaret singers and child stars from the 1940s. For decades, the sight of Joe Franklin ambling through midtown would be a quintessential

New York moment, as iconic as the Empire State Building or a Sabrett hot dog in dirty water. Rattling off questions to Bela Lugosi's co-star or Bela Lugosi's barber held equal weight in the middle-of-the-night Joe Franklin universe, so it was natural that Sammy and Joe traveled in the same faded Times Square circles. Sammy ended up on Joe's talk show several times throughout the years.

"So Sammy calls Joe on the phone," Martin continues, "and I'm saying, 'You're full of shit,' 'cause he was always joking, and in less than twenty-four hours I was sitting in the studio. Joe asked him if he was plugging anything and Sammy said yeah—something generic like, 'I'm gonna be at the Airport Club.' The reason I say the Airport Club is because that was the most gangsterish of all them. That was a real mafia nightclub."

Despite all of these engagements, Sammy still had trouble paying the bills. "Sammy did anything to make a living because he only worked on the weekends in these nightclubs," Martin says. "Sometimes we would go from store to store in Manhattan selling whatever we had to sell, whether it would be fake perfume ('Smells just like it!') or Santa Claus bells and inflatable Christmas toys." Despite his dislike for driving, Sammy drove taxis and limos for Martin's upstate chauffeur business.

In June 1967, at a burlesque show at the Red Carpet in Pompano Beach, Florida, on a "7 Night a Week" bill with a "smashing exotic dancer" named Tatasha, the comedy team of Sammy Petrillo and Lady Mary debuted. Lady Mary (Cochran), a divorced dancer and stripper with little interest in comedy acts, was selling 8mm stag

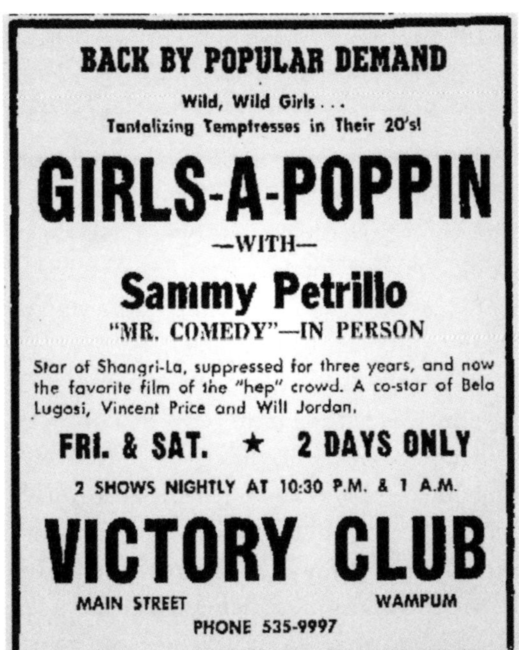

Cashing in on *Shangri-La*. *New Castle News*, May 19, 1967.

movies in her shop in San Francisco when she met Sammy. He convinced her to travel with him as his comedy partner and to let Don D'Carlo book them. "I got talked into it," Lady Mary said. "Sammy did that, yeah. I didn't do comedy until I met Sammy." When asked if she had had a romantic relationship with Sammy during this period, Lady Mary said, "Yeah, yeah, I did. We were together for a couple of years." With prearranged hotel accommodations in every city and state, Sammy and Lady Mary toured the circuit with a troupe of three or four other performers, staying in town usually for a week, but never more than two. "He was a loner," she said:

> When you're on a troupe show, you always have a comedy and a straight man. Well, he didn't have a straight man or anything, so he just chose me, and we just got in together. And I wasn't never really a star of the show. I was just there to help out in different situations. Sammy was never onstage with me when I was stripping. I just did my thing. I would get dressed again and come back on with Sammy afterwards. He didn't really do no Jerry Lewis. He had his own comedy, even though he looked exactly like Jerry Lewis [laughs]. The last time I saw Sammy was in upper New York when Sammy found his wife. He found her and he left with her. And what year that was is beyond me. I haven't the slightest idea. I never met her. We split up because Sammy was gonna go back to his wife.

Between 1962 and 1967, Elaine and Sammy became the parents of four sons—Shawn, Jeffery, Mark, and Kurt. The boys' memories of Sammy are sketchy at best. Shawn, the oldest, has the clearest recollections: "Sammy would make up funny stories. I remember laughing really hard at that. He would do the typical guy thing where you would put your hand under your armpit and make fart sounds.

"One time it was during the summer in Texas. We all had shorts on and Sammy was putting us to bed. He took a glass bottle of Mercurochrome [antiseptic] and, with the eyedropper, drew red lines down our sternums and down our ribs and he made us into skeletons with the Mercurochrome. I'll always remember looking at my brothers and looking at myself and we thought that that was the greatest thing, that he made us into skeletons."

When Sammy and Elaine worked as a team in the early days, occasionally they would have to come up with a last-minute babysitter option. Shawn remembers that one time "They couldn't get a babysitter for me so I sat on the drummer's lap while they did their show. I don't remember the act exactly, but I remember seeing the back of Sammy and

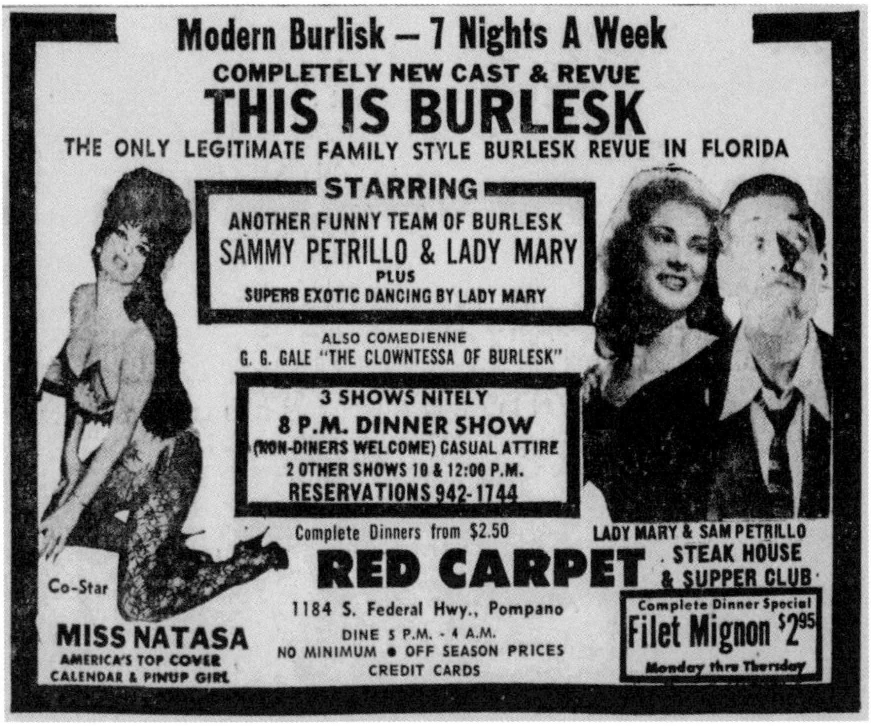

Debut of Lady Mary: Sammy's girlfriend and foil. *Fort Lauderdale News*, June 30, 1967.

seeing the lights coming through. Sammy was facing the audience, and it was probably part of the act, but I remember the audience booing him. It might've just been because he told a corny joke, but I remember that it made me cry because they were booing my dad. I remember Sammy saying, 'No, no, it's okay, everything's okay. It's gonna be all right.'"

APTER 17

KEYHOLES ARE FOR PEEPING

He told me that when he did *Brooklyn Gorilla* he was mobbed in the bathroom at the premiere, which was on Broadway. Then he told me that when he did *Keyholes Are for Peeping,* it was just him and Doris Wishman and the guy who owned the theater. They were the only people in the audience for the premiere. And that was on Broadway, also. Or 42nd Street. One of those.

—Stephen Kroninger, artist and friend of Sammy's, 2013

Sammy's youngest son, Kurt, who was three and a half years old at the time, tells the story as it was told to him: "One day Sammy left for the store—and left my mother and four kids with less than a dollar to their name and never came back."

"I remember as kids being at a bench in a park and when my mom took us home, he was gone," says his oldest son, Shawn. "And we called the landlord [looking for him] and he said, 'No, Sammy left.' We couldn't believe it. We all went to a phone booth, because that's what you did at that time, and made calls and, sure enough, we found out that he did move back to New York. I don't remember if it was in my head for dramatic effect or if it's true, but I remember that all we had was one dollar. We had nothing."

Elaine and the kids received assistance from the Jewish community center, who brought them groceries and household items. Free clothing was provided by the Salvation Army. Back in Monongahela, Pennsylvania, Elaine's family owned a flower shop where Elaine had worked part-time.

This experience landed her a job with a local florist, in addition to a second job as a secretary for a plumbing company. "She would do anything to make it so that we could actually just get by," Shawn says. Sometimes the kids were sent to live with Sammy's parents, Anna and Skelly, in their apartment in Miami. "All the while," Kurt adds, "no contact from 'Dad.' No birthday calls or cards—nothing."

Sammy didn't remain in New York for long. In early April, he was headlining at the family-friendly Four Seasons Supper Club in Brentwood, a suburb twenty minutes south of Pittsburgh. A week later, Sammy was in McKees Rock, an iron and steel mining town north of Pittsburgh, at the Go-Go Lounge, sharing the bill with a stripper and "Woman's Lib Leader" named Amber Mist. The following month, the *Pittsburgh Press* broke the news that Sammy was back in the movie business:

> Comedian Sammy Petrillo, who calls Pittsburgh the "film capital of the world," finished his latest epic, "Off the Wall," and brought it in for less than $100,000. Drummer Buddy Rich, who does comedy in the picture, is the only big name but Sammy has all his night club buddies in the film. Speaking parts have been given to the Jaggerz [who scored a gold record with "The Rapper" in 1970], Zorran, the Man of Mystery, Smokey Joe, the fire-eater, singing comedienne Sandy Polo, comedian Bobby Jones, the Country Belles and, as a heavy, agent Don D'Carlo. Don was also casting director. The movie was shot in Carnegie Museum, the Go Go Lounge in McKees Rocks and other locations. Interiors were filmed in the studios of WPGH-TV.

One week later, *Variety* reported that Sammy had spent the previous two weeks *casting* "his new picture, *Off the Wall,*" a movie which the *Pittsburgh Press* reported as completed. "Buddy Rich is in the film in a character part," *Variety* wrote, "and will not play the drums." (Rich, a wildly talented and volatile drummer, had appeared uncredited in Jerry Lewis's *Visit to a Small Planet* in 1960.) "Petrillo and his partner, Bill Gyorfy of Detroit, who owns the Eagle-Lion film lab there, will finish shooting next week in New York and expect to have a finished print within two months."

A finished or unfinished print of *Off the Wall* has never turned up, even though Sammy referred to it through the years. "Sammy was always talking about a movie that he was working on with Buddy Rich," his nephew Stuart says. When Buddy Rich's daughter Cathy, who carries on her father's legacy with her own version of the Buddy Rich Band, was asked about *Off the Wall,* she reported "no knowledge of it."

Sammy wrote a screenplay called *The Army Needs You, Marvin,* which he had submitted for copyright as a "motion picture dialogue script." With all of the subtlety of an episode of *Laugh-In,* the script opens with a Black man getting arrested after urinating against a wall while an unseen narrator intones, "America . . . land of the Free . . . land of equal opportunity . . ." After a few blackout gags about corrupt politicians and wife-swapping parties, a nebbish named Marvin Grossclose is introduced as he receives his draft notice. Marvin was written to be played by Sammy, as he embodies all of Sammy's usual comic bits as a whiny schlemiel. Hanging out with a familiar Bowery Boys–type gang at a soda shop, Marvin and the gang brainstorm ideas on how he can avoid the draft. The barebones plot is merely a clothesline to hang the usual racist, sexist, and homophobic jokes that were second nature to Sammy. Along with missing-denture gags, scenes from *Brooklyn Gorilla* are evoked: Marvin gets literally carried off by a smitten, overweight heartthrob, and a doctor in a dream sequence turns into Bela Lugosi, complete with "cape, fangs, and bushy eyebrows." To save himself, Marvin holds up a big cross, to which the Lugosi doctor responds, "That won't help you . . . I'm *Jewish!*" *The Army Needs You, Marvin* was uncovered by Marco Joachim in 2025 while going through his father Larry's papers. The script remains unproduced.

Sammy returned to Dallas in 1971 to appear on a bill with Art Riley, with whom he had worked in the USO ten years earlier. The show was at the Rex Theater in the Oak Cliff section of town. Riley's good pal Robert McCandless, who, though underage, was able to sneak into the show, gave an eyewitness account years later:

> The lights went out and a drumroll was followed by Art's voice: "Ladies and gentlemen, welcome to the Rex Cinema Review, featuring your host Sammy Petrillo; comedienne Dianne Durette, the beautiful and vivacious Bubbles Cash with the Nick Nicholas Trio." Music began and out from the exit curtain came the guy that looked like Jerry Lewis. He welcomed everyone and introduced himself as Sammy Petrillo, then went into some one-liner risqué jokes. Each time he didn't get a response just as he wanted, he would make a face and talk like Lewis. The guy was really funny.

After a few more comedy segments and singers, the Nick Nicholas Trio eased into a bump-and-grind beat. Miss Robin Lee appeared in a full sequin gown and gloves before paring down to a G-string. "Her tassels gyrated in opposite directions," said a still-impressed Robert. "The show continued with a guy doing a bullwhip act in which he popped a bunch of balloons and ended by taking a cigarette out of his beautiful assistant's mouth at about twenty feet.

"It would be several years before I would realize this was one of the last-ditch attempts at keeping burlesque alive," Robert said. Later that evening, he dropped by the Rex's sister venue, the Lido, to catch another performance featuring the same cast.

Billed as "A Refreshing New Comic," Sammy spent a few weeks in Tampa, Florida, in April 1972 for three shows a night at an "All-Star X-Rated Show" at the Tiger's Den. Headlining was Princess Tenoka ("Don't Miss Her Exotic Indian War Dance"), along with "Sensational Exotic Janeen" and "Tampa's Wildest Go-Go Girls." The following weekend the cowgirl-clad "X-Rated, Dynamic, Exotic Diane Does (And How!)" replaced Princess Tenoka. In May, Sammy supported a wholesome girl singing duo called the P. J.s at the San Su San in Mineola, Long Island.

That week, *Backstage* announced the progress of Sammy's other ventures:

> Petrillo's 2 Features: Former comic turned film producer Sammy Petrillo is in New York for an indefinite stay to negotiate distribution arrangements for two ninety minute feature films he has completed. Films are in the rough cut phase, and will be available for screening during the next few weeks. Films are titled "Off the Wall," starring Buddy Rich and featuring Rose Scorza, and "All You Want To Know About Sex, But Were Afraid To Ask A Jewish Mother." Production company is Eagle-Lion Film Enterprises with offices in Pittsburgh and Miami, but Petrillo can be reached in New York at the Sutton-East Hotel.

Neither of these movies was released, if even completed. Little is known about *All You Want to Know about Sex, but Were Afraid to Ask a Jewish Mother* beyond the title. Sammy's cousin Martin offers a possible explanation for the missing movies: "Sammy would drive around with reels of his films in the trunk of his car. Then he put them in storage, but he couldn't pay the storage fees and lost his reels of film."

One Sammy Petrillo movie not lost to storage fees was the Doris Wishman–helmed *Keyholes Are for Peeping; or, Is There Life after Marriage?* The pioneering filmmaker Doris Wishman wrote, produced, and directed over thirty feature-length movies, starting with the 1960 nudist-camp gangster thriller *Hideout in the Sun*. At the time, nudist films were allowable under the censorship laws provided they depicted real-life nudists. Doris pushed the limits of the skin-flick industry with the genre-stretching *Nude on the Moon, Diary of a Nudist,* and *Blaze Starr Goes Nudist*. Switching to sexploitation in the mid-'60s, Doris filmed a series of "roughies"—harrowing and violent exercises in the seamier side of life. *Bad Girls Go to Hell, Indecent Desires,* and *Another Day, Another Man* typify her output at the time. After *The Amazing Transplant,* a brutal depiction of a sex change gone wrong, Doris was contracted by Bill Gyorfy to edit his unfinished comedy *Gas Is Best*. This was how Doris met Sammy.

"[Doris] said, 'Would you like to make a movie with me as a partner?' and I said yes," Sammy recalled. "She said, 'Would you [first] finish a movie for me?' She said, 'Since we're gonna make this other movie together, maybe you can help me with this one? I have a lot of stock footage.' I didn't know what kind of footage she had. She said, 'See, I'd like to roll this into a movie,' and I said fine."

The new scenes were shot over a weekend at Doris's apartment near the United Nations. Afterwards, Doris inserted several minutes of nudie footage left over from her previous movies. "I didn't mind that there were girls nude in the movie," Sammy said. "That was hip enough. Marlon Brando was in a movie with a nude. Who cares? So that didn't bother me. But when I saw other footage and I saw the movie . . . I didn't expect it to be *Gone with the Wind* . . . I figured it's a prelude to making my other movie, right?"

Sammy introduced Doris to Don D'Carlo to work out the arrangements for the next movie. D'Carlo also handled Chesty Morgan, a stripper whose 73-32-36 physique gave Doris an idea. This led to a move that Sammy described as his "demise." "The next thing I know is, instead of making a movie with me, she's making a movie with Chesty Morgan. I did [*Keyholes*] for peanuts figuring that I was going to make another project with her."

Deadly Weapons and its sequel *Double Agent 73*, both starring Chesty Morgan as a secret-agent stripper who smothers enemies with her massive breasts, are sleazeball classics that have cemented Doris Wishman's place in cult movie history. During her "roughie" period, Doris used unusual camera effects to avoid an X rating, a gimmick that gave her work an arty quality: she would cut away from a rape or a murder to a random static shot, evoking silent-era montage filmmaking, a technique that didn't go unnoticed by observant critics. Her empathy for her characters, no matter how perverse, was also a thumbprint that distinguished her films from other grindhouse fare. Celebrated and studied at the Museum of Modern Art and London's Institute for Contemporary Arts, Doris Wishman challenged the notion that a Z-budget skin flick couldn't also have artistic merit. Despite having no greater aspiration than to churn out cheap, exploitative quickies, Doris Wishman is rightfully regarded as a pioneer of independent cinema.

If *Shangri-La* is a nudie-cutie, then *Keyholes Are for Peeping* is a nudie-ugly. Unfunny, tasteless, and charmless, it's a Doris Wishman misfire that inhabits a place in her oeuvre as possibly her most unwatchable movie. In later years, even Doris would distance herself from *Keyholes*. "I made one comedy and it didn't make money, so I'll never make another," she said.

Sammy plays a marriage counselor named Stanley Bebble who lives with his mother, also played by Sammy but with Doris Wishman's voice dubbed in. Sammy, billed as Samuel Petrillo, sports long, greasy hair and is outfitted in the fashions of the day, likely plucked from his own closet—a jacket with wide lapels, oversized buttons, and a wide tie. Stanley's mother wears a blonde wig and a frowsy housecoat. The two Sammys share a scene near the beginning of the movie through a clumsy split-screen effect. The plot and all the dialogue are clearly improvised.

Sammy almost comes up with a funny bit in a breakfast-table scene. He pats his face with a slice of rye bread as if it were a powder puff, then does his Claude Rains impersonation: putting a pair of glasses over a white paper napkin that's draped over his head, he says, "I don't take up much room—I'm invisible." He caps this off with a brief Porky Pig ("Th-th-th-th-th-th-that's all, ma!"), leaving *Keyholes* with only two celebrity impersonations. In another scene, Sammy, in close-up, is wearing glasses and psychoanalyzing a patient: "You tell me that your husband called you a bitch and he likes to make love in the park? He likes to do it only dog fashion? How degrading! You just tell him that he's barking up the wrong tree!" A camera cut reveals the bemused dog that Sammy's been analyzing.

The balance of *Keyholes Are for Peeping* is abrasive and unfunny—seventy painful minutes of nagging-girlfriend, nagging-mother, and nagging-wife sketch comedy, punctuated by almost a dozen garishly tinted softcore sex scenes. Looking to skirt an X rating, the stock footage features couples rolling around on top of each other and randomly pawing at mostly non-erogenous zones. The soundtrack is groovy, muddy make-out music with flutes. In a sixty-nine position, lovers grasp at each other's ankles.

One-time collaboration between Sammy and cult movie director Doris Wishman.
Promotional poster, circa 1972.

There's a close-up of a nipple undulating against a hairy armpit. The screen fills up with a tongue going into an earhole. A shot of a man fondling a woman's breast is accompanied by the sound of a cow mooing. With a Beethoven score, the sex scenes wouldn't be out of place in *A Clockwork Orange*'s eyes-clamped-open sex-aversion-therapy sequence. Taken as a whole, *Keyholes Are for Peeping* is one hour and ten minutes of rotten business—a movie best viewed through a keyhole, if at all.

Despite his efforts, Sammy's future would not see him starring in any more motion pictures. The live stage, and in particular a nascent burlesque revival, was calling.

And the boys don't understand, either . . . *Greenville News*, April 8, 1976.

APTER 18

BURLESK IS MY THING

SAMMY: Where am I?
DUKE: *Where are ya*? You're in our dressing room at the Jungle Hut in Passaic, New Jersey, and we're on next!

—*Bela Lugosi Meets a Brooklyn Gorilla*

In the late 1930s burlesque was at its peak, with its most popular booking agency, the Minsky brothers, branching out into more than a dozen legitimate theaters in New York, Philadelphia, Pittsburgh, and Baltimore. Burlesque was a stepping stone for a handful of comics that would find major success in radio, movies, and television. Abbott and Costello, Phil Silvers, Jackie Gleason, Red Buttons, Red Skelton, Bert Lahr, Pinky Lee, and others created their personas on the burlesque stage before breaking into the mainstream. Several burlesque stars who were giants in their field would never ascend the heights: Loney Lewis, Hap Hyatt, Vic Purée, Peanuts Bohn, and the bald, toothless master of the spit-take, Billy "Zoot" Reed, to name a few. In a cost-cutting move, burlesque shows were whittled down to striptease acts, eschewing the more elaborate musical numbers. The whole industry came crashing down with Mayor La Guardia's 1939 clampdown on obscenity, which banned burlesque from New York theaters. Other cities followed suit. Burlesque found an afterlife in nightclubs where strippers and showgirls were now required to go out in the crowd when not onstage and try to get the men to buy them champagne. The striptease acts upped their novelty quotient to compensate for the lack of show-stopping numbers. Rosita Royce had trained doves to remove her clothing piece by piece, while Yvette used parrots. Some strippers relied on snakes, trained dogs, and even monkeys to remove their garments. After World War II, burlesque was relegated to seedier nightspots and considered to be the bottom rung of showbiz. The "burly Q" was the place where a performer went when all other options had dried up. One stripper, Beverly Arlynne, remembered that the comics at this time were "mean, vicious, angry, frustrated. They had tried to make it in show business, probably on Broadway or in vaudeville, and they couldn't do it, so they were relegated to burlesque." It was a hardscrabble life, with performers cooking spaghetti in backstage coffee pots and carting their belongings around in shopping bags. In the 1950s, television gave burlesque another kick in the groin. Funny men became glorified emcees, existing mainly to introduce strippers and exotic dancers, and the comics that were left were aging out. There was hardly anyone stepping up to replace them. This was the level that burlesque had sunk to when Sammy came aboard in the mid-fifties. By the late '60s the chorus girls were gone, and so were the live bands. Girls were now stripping to tapes of music. X-rated movies and peep shows, along with the rise of women's liberation, helped snuff out almost whatever life was left in burlesque. Sammy and a small clutch of putty-nosed, baggy-pantsed funnymen continued, filling time between striptease acts in dive bars across the land.

Don D'Carlo and other agents kept Sammy working through 1972 and the first half of 1973. At the Roxy Night Club in Lima, Ohio, he appeared with an "Exotic Dancer," Delphine Felice, on a stage that promised "Continuous Go-Go Dancing Daily from 3 PM to 9:30 PM." Billed as "The Today Comic With All the Experience of Yesterday" and "A Totally New Exciting Act!", Sammy did three shows a night at Mr. B's, an hour and a half east in Marion. In addition to a go-go girls act, Pam & Geri, were "Old Time Movies Including Charlie Chaplin, Keystone Cops [*sic*], etc. All at Mr. B's." By the summer, Sammy was in Hackensack, New Jersey, at the Flamingo Pub and Club, on a bill with the movie *Deliverance*.

There was a shift in the show-business landscape in the early 1970s besides wide collars and bushy sideburns. Charlie Chaplin movies in titty bars was a signal that pop culture was moving forward and backward at the same time. Head shops were selling posters of W. C. Fields and the Marx Brothers. Retro movie theaters were making bank on classic black-and-white double features. Woody Allen's hit Broadway play and movie *Play It Again, Sam*, charmed a public weary of Vietnam and Nixon, ready to luxuriate in a more innocent age. The kids and the middle-aged kids wanted nostalgia, and Sammy knew that he could serve it up for them.

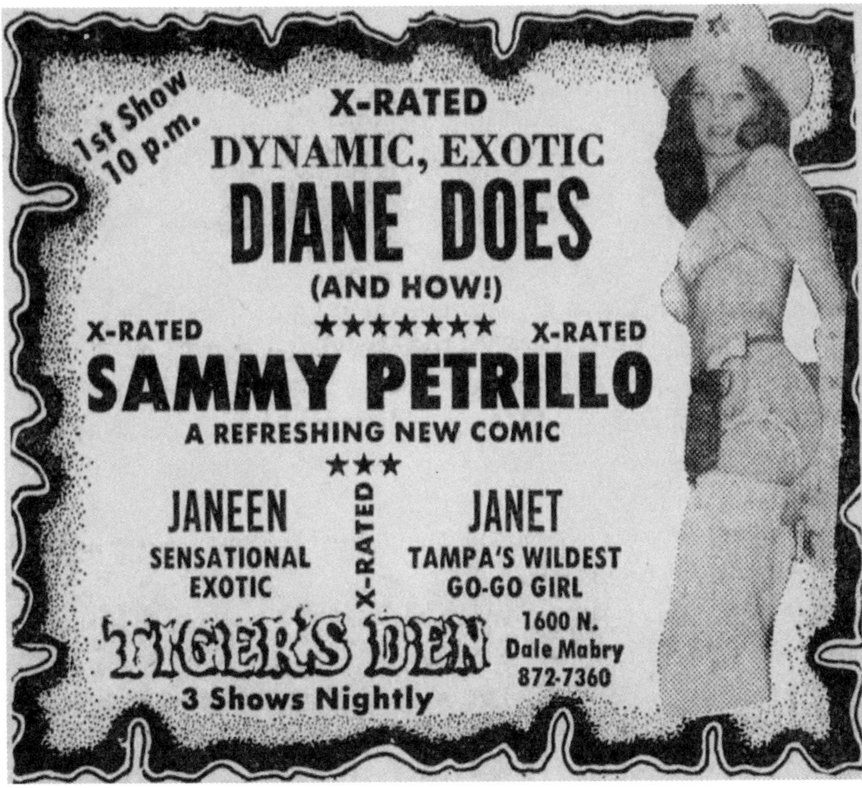

Tiger's Den, *Tampa Times*, April 21, 1972.

In August 1973, a burlesque show was booked into the seedy Capitol Theatre in downtown Passaic, New Jersey. A grand vaudeville house in the 1920s, this 3,200-seat venue was now showing X-rated movies and staging rock concerts booked by its owner, John Scher. The Capitol had recently been raided for allowing kids in to see *The Devil in Miss Jones*. Scher paid the fine and promised to bring family-friendly acts into the venue.

The stripper Hope Diamond was touring with a show that kept its pasties and G-strings on, called *Burlesk Is My Thing*. It was an act just smutty enough to not lose the raincoat crowd, while keeping John Scher out of jail. Hope promised that the show was "camp and nostalgia—good, clean family fun," adding, "The nude scene was just not my bag." The live acts were broken up by movies—chapter one of the 1944 Republic serial *Captain America* and Bela Lugosi in Ed Wood's 1955 *Bride of the Monster*. Joining Diamond was a nine-member musical group led by her husband

Al Beldini, six chorus dancers who weren't strippers, a handful of actual strippers, and Sammy Petrillo.

Burlesk Is My Thing opened on August 6th to about 100 mostly middle-aged men, disoriented by the corny schtick and B movies among the bumps and grinds of the strippers. Also in attendance was Passaic County's first assistant prosecutor, John T. Niccolai, who was ready to shut the revue down for the slightest act of lewdness. He left halfway through the show, finding nothing objectionable; however, he did restrict admission to age eighteen or over, significantly cutting into the "family-friendly" crowd. The *Asbury Press* reviewed the show as "standard stuff of the old days of Newark's Empire Theater and Minsky's" but singled out Sammy in a *Honeymooners*-like sketch about a husband fed up with his dowdy wife and life: "His lines were original and sparked some good laughs among the reporters and photographers."

After a couple of weeks, Diamond and Beldini left town, but the stock company remained, with Ricki Covette, Liz Renay, Ann Corio, Kitty Kovac, and other striptease royalty changing up the bill every two weeks. The rebranded Capitol Burlesk promised "Adult Family Entertainment The Way You Like It" and featured Tony Pischado's Capitol Cuties.

The future screenwriter and film historian Henry C. Parke was a student at New York University's film school in the early 1970s when he was allowed backstage access to the burlesque shows at the Capitol. On assignment from NYU's literary magazine, *Cold Duck,* Henry struck up friendships with the cast and crew, including Sammy. "He was a very funny guy," Henry said. "I think that the reason that Jerry was so awful to him was that Jerry realized that Sammy could do him funnier than he could. I think Sammy's timing was better."

Sammy was now folded into an act called the Hilarious Kapitol Komedy Korps, along with old-time comics such as Frank Silvano, the husband-and-wife team Naples & Vance, and Eddy Black. Frank Silvano was married to Jill Harris, a stripper, who also acted as a straight woman. Charlie Naples played a violin made out of a cigar box and did the same Chaplin imitations that he had been doing since Chaplin was making silents. According to Henry, Eddie Black, in his eighties and still taking pratfalls, was the one who was really running the show. As a young man, after "getting a girl in trouble," Eddie Black escaped town in blackface and joined the Honey Boy Minstrels, thus kicking off his showbiz career.

Since the theater was still showing *Deep Throat* and *The Devil in Miss Jones* multiple times a day, it was decided to combine porn with burlesque for a retooled burlesque experience. The porn industry had fallen upon hard times since the Supreme Court had updated obscenity standards earlier that year. In *Miller v. California,* hairs were split over what was legally considered erotic and thus protected by the First Amendment, and what was obscene with no redeeming artistic, literary, scientific, or political value. X-rated movies fell into the latter category, and the "porn chic" era was over, with careers and movies pushed out of mainstream theaters and back into the peep-show district. The adult film stars that had shot to stardom in *The Devil in Miss Jones*—Marilyn Chambers, Harry Reems, and Marc Stevens—were sidelined and looking for any kind of work. All three joined the cast of Capitol Burlesk, now retitled Skin 'n Grin.

Opening night, December 5th, brought news services and reporters from *Playboy, Screw,* and *Time* magazine. A searchlight scanned the Passaic sky as curiosity-seekers queued up to see what their favorite porn stars would do with their clothes on. Marilyn Chambers opened the show with a song and dance and then sat down on an oversized box of Ivory Snow and wistfully sang "(I Can't Get No) Satisfaction." (Before her porn career, Chambers was known as the Ivory Snow Girl for appearing on boxes of Ivory Snow soap flakes.)

"I remember Sammy doing Jerry Lewis schtick with Marc Stevens," Henry said. "It was a bit called 'Do What I Do.' The whole point of the gag is that the guy shows how to be suave when the girl walks by and the comic tries to do it and does it badly. The guy who's trying to teach him says, 'Well, here, I'll be the girl and you do this,' and then that was an excuse for doing a lot of gay jokes. I remember Sammy saying, 'Anyone got change for a three-dollar bill?'

"I watched the show from the wings," Henry said, "and I thought it was really funny. It was a very good show. However, having Marilyn Chambers, Marc Stevens, and Harry Reems really destroyed it. The porn people expected something dirty and it wasn't—it was just risqué. The regular burlesque people didn't go because they thought they'd get something dirty. It didn't make anyone rich, I'm afraid."

Sammy took a liking to Henry and offered him a job for $75 a week as a personal assistant that he could call on night or day. "My main duty, he told me, would be apologizing for him," Henry recalled. "People did get irritated at him. He was kind of brash and pushy without meaning to offend. He needed someone who could call people up and say, 'Sammy's a nice guy, and he didn't mean that the way it sounded.' Needless to say, I jumped at the opportunity to smooth ruffled feathers for $75 a week."

Sammy also offered Henry a job as a general assistant on four shows he was producing at the New York City radio station WHBI. "The station was so high up on the FM dial [105.9] that only dogs could hear it," Henry said. "It had no signal. It was so small-time that Sammy used to buy the airtime directly for cash and then sell it to other people to do their shows." Henry's primary job was to collect the money before letting them on the air. "I would stand in the doorway with my hand out, moments before showtime, and say, 'Your check bounced. I need $125 in cash, or they broadcast dead air for the next hour.'"

The judo entrepreneur Jerome Mackey's *Protect Yourself* was one of the stranger shows that Sammy produced, the first and possibly only martial-arts instructional radio show. Mackey had operated more than two dozen judo schools in New York and Miami, and his commercials were a staple of late-night television. Standing with a child, he'd say, "Hi, I'm Jerome Mackey and this is Scooter. He is the wrong person to attack." The judo business collapsed in 1974 due to some creative bookkeeping, and a year later Mackey was convicted on federal mail-fraud charges for selling pirated cassettes and eight-tracks. By Henry's account, Mackey was a large and good-natured black-belt instructor from the Deep South.

Sammy hosted a light-hearted hour-long call-in show called *Out to Lunch,* often with his new girlfriend—soon to become a longtime partner—Suzie Perkovic. When the phones were dead, one of Henry's jobs was to run into another room and call the show as different people. "I would occasionally be interviewed on the show myself, if guests didn't show up on time. I'd be impersonating whoever was supposed to be there."

Mark Buniak, an engineer and host who started at WHBI in the early 1970s, recalled his time there with Sammy:

> When I was doing news and stuff, I used my real name because my parents loved hearing it, but when I was playing music I used the persona of Chris Scott. Sammy was buying airtime from the station to do his own program and I had seen the gorilla movie, so I knew who he was. As a little kid, I thought Jerry Lewis was funny, but he never changed. As I grew older, he didn't, and I just found him to be irritating. Sammy did the Jerry Lewis thing, which really irritated me. He didn't do a very good program. I don't remember exactly what he did, but it was stupid. On my music program, I would make a little bit of fun of him, and at one point he approached me as Mark and asked me, 'Who is this guy, Chris Scott?' and I said, 'He's some

guy that does a program overnight,' and he says, 'Can you talk to him? I want to talk to him about having a Jack Benny–Fred Allen feud going on between us because of the things he was saying,' and I said, 'Well, when I see him, I'll mention it to him.' So when I saw myself in the mirror that night I mentioned it to myself. He never discovered the difference between me and my alter ego as Chris Scott. When I would engineer his show, he would bitch to me about this other guy, Chris Scott, so it was like three different people—me, myself, and Petrillo. I didn't want anything to do with him because I really didn't like him. Maybe it was because of the dislike I developed over the years about Jerry Lewis.

Commuting between Passaic and the city, Sammy juggled his multiple ventures, with the hope that one of them would hit paydirt. "He was doing burlesque at the same time that he was doing four radio shows," Henry said, "and at the same time he was producing a cable TV show, which I know some segments were shot at the Capitol. I never saw anything because I didn't have cable TV. Nobody had cable TV then."

Another one of Henry's duties was to track down 16mm public-domain Bela Lugosi movies. "Sammy knew the burlesque thing was not gonna go on forever, and he had this whole thing in his head that he was gonna do this national college tour talking about Bela, which would've been something that me and six of my friends would've loved to have gone to."

After working together for a few months, Henry and Sammy became good friends and would frequently go out to lunch, with Sammy buying Henry his first pastrami sandwich. "Eventually, the burlesque show closed," Henry said. "Sammy left town, and my job was over."

Skin 'n Grin's last show was on New Year's Eve 1973, leaving the cast scattered and looking for new employment. Marilyn Chambers found success in a Las Vegas dinner-theater production of *The Mind with the Dirty Man*, which ran for fifty-two weeks, making it the longest-running play in Vegas history, and earned Marilyn a key to the city from the mayor.

In February 1974, *Backstage* announced that Sammy would be producing vaudeville shows at the historic State Theatre in New Brunswick, New Jersey, and that he was on the lookout for variety and novelty acts. Sammy's old pal Joe Franklin was roped in to emcee what became a weekly Sunday show that featured seven acts, including a Clown Dog, an Obedient Cat, a magician named the Great Raydini, and an escape artist named Vancinni. Showtimes were 2, 5, and 8 p.m., and tickets were sold at the "1940s prices" of $3 for adults and $1 for children.

"We're not reviving something and putting it in a new setting," Sammy told the *Central New Jersey Home News,* referring to the State Theatre's association with the Keith vaudeville circuit in the 1920s. "We're returning it to its real home. Vaudeville never really died. Audiences need vaudeville. They sit in front of their television sets and watch an endless parade of people having their gallstones taken out. People are getting alienated from each other. This kind of show gives them a chance to mingle, without going broke."

Unfortunately, Sammy was the one who went broke producing the show. After a few Sundays, the afternoons were packed, but the turnout in the evening remained dismal. Joe Franklin could only work the afternoons, so he could head back to New York to tape his TV show, leaving Sammy as the nighttime emcee. At this point, the bill included local talents such as the Harmonikings, a magician named "Count" di Matiazzi, and a juggler, Jay Green. After Green finished his act one night, Sammy, looking out at the empty seats, remarked, "You think that was something? Wait'll you see us juggle the books after a crowd this size!"

A few blocks away from the State Theatre was Cheap Thrills, a record store co-owned by Steve Kaplan. During the run at the State, Sammy dropped in on Steve and tried to sell him a machine that would press glittery rock-star photos onto T-shirts. Steve didn't recognize Sammy, but he had run into him seven years earlier at a film screening at the McBurney Y in New York, hosted by Calvin Beck, the editor of *Castle of Frankenstein* magazine. Sammy had shown up that night with a remarkably sober Lawrence Tierney. "Lawrence was funny and articulate," Steve said. "They did separate talks, but they were conferring with each other. They were pals."

Steve wasn't interested in the T-shirt machine, even though he ended up buying a new one from a dealer a few months later. ("It was not successful, by the way," he added.) Before leaving, Sammy noticed the old movie posters hanging on the walls and told Steve that he used to be in movies. "I'm looking at this guy and he was essentially pretty sloth-like," Steve recalled. "His hair was greasy. He needed to shave. He was not dressed well. He said, 'I used to be in the movies,' and I'm thinking to myself, 'Oh yeah, this guy was in the movies.' So I said, 'Oh yeah, what movies were you in?' He says, 'My most famous picture was *Bela Lugosi Meets a Brooklyn Gorilla.*' And my jaw dropped, and I said, 'Oh my god, you're Sammy Petrillo!' He was so excited that I recognized him. That someone knew him. I said, 'Oh, man, Sammy, I'm so happy to see you.' I called up a lot of people."

When Joe Franklin and Sammy Petrillo worlds collide.
Central New Jersey Home News, February 17, 1974.

A week later Steve caught the State Theatre show and was underwhelmed. "It was not X-rated . . . it was pretty puerile. There was song and dance which was rudimentary and not particularly good. I just dealt with it." Steve took Sammy out to dinner with some friends at an upscale steakhouse, the Wooden Nickel. Sammy arrived with his girlfriend (possibly Suzie, possibly not), whom he was living with a few miles away in South River. "She was very attractive and much more refined than he was. What she was doing with him . . ." Steve's voice trails off.

Sammy had Steve's home address and often would pop up uninvited. "I would come home from work sometimes, exhausted at six-thirty or seven o'clock at night and Sammy would be sitting on my doorstep. He would say, 'What are you doing for dinner tonight?' He was always looking for a free meal. I don't want to say *always*. My impression was that he wanted to have a meal. There was no way that I could say no. So, whatever I did for dinner, whether I went to someplace in New Brunswick or if I went to the Wooden Nickel, I would always have to take him."

This went on for about six months. Steve's girlfriend Diane was beginning to get sick of Sammy hanging around, "which I could understand," Steve said, "because Sammy's an acquired taste." He was wearing dentures at this point, and would ask permission to remove them among friends, because they were uncomfortable. Sammy would stash the teeth in an empty Marlboro box for safe keeping. One time Diane spotted the cigarette box on the kitchen table and threw it into the incinerator. "Sammy went for weeks without teeth," Steve said.

Sammy brought Steve a script that he was working on called *Jewish Mother Centerfold* to see if he knew any available cameramen who would work for cheap or free. Steve's school pal Warren Marcus said that he would shoot it for free with his 16mm Bolex if they only shot on the weekends. "Sammy did everything in the movie. He wrote it. He directed it," Steve said. Bill Gyorfy was the producer. "Gyorfy was an ordinary guy. I thought that Sammy had probably sold him a bill of goods."

Jewish Mother Centerfold was shot silent in the Jersey Shore town of Belmar, or possibly nearby Bradley Beach, with the intention of dubbing sound in later. Sammy played several roles, including an Old Mother Riley type of character in drag. Steve was given a small role. "I played a homosexual sailor. A real swishy limp-wrist guy. He gave me an obscene line to do. They were singing a song called, 'Cock-A-Doodle-Doo, Cock-A-Doodle-Doo.' And he said you're going to say, 'Any cock will do!'"

Even though he was in only one scene, Steve saw a few days' worth of rushes on a Moviola. "Sammy knocks on a door that says 'Cat House,' which was really an outhouse," Steve said. "In the next shot, which was filmed in Warren's basement, Sammy walks into a room where someone is supposed to be singing and playing a piano. The camera pans over to the piano, and there's a cat sitting on the piano with a tiara on her head. A real cat. And Sammy and the cat have a dialogue. Then, in the last shot of the scene, Sammy is walking out of the outhouse, I mean the cat house, and that's the end of the scene. I never saw any more of the film than that."

After two and a half weeks of hemorrhaging expenses, the burlesque show at the New Brunswick State Theatre shut its doors. Sammy publicly thanked "all the people who helped bring a few moments of sunshine and glitter into a somewhat cold and chaotic world." Privately, he blamed the failure on the public's general fear of downtown New Brunswick. The theater's owner, Jeff Gerstin, pointed to its other sold-out attractions, such as Cheech and Chong, and commented, "Times have changed, and you have to give people entertainment in tune with the tastes of today." Sammy insisted that he was not "beating a dead horse" and told the *Central New Jersey Homes News,* "They say times change. But they really don't. Audiences have to get used to something and then it finally works." Undaunted, Sammy vowed to talk to other theater owners and "try to sell them on the idea that six or seven acts plus a movie, at supermarket prices, could get to be a good habit." A meeting was set up with Joe Franklin to discuss bringing burlesque to New York City, as well as exploring theaters in the nearby suburbs. "If the suburbs won't come to us," Sammy said, "we'll have to go to the suburbs."

On March 1, 1974, one week before the burlesque show closed, Sammy established a for-profit corporation with the New Jersey Division of Revenue, known as the Camptown Vaudeville House. Set to open in a 350-seat theater in South River, about twenty minutes south of New Brunswick, the auditorium was expected to house a vaudeville museum with articles of clothing to be gifted by Milton Berle and Sammy Davis, Jr. Amid the "psychedelic" and "Art Deco" motifs, there would be a Memory Lane Room, where fans could listen to old-time radio shows on headphones while thumbing through classic comic books. Aside from sharing the space with Polish, Hungarian, and Italian language movies on Mondays, Tuesdays, and Wednesdays, the theater would show hip, youth-oriented "camp" movies such as *Marihuana: Weed with Roots in Hell.* Friday night would be dedicated to classic horror films starring Bela Lugosi, Boris Karloff, and

Lon Chaney, with kiddie matinees of *Gulliver's Travels* and *The Wizard of Oz*. Saturday nights were reserved for "baggy pants burlesque," animal acts, song-and-dance, and ESP and mentalist acts. Sunday nights were "dish nights," with assorted crockery gifted to the female patrons.

"When things get rough on the national scene, and everyone's worried about money and things like inflation, that's when people need entertainment," Sammy said in a press statement. The Camptown Vaudeville House was set to open in August 1974, but, by all existing accounts, it never did.

After a few months, Sammy asked Steve if he would mind holding onto his steamer trunk until he was settled. Sammy also asked for and got a $90 loan. Steve put a tablecloth over the trunk and used it as a coffee table. After a few weeks, a god-awful stench emanated from the trunk. "I was forced to break the lock," Steve said. "In addition to dozens of eight-by-tens, flyers, and clown's feet, Sammy absent-mindedly packed a sandwich, which was now green and rotting." One day, Sammy called Steve and asked him if he could UPS him the trunk. "I said, 'No problem. How are you?' I guess he must've given me a positive answer. I sent him the trunk and that was it. He was basically a fair-weather friend."

Steve saw Sammy once after that, fifteen years later, at the Chiller Theatre Convention at the Hilton Parsippany in New Jersey. Recently divorced, Steve had lost the record store and was dealing with some financial hard times. He saw an ad that Sammy would be appearing and hoped that Sammy might be able to pay him back the $90. "That $90 would have made a world of difference to me. That's how bad off I was." Sammy claimed to only vaguely remember Steve, which was hurtful after all the time they had spent together in New Brunswick, and *definitely* did not remember the $90. Sammy told Steve to see him after the show. Steve helped Sammy gather up his stuff (autographed copies of *My Son, the Phone Caller*) and carried it out to Sammy's car in the parking lot. "When I saw what condition his car was in, my heart sank. There was not one square inch of the car that did not have a scratch or a broken part on it. The back seat was torn out—not torn out, like, removed purposely, but a mess—everything about it. There was nothing right about the car. I didn't mention the money again. Obviously he was bad off, if not worse off than I was. At least I was driving a nice car.

"I said, 'Sammy, give me a card or something.' He gave me a card. The front of the card said 'Sammy Petrillo—paralegal,' which I didn't know anything about. I said, 'Okay, maybe we can get together. I'll come into New

York.' I meant that sincerely, because I was so happy to see him. I put the card in my pocket. About a week or so later, I said, 'You know what—I'm going to New York and I'll give him a call and I'll take him out to eat.' I looked at the card and there's no phone number. I turn it over to look at the other side—no phone number. 'Sammy Petrillo—paralegal.' That's the only thing that it said on the card. There was no way to get in touch with him. No address. No nothing. I'm sure that was by design."

The Palace, *Pittsburgh Press*, May 25, 1976.

CHAPTER 19

THE NUTHOUSE

I saw him a couple times as a kid. We had a lot of arts festivals, New Year's Eve, etc., and he would be at these things. He would have a ten-minute spot. I remember it was this wild whirlwind of random silliness. When he performed for kids, it was very over-the-top, very Jerry-Lewis-esque. I think it became a thing that was expected of him. He had the appearance, even if he tried new material. It was like a band that had new material—all people want to hear is the hits. He just happened to be a cover band, and people wanted to hear Jerry Lewis's greatest hits!

—Joe Wos, Pittsburgh historian, 2019

Nineteen seventy-four and 1975 were a blur of burlesque activity. Sammy took up with Hope Diamond and her *Burlesque Is My Thing* (formerly *Burlesk*), which criss-crossed the tri-state area. They hit the Apollo Burlesk Theatre in Atlantic City, the San Su San and Holiday Inn in Long Island, and the Chateau de Ville Dinner Theater, the Four Seasons Dinner Theater, and the Hidden Valley Cafe, all in Connecticut. Advertised as a "Spicy Musical Revue," Sammy shared the stage with a "Glo-Girl," Toni Rose, "Beautiful Exotic" Jan Julianne, and Lady Erika, as well as some fellow top bananas—Irving Selig, Joey Faye, Tom Poston's brother Dick, and his old pal Will Jordan—all under the musical direction of Hope Diamond's husband, Al Beldini.

Sammy returned to Pittsburgh in April 1976 to work for Gibby Katz, who operated adult movie houses in town. Katz refurnished the decaying L'Amoure Theatre downtown on Liberty Avenue into a "burly Q" known as the Palace. Don D'Carlo booked the talent, and a runway was installed down the middle of the 150-seat theater, inviting patrons to sit on either side for a more intimate experience. An X-rated movie would rotate with four or five stage shows a day: 12:30, 5, 8, and 10 p.m., with midnight shows Fridays and Saturdays. Sunday shows were at the respectable hours of 1:30, 4:30, and 8 p.m.

D'Carlo stacked the venue with strippers, employing, at various times, Joy Sweet, Michelle Lamor, Christy, Sharon Starr, Camille 2000, Lucky Seven, Laura Stevens, Gin Dilder, Alexis Wilder, Virginia Dare, Sandy Dune, Renne Marquee, Terry Robins, Virginia Lee, Sugar Sweet, Mahogany, Lenora Leah, Wonder Woman, Stephanie Plum, Heanne Harding, Dora Deven, Tiffany Day, Tammy Taylor, Susy Field, Arlene Light, Miss Nude America, and the World Famous Gorgeous Gibby Girls. Down-on-their luck porn stars such as Blaze Starr, Georgina Spelvin, Candy Kim, Morganna, and Jacquie Brody bolstered the already top-heavy bill. Don D'Carlo's meal ticket, Chesty Morgan, was also added to the festivities, fresh from filming—and eventually being excised from—Federico Fellini's *Casanova*. And then there was Sammy. The "burly Q" was alive and well in Allegheny County, where the Palace billed him as the "King of Comedy."

Joe Wos is a syndicated cartoonist and a Pittsburgh historian. "I've lived in Pittsburgh my whole life," Joe says, "and I became interested in what I call 'Pittsburgh's characters,' people who really captured the quirky spirit of Pittsburgh. [Like] Uncle Milton, who invented the ant farm—he's from Pittsburgh. Quirky people who either were born here or ended up here or drawn to here, and Sammy Petrillo is one of those. He's one of those characters who became part of Pittsburgh's rich tapestry of characters.

"Sammy was sort of a fixture in Pittsburgh. He would do a lot of emceeing for charity events. He would show up at these kiddie shows in the afternoon, and then in the evenings he was an emcee at strip clubs. He could take whatever work he would get. He played all over Pittsburgh. At the opening of an envelope he was probably there."

Sometime in the early to mid '70s, Sammy revived "the Nuthouse," a showbiz brand that was particular to Pittsburgh and its environs. The Nuthouse had its roots in 1933 in a small bar across the Allegheny River in Millvale, minutes from Pittsburgh proper. Working for tips, a team of comics entertained the working men that dropped in with a barrage of zany skits and routines. More funnymen were signed on, including Boogie Woogie Sherman, Paddy Buchanan, and "Mousie" Powell and His Seven Screwballs. Mel Farber, Morris "Rummy" Spector, and Joe Gottlieb were added to the bill in the late 1930s and performed as the Bishop Brothers,

Headshots. Date unknown.

an act that lasted until Rummy Bishop was drafted during World War II. Joe Gottlieb put together a solo act using the name Joey Bishop, was spotted by Frank Sinatra at New York's Latin Quarter, and became Sinatra's opener and gag-writer for several years and a member of his Rat Pack. In the early '40s, the Nuthouse moved to a larger space in the Wolfendale Hotel with the promise that "Everything was new but the name" and provided wacky entertainment until closing down in 1960.

Sammy's ace in the hole for resurrecting the Nuthouse was the possibility of bringing in the former Nuthouse regular Rummy Bishop. Insisting on $1,000 a week, Rummy was out of Sammy's price range, so the more affordable Bobby Paul was hired as second banana. At state fairs, Bobby's routine would involve him trying to sell a tomato slicer: "The slicer is so sharp, I use one tomato all summer long!" Partly scripted, partly improvised, a night at the Nuthouse would invariably involve audience participation, and Bobby Paul was up for the challenge.

The elusive Rummy Bishop.
The Pittsburgh Press, April 6, 1978

Sammy brought his revived Nuthouse to the Carousel Club down on Stanwix Street. After failing to get the staff to take part in a breaking-the-fourth-wall, *Hellzapoppin'*-like show, auditions were held to bring in ringers who pretended to work there. The Nuthouse eschewed the usual T & A for more of a "continuous fun" atmosphere supplemented by a hot and cold buffet. On occasion, Sammy was double-booked at the Palace and the Carousel and would hustle the half-mile between the two venues to fulfill his commitments. After the Carousel closed in August 1977, Sammy brought the Nuthouse to the Vibrator Club with his "Old Nuthouse Regulars." When that proved untenable, he was able to snag a now-moderately-priced Rummy Bishop as the Top Banana at a club called Encore II. For Sammy, the Nuthouse proved to be less a place than a state of mind. For the next few years, the Nuthouse bounced around from the Encore II to the Stage Door to the Piano Bar to the Char Bar with a revolving cast of Nuthouse regulars. One such regular was Sammy's girlfriend, a former Penn State theater major named Suzie Perkovic.

A Pittsburgh native, Suzie grew up putting on shows for other kids in her Butler Street neighborhood, returning after college to work with the Fox Chapel Players and other community groups. Sammy was twenty-one

Suzie & Sammy in a Nuthouse promotional photo, circa 1980s.

years older than Suzie when he hired her at a Nuthouse audition.

"Sammy wanted to be my partner," Suzie said. "He was older than me. He was smarter than me. He was more established than me. I looked up to him 'cause he was a star."

It was Suzie's first professional break, creating a bond between them that would last for more than thirty-five years. "Sammy was in the business so long that it was second nature to him," Suzie said. "If I messed up a punchline, he would be right in there—boom boom boom—to fix it."

Sammy and Suzie were an item, both romantically and comedically, with at least half of Sammy's solo gigs replaced with the new team of Suzie & Sammy. "Whoever Sammy was going out with, they were part of the act," his nephew Stuart says. "If they had the abilities, or he gave them the lines, they could do it, you know? Suzie was a theater major or something, so he had this opportunity for her."

Together they wrote a one-off syndicated column that ran in a handful of East Coast newspapers. The half-page "My Favorite Jokes" is accompanied by a charming double headshot of the authors. Suzie is seen smiling and leaning her head on Sammy, whose closed-mouth idiot grin evokes Stan Laurel. His eyes are crossed. An Editor's Note introduces readers to the comedy team and the stars of the soon to be released *Gas Is Best*.

A sampling of their jokes:

SAMMY: I'm telling you, my dog can talk. Yesterday I asked him what three minus three was.
SUZY: What did he say?
SAMMY: Nothing.

And:

SAMMY: After the boxing match, they gave me a silver cup.

SUZY: They gave you the cup because you won?

SAMMY: No, to keep my teeth in.

Sammy and Suzie also offered comedy workshops with tips on mic technique, delivery, ad-libbing, and overcoming stage fright. One outstanding student would get a paid, one-night engagement at a Pittsburgh comedy club. The blurb for the course credited Sammy with "writing comedy for over 30 years for such stars as Dean Martin, Frank Sinatra, Buddy Rich, Maxie Rosenblum, and Richard Pryor."

A musical drama, *Who Killed Vaudeville?,* written by both of them and to be directed by Suzie, was scheduled for a four-week run at the Beverly Hills Playhouse in Ross Township. The production appears to have been canceled due to a lack of technicians and available talent. Years later, Suzie would say, "You know the ending? The ending was: nobody killed vaudeville. Vaudeville is still alive today."

In 1976, a full ten years after starting *Gas Is Best,* Bill Gyorfy and Sammy formed Giggles, Inc., to finally finish the movie. They had already shot footage in Detroit, New York, New Jersey, and Tampa, with at least three different cinematographers, and Gyorfy was deep in debt to his in-laws for production costs. They hired a seventeen-year-old kid to resume shooting in Pittsburgh until they ran out of money. Four years later, in 1980, Sammy and Suzie moved to Los Angeles, presumably to raise completion money for *Gas Is Best*. His old pal Larry Joachim needed someone to manage the West Coast branch of his distribution company, Transcontinental Film Corporation, so Sammy took on the part-time work.

In one last stab at conquering Tinseltown, Sammy tested for a role on the top-rated ABC-TV show *Mork and Mindy*. They were looking for someone to play a Jerry Lewis knockoff, Jerry Looney. "We needed the money so friggin' bad," Suzie remembered. "Sammy was in an audition and he was throwing lines. It was going well, but his teeth fell out when he was talking to someone. He didn't get it." The comic Jeremy Vernon won the part and turned in a superb 1950s-era Jerry Lewis impersonation.

Sammy picked up some extra work dubbing in a short speech in Roger Corman's *Humanoids from the Deep*. Quickly filmed to cash in on the Italian horror movie *L'umanoide* (*The Humanoid*), *Humanoids from the Deep* is a sludgy, rubber-suited mess, with workmanlike performances from two former stars, Vic Morrow and Troy McClure. Near the beginning

Original title for *Massacre Mafia Style*. Newspaper advertisement. Circa 1974.

of the movie, Sammy loops in sixty seconds of a portly, older man giving a corporate spiel at a town hall meeting. Even with his voice pitched down slightly, Sammy's raspy line-reading is immediately recognizable.

While working for Larry Joachim, Sammy also reconnected with his most famous ex-partner. "Duke would visit me at my office every day and we'd hang around together," Sammy told *Filmfax*. "Duke had written, directed and starred in a film called *Massacre Mafia Style* [a.k.a. *Like Father, Like Son* and *The Executioner*] and he wanted me to distribute it for him."

Duke had weathered the years well, from headlining at Dino's Lounge on the Strip to buying a controlling interest in Ciro's Restaurant in L.A.

to releasing novelty 45s featuring his kids. He even videotaped a tribute to his idol, Jimmy Durante, fake nose and all. The TV special, *Goodnight Mrs. Kalabash!*, never aired, though a soundtrack album was issued. Duke died from lung cancer at age fifty-five with his second gangster epic, the idiosyncratic *Gone with the Pope*, still in the can. In 2011, the filmmakers Bob Murawski and Sage Stallone meticulously reconstructed *Pope* and released it theatrically, gaining it its deserved cult status.

"Petrillo tried to float a story after my father's passing that there was a reconciliation," Duke's son Jeff says. "*Nothing* could be further from the truth. My dad didn't want him in his life. He was done with him after that movie. He didn't like this Jack Broder, either, and he hated Maurice Duke 'cause Maurice Duke had my dad's management and he could make him do anything. As a matter of fact, my father started his own management company and never had another manager again, except for himself."

"Sammy and Duke were friends," Sammy's nephew Stuart says. "They weren't close, but they used to talk on the phone once in a while."

"We talked about making another film together," Sammy told *Filmfax*. "*The Team*, about a famous comedy team who split up. It shouldn't be too difficult who we based the story on. [laughs] But before any of this happened, Duke passed away, may he rest in peace. He was a great guy."

Sammy reconnected with another old friend in L.A.—Henry C. Parke, the NYU student whom Sammy had hired as his personal assistant and professional apologizer. "I was just reading the *Variety*," Henry said, "and there was an article about some small distribution outfit that had picked up a couple of martial-arts films, and whoever was in charge was Sammy Petrillo. And I thought, 'Holy shit!', 'cause I had not heard from Sammy in decades. When I called him and identified myself, his first words were, 'How much money do I owe you?' I told him, 'Not a dime.' He said, 'You're kidding! I'll buy you lunch!' We went to the Farmer's Market, where we had a nice Italian meal served to us by Dean Martin's aunt. The film distribution company went under a little while later, and I never saw Sammy again."

In 1979, Sammy formed a partnership with two heating and air-conditioning contractors to promote a cost-cutting system known as the Energy Machine. Advertised as "your own utility company at home," the Energy Machine promised consumers free hot water and a 50% reduction in their electric bills. In an interview, Sammy weighed in on the ecological implications: "The sun is 90 million miles away, making it the safest nuclear power plant we have. More sunlight falls on the earth in just over two days' time than we have fossil fuels on the entire planet." The miracle answer to America's home fuel problem went out of business months after being introduced.

In November 1980, *Variety* reported that Sammy had "ankled his post as west coast branch manager Trans-Continental film distrib to produce cable TV show *That's Funnie* with Al Jackson and Sandy Brown." Sammy and Suzie were back in Pittsburgh.

"Sammy widely regarded Pittsburgh as his adopted hometown," Joe Wos says. "You spend ten years somewhere, especially towards the end of your career, it becomes a big part of you. And Pittsburgh really loved him. I mean, they really did."

Billed as "The Best Comedy Team Since Burns and Allen," Sammy and Suzie brought their Nuthouse Revue to several clubs over the next few years with the *Pittsburgh Press* raving that their show was "funny, corny, old and dated and certainly a riotous evening of fun, if you haven't heard the material before." In addition to returning to old haunts such as the Piano Bar and the Char Bar, they appeared at the Tree Tops, the Wexford Inn, the Funny Farm, the Limeliter, and the Holiday House with great regularity. "All of the clubs were allegedly run by connected men," says Joe Wos. "They all would book acts at the Holiday House and down at the strip clubs. There was a transgender mob boss named Tex here in Pittsburgh who owned a bunch of massage parlors and would hang out in the strip clubs."

Sammy would headline Nuthouse bills with up-and-coming-entertainers, including the future *Saturday Night Live* comedians Dennis Miller and Kevin Nealon. Bob Zmuda, Andy Kaufman's best friend and sometime alter ego as Tony Clifton, performed as a magician on one of these bills. Among the more interesting cultural crossovers was Don Brockett, who, with his wife Barbara, was responsible for a good portion of broad burlesque comedy in the Pittsburgh community. Brockett also appeared as "Chef Brockett" on 135 episodes of *Mr. Rogers' Neighborhood,* which taped at the local PBS station, WQED. David Newell and Betty Aberlin (Mr. McFeely and Lady Aberlin on the show) also worked the "burly Q" houses.

"Sammy probably lived downtown," Joe Wos guesses. "Pittsburgh was a filthy cesspool. That era when he was popular in Pittsburgh, he was in the heart of the red-light district. It was strip clubs, massage parlors, a few nightclubs, and it was a pretty seedy area."

Raymond T. Book became an important colleague to Sammy during this period. Partnered with a much older Rummy Bishop, Ray crossed paths with Sammy and Suzie at a show at the Twin Coaches and an enduring friendship was formed. Ray's mother was a dancing girl who worked for Don D'Carlo as a secretary, where she wallowed in a tornado of an office whose only rival in disgustingness was Joe Franklin's Times Square pigsty. Having developed an early taste for the business, Ray auditioned on the revival of *Ted Mack's Amateur Hour* and pursued a career as a comic with some singing on the side. Years later, Ray roomed with Sammy in Westchester, and his respect for Sammy's showbiz experience never wavered. "You know who called on his answering machine?" Ray asks. "Milton Berle! Sammy knew people—he had contacts." Sammy considered Ray his "second-best friend after his brother" and told Ray so. "A lot of people just think that he did Jerry Lewis. That's not true. He was a great ad-libber. He would go in the audience and talk to people and just ad-lib."

Sammy enlisted Ray to go back to Brooklyn with him to help finish filming *Out to Lunch,* a movie that Sammy had abandoned a dozen years prior due to a lack of funds. "We filmed it at the Crazy Country Club in Bay Ridge, off of 65th Street. The Crazy Country Club used to have toilet seats hanging from the ceiling. If a woman walked in with a dress the air would blow from the floor like Marilyn Monroe." Unlike Sammy's other film projects that were victims of unpaid storage-fee bills, *Out to Lunch* appears to have had a one-week theatrical run before disappearing into the ether.

In an event as arbitrary as it was unexpected, on Tuesday morning, October 5, 1982, Sammy Petrillo appeared on nationwide television, putting him back in the showbiz zeitgeist.

ENLIGHTENED ENCOUNTERS

CHAPTER 20

It's like that old joke about the guy that shovels elephant shit and his wife says, "Why don't you just quit?" and he says, "What? And leave show business?"

—Shawn Patrello, 2019

Jerry Lewis, smoking like a chimney, fidgeted in his chair. It was two months before his second heart attack in December 1982, and Jerry was looking to turn his life around. Morphing from Total Filmmaker into Elder Statesman, Jerry sat on the set of *The Today* Show across from Bryant Gumbel, waiting for Willard Scott to finish the weather. Not long ago, Jerry had been the highest-paid movie and TV star in the world, but the past two decades had been a slide down to Nowheresville. The 1960s had started out promising enough, with money-makers such as *Cinderfella*, *The Ladies Man*, *The Errand Boy,* and *It's Only Money*—half of them directed by Lewis, half by his beloved Frank Tashlin. In *The Ladies Man*, Jerry created a four-story cutaway set of a women-only boarding house, lovingly filmed with gliding crane shots peeping into all of their rooms. Paramount spent a half-million dollars knocking down its studio walls to accommodate Jerry, and it was money well spent. *The Nutty Professor* is Jerry's acknowledged masterpiece—funny, dark, and well-constructed, it's a brilliant satire of Robert Louis Stevenson's *Strange Case of Dr Jekyll and Mr Hyde*. Jerry plays a schlubby, buck-toothed professor, Julius Kelp, who invents a serum that turns him into a narcissistic sleazebag, Buddy Love. Far from being a dig at his former partner, which some had surmised at the time, Jerry has stated that Buddy Love was based on "every obnoxious, self-important, hateful hipster he ever knew," a description that sounds suspiciously like the real Jerry Lewis. Artistically and commercially, Jerry had climbed to the highest peak of his career.

Television had proved to be a tougher nut to crack than the movies. Performing on TV without Dean resulted in random appearances on specials and game shows for several years. It wasn't until he successfully guest-hosted *The Tonight Show* for a two-week stint in the summer of '62 that he was taken seriously as a host. The gig would be Johnny Carson's in the fall, and Jerry and several other entertainers were serving as substitutes until Carson's contract with a rival network lapsed. ABC won a bidding war for a Jerry Lewis talk show and gave Jerry a blank check and two hours of live airtime every Saturday night. They also threw in a refurbished burlesque house—the El Capitan near Hollywood and Vine, which was renamed the Jerry Lewis Theater. At great expense, Jerry's onstage desk was wired up to the control room so he could override the director and choose different shots on the fly. The show debuted on September 12, 1963, and was a catastrophe—a night filled with equipment malfunctions and deadly unfunny moments. Subsequent shows retained the stench from the first episode. Jerry floundered under the hot lights for two hours every Saturday night until ABC, in an act of mercy, pulled the plug in December. Near the end of the last episode, Jerry sang "Smile," the mawkish theme from Charlie Chaplin's *Modern Times,* to a look-alike hand puppet of himself.

By 1965, Jerry was washed up in the States, but France adored him. In their film magazines, *Cahiers du Cinéma* and *Positif,* intellectuals deemed him an auteur and saw his self-indulgence as integral to his brand of high-level satire. Despite the overseas accolades, the clock was running out on his screaming idiot persona. Acting like a moron all of the time was a young man's game. As Rick Saphire, who knew Jerry all of his life, said, "Jerry hated his image. His image as a jerk, as a clown, as a nut, whatever. He hated that even before he broke up with Dean Martin. He was finished with that image, but that's what sold tickets." At this point, he wasn't even selling tickets. Meanwhile, Jerry's wife Patti was financing Gary Lewis and the Playboys, their son's rock 'n' roll band, which had just scored a hit with "This Diamond Ring," a development that Jerry warily applauded.

It had been a tough twenty years. Jerry had endured a series of self-inflicted agonies, both physical and mental, which furthered his downward spiral. On an *Andy Williams Show* appearance, he slipped on a pool of water, fracturing the base of his skull. A few weeks later, a miscalculated pratfall off a piano at the Sands put a dent in his spinal column. He was introduced to Percodan, which spawned an opioid addiction that kept him foggy for the next thirteen years. On the night of his twenty-ninth wedding anniversary, Jerry locked himself in his private bathroom and stuck the barrel of a .32 halfway in his mouth. According to Jerry, it was only after hearing some of his kids laughing and chasing each other down the hall that he put the gun back into a locked drawer and continued the fight.

Jerry involved himself in business ventures that could keep him out in the public eye. He invested in a chain of Jerry Lewis movie theaters that went bankrupt a few years later due to his insistence on only showing G-rated pictures. In 1972, the same year that Sammy appeared in *Keyholes Are for Peeping,* Jerry was presented with what he saw as a message from above that, if successful, would be the artistic achievement of his life. *The Day the Clown Cried* would become the most famous movie that nobody has ever seen.

When pitched the story of a clown in a World War II death camp enticing children into the gas chambers, Jerry believed that he was the one to pull this off. Shot in Stockholm, using much of his own money, Jerry acted in his first fully serious role, albeit laced with slapsticky clown schtick. Pushing himself physically and nursing an opioid habit, if there were any wrong choices to be made filming the movie—and there were many—Jerry made them. Blue-eyed, blonde-haired Swedish kids playing Auschwitz inmates was a particularly poor decision. Wrongheaded and insultingly bad (according to the handful that have seen it), *The Day the Clown Cried* never got past the editing stage and remains one of the great cultural enigmas of the twentieth century. Addressing *The Day the Clown Cried* in his autobiography, Jerry insisted, "One way or another, I'll get it done," and, as long as an alleged full videotape copy of the movie exists, then Jerry might get it done from beyond the grave.

The '70s rolled on. Jerry's dream stage project, a Broadway-bound revival of *Hellzapoppin',* imploded out of town amid fights with the director and the other cast members. Frank Sinatra escorted Dean Martin onto the 1976 Muscular Dystrophy Telethon for a rare public reunion, and Jerry was so looped out on goofballs that he barely remembered it happening until he saw the replay. In 1977 there were accusations in the press about him profiting from the annual telethon, which enraged him. Jerry's father Danny had suffered a stroke in 1972, which left him still able to sing Jolson songs but unable to say what he had for lunch. After a long illness, Danny died in 1980, leaving his son wondering whether his father ever really approved of him. The following year, Jerry kicked the pills, and *Hardly Working,* his first movie since *The Day the Clown Cried,* was actually doing well at the box office. Then Scorsese came calling.

Martin Scorsese and Robert DeNiro's latest movie, *Raging Bull,* an intense biopic about the boxer Jake LaMotta, was their greatest critical success yet. Searching for a new project to do together, DeNiro opted for a comedy after the physical and mental strain of *Raging Bull*. Conceived as a meta-parody of *Taxi Driver*, which was recently used as evidence in John Hinckley's trial for the attempted assassination of President Ronald Reagan, *The King of Comedy* was another tale of an outsider looking to get in. DeNiro would portray Rupert Pupkin, an amateur stand-up comedian whose only goal in life was to do a tight five on the Johnny Carson–like *Jerry Langford Show*. The plot involves Rupert and a celebrity-stalker named Masha (Sandra Bernhard) kidnapping Jerry Langford, offering to free him only in exchange for Rupert getting a spot on the show. Casting Jerry Langford was problematic—Johnny Carson, Sammy Davis, Jr., Dick Cavett, Joey Bishop, Orson Welles, and Dean Martin had all passed on it before Jerry signed on. At fifty-six years old, he was the perfect choice to capture the earnestness of a weary showbiz veteran. Jerry plays the role absolutely straight, wearing his own clothes and seemingly not having to stretch himself much as an actor. "It was the easiest job I ever had in my life," Jerry said. "I didn't have to do a fucking thing but show up. All I had to do was play the character, read the dialogue."

An indelible image near the end of the movie is Jerry looking at a wall of TV sets in an appliance-store window, all showing the imposter that took his place. His reaction shot is chilling. Playing a character not unlike himself, Jerry didn't have to dig deep to come up with an appropriate scowl. It's the expression he might have had seeing Sammy on TV with Eddie Cantor on *The Colgate Comedy Hour* or seeing Sammy tear him a new one on *The Steve Allen Show* or seeing Sammy steal his act for an hour and ten minutes in *Brooklyn Gorilla*—or just about any time Sammy Petrillo ever crossed his mind.

The King of Comedy would turn out to be a box-office flop, but Jerry's performance impressed the critics, and offers were coming in again. In order to get ahead of his deserved comeback and any possible negative press that might accompany it, Jerry rushed out an autobiography, *Jerry Lewis—In Person*, co-written with Herb Gluck. With the buzz-worthy *King of Comedy* not to be released for another four months, Jerry hit the talk-show circuit touting the cleaned up version of his messy life.

So, on the *Today Show* set, Jerry lit another cigarette as Willard Scott wrapped the weather and threw it back to Bryant Gumbel. "For some people, it's a mystery. For others, it's a gift," Bryant said to the camera. A black-and-white kinescope rolled with Bryant's prerecorded narration: "The young man you see here making a cameo appearance with Eddie Cantor on the

Bryant Gumble and Jerry Lewis. The *Today Show* debacle, NBC, October 5, 1982.

old NBC *Colgate Comedy Hour* first burst on the Hollywood scene with the following notice: 'This freakishly built and acting young man has genuine comic quality. The swift eccentricity of his movements, the howling features of his face, and the squeak of his vocal protestations have flair.'" There was only one problem—that wasn't Jerry Lewis on the TV screen. During Bryant's entire spiel, NBC had just televised the entire Sammy Petrillo appearance with Eddie Cantor, complete with Sammy looking into the camera and aping Jerry's trademark line, "I like it! I like it!"

At the end of another minute of clips that actually feature Jerry, an offscreen voice yells, "We're on air!" which probably shut down any discussion held between Jerry Lewis and anyone within shouting distance. The camera cuts back to Bryant reciting some more biographical information off a cue card, as the screen clouds up with Jerry's cigarette smoke. Bryant nervously winds it up:

BRYANT: As I welcome you here and say good morning, we do it with egg on our face.

JERRY: Let's not forget I open at Wendy's Friday.

BRYANT: The tape we just saw was the best "I like it! I like it!" that anybody has ever done.

JERRY: Best impression I ever saw in my life.
BRYANT: You caught us. It was not Jerry Lewis.

At this point, Jerry constructs a Sammy origin story, giving him the opportunity to swing through the snafu and own the moment:

JERRY: It was Sammy Petrillo. A kid that I found walking on 53rd Street here in New York, and I brought him out to Hollywood to work in a sketch with Dean and I, and then he worked with Eddie Cantor two weeks later.

NBC then re-airs fifteen seconds of Sammy while Jerry and Bryant talk over it:

BRYANT: This is not Jerry Lewis!
JERRY: I have a hunch I know for sure.
BRYANT: And you never worked with Eddie Cantor.
JERRY: Well, not only that, but I was never quite that good-looking. [laughter]

After a few minutes of plugging Jerry's upcoming projects and the memoir, Bryant brings it back to Sammy Petrillo:

BRYANT: What can I say? I apologize for the false Jerry Lewis we put on up front.
JERRY: I love it. I love it. NBC did it again. [laughs]
BRYANT: I will guarantee you that that clip will be the discussion of the office beyond nine o'clock.
JERRY: I would love to be there.
BRYANT: I would love to miss it.
JERRY: "Hello, I'm from research!"

Sammy never saw the episode, but others told him about it. "Jerry said some very nice things about me and I was very shocked," Sammy said. "He said, 'I was never that good looking,' which I think was pretty funny."

Jerry was slated to appear later that evening in the same building on *Late Night with David Letterman*. Sammy's old buddy, Henry Parke, got an urgent call from one of Letterman's writers, Karl Tiedemann. They were desperate for Sammy to do a surprise walk-on in the middle of the interview. Henry tracked Sammy down at the Nuthouse. "It was a great idea," Henry said, "but they couldn't talk Sammy into it. He was too bitter about Jerry to ever want to be onstage with him again. I couldn't blame him, but I was disappointed. It would have been the biggest break Sammy'd had in forty years."

Sammy could have used that break, considering that, with the freakish exception of *Sugar Babies* on Broadway, the rumpled corpse of burlesque wasn't springing back to life anytime soon. Sammy filled in the gaps between increasingly infrequent shows by taking jobs, and a lot of them. "Sammy did telemarketing for a remodeling place," his partner and girlfriend Suzie said. Suzie often attributed many achievements and qualities to Sammy, sometimes to the point of incredulity. "Sammy was also an acupuncturist," she said. "He got a paralegal degree and a degree in Bible law. He loved studying. That's all he did was read, study, and get degrees. He got a computer degree in DOS. Sammy sold furniture. He used to flip burgers. He sold insurance. The guy was always working." When Sammy was in the New York area, he could usually depend on his cousin Martin to throw him some work as a cab driver. When Martin opened a used-car lot on Central Avenue in White Plains, Sammy manned the office and did odd jobs. Sammy also dipped his toes into the nascent and relatively inexpensive world of cable TV. He produced thirty-minute infomercials for the American Legal Access Company and other clients. "We had a real-estate show," Suzie said. "We had a lawyer show. See, if Sammy couldn't do things in show business, he would look to use show business in other businesses."

Settling into his role as comic emeritus for the local Pittsburgh scene, Sammy took part in events that acknowledged his long history in the business. He judged a roomful of young comics in a show titled *Operation Laughs* at the Tickles club in the Holiday House. Sporadic bookings continued for Sammy & Suzie in family-friendly venues such as the Courtyard Restaurant and Comedy Club, the Galleria, and the Copa Banana Room at the Holiday House. Later that year, Sammy and Suzie appeared in blackout sketches on an episode of the late-night talk show *Thicke of the Night,* starring Alan Thicke. Designed to rival Johnny Carson's *Tonight Show, Thicke of the Night* struggled for viewers and was canceled after one season. "The show was ahead of its time," Alan Thicke commented. "It should've been on in 2084, when all of us are dead."

In the mid-'80s, with the proliferation of cheap public-domain videocassettes, pop culture from the past was being amusingly reassessed. Leonard Maltin cited *Brooklyn Gorilla* as "One of the all-time great bombs" in the

1985-86 edition of *TV Movies,* coupled with the advice to "Proceed at your own risk." Maltin also picked *Brooklyn Gorilla* as his "holiday turkey" on the syndicated TV show *Entertainment Tonight,* exposing the concept of a Martin and Lewis knockoff act to a new audience. When asked to comment on *Brooklyn Gorilla*'s resurgence in the news cycle, Sammy said, "It's not *Othello.* When it was released, people laughed *with* it, not *at* it. It's still making me money in a way."

Johnny Martinelli, Sammy's agent for the Bronx and Westchester, hooked Sammy up with his other clients, Tiny Tim and "Grandpa" Al Lewis, for a proposed TV pilot called *The Sammy Petrillo Show.* Sammy's pal Ray Book was also involved with it. "It was a grade-B *Benny Hill* type of show," Ray said. "He had Miss Yonkers in it. She was nice and very pretty, but she really wasn't that good. Sammy still wanted to use her. Judy Carne (former *Laugh-In* "sock it to me!" girl) was supposed to be in it, but she had problems and bowed out. In one of the skits, I was playing some guy that was interviewing Sammy for a job, and Sammy insisted that I ad-lib, which scared me. I was insecure, but Sammy had faith in me, and it turned out to be much funnier than what was written. He made me look so good." Sammy shipped the raw tape down to Florida, where he was supposed to get a deep discount on the editing. "So he sends it to these people in Florida and never sees it again," Ray said. "This is stuff that would happen. It's a funny story, but it wasn't funny at the time."

Sammy appeared on *Beyond Vaudeville* in 1988, an inspired Manhattan public-access TV show that ran for ten years before it was briefly picked up by MTV and renamed *Oddville, MTV* for one season. A hilarious time capsule of New York City–centric B-listers, *Beyond Vaudeville* was set in a cramped rec room of a set, populated by oddball puppets that peeped out from behind the couches during the interviews. The comic and writer Rich Brown created the nerdy persona of Frank Hope, the stammering, bespectacled host who butted heads every week with his belligerent, mostly silent sidekick David Greene as they welcomed the likes of Larry Storch, Quentin Crisp, Joe Franklin, Brother Theodore, Benny Bell, Kaye Ballard, Jimmy Breslin, Pat Cooper, Joey Faye, and many others. Some of the celebrities were in on the joke and some weren't. "Sammy couldn't have been more gracious and friendly," Rich says. "He definitely rolled with it." Sammy riffs on the stoically stupid co-host David Greene ("How long has this man been dead?") and tells a couple of jokes—"What did one casket say to the other? Is that you coffin?" When asked what he was up to, Sammy says that he's "Playing nightclubs, doing a few television things here and

Beyond Vaudeville TV show, 1988. Courtesy of Rich Brown.

there. I have a movie coming up that I'm supposed to star in and I'm looking for a job." The episode ends with Sammy dancing a jig with Joey the Monkey, an absurdly tall monkey-masked man in a long red robe and oversized gloves. Sammy is 100% invested in the gag as he shuffles across the floor with the giant monkey.

Sometimes *Beyond Vaudeville* presented live shows at the NYU Loeb Student Center, which the artists and best friends Mark Newgarden and Stephen Kroninger would attend. The shows were padded with eccentric personalities: UFO experts, tap dancers, comedians, memory acts, and occasionally Underdog Girl—a woman whose goal in life was to rehabilitate the image of the cartoon character Underdog. According to Stephen, Ray Book also performed there, as Sammy's sidekick: "Sammy would always go, 'Raymond!' [raspy voice] like the way he'd yell, 'Dukey!'" Ray was also in the comedy team Book-n-Martino, releasing a small pressing of an LP called *Interview with Dracula and 5 Other Skits*.

"*Beyond Vaudeville* would find these unbelievably untalented people, but when you put them all together for an hour it was the greatest night of entertainment," Stephen said. "My wife was friends with Rita Dove—the [Pulitzer Prize–winning] poet. It was the first time that I met her. Anyway, she gets off a plane and comes with us to see Sammy Petrillo. He was doing impressions and throughout the whole thing, people would be yelling, 'Jerry Lewis! Jerry Lewis!!' and he didn't want to do Jerry Lewis, but he eventually gave in to Jerry Lewis. The funny part is, it was a benefit for a homeless shelter or something. So he did his Jerry Lewis impression and he must have thought that he was really Jerry Lewis, 'cause at the end he said, 'Folks, this is a great cause. Please give generously'—like Jerry Lewis from the telethon, not knowing he was doing Jerry Lewis from the telethon."

After the show, Sammy signed Stephen's copy of the *My Son, the Phone Caller* record and they walked him out to a bus stop to go back to wherever he lived. "It was a rainy night and Mark Newgarden said, 'That's a Drew Friedman drawing—a sad guy in a raincoat, all by himself, who was once the toast of Broadway.' This was the Sixth Avenue and West 4th Street station. That's how I met Sammy."

Stephen recalls around this time seeing Sammy and Suzie on *The Joe Franklin Show* promoting their *Hellzapoppin'*-esque club show. Suzie would say to Sammy, "Doctor, doctor, I have a cataract!" Sammy, as an Asian doctor, in full stereotype mode with false bucked teeth, would reply, "Oh, that OK! I own Rincoln Continental!"

"So then Sammy started to hang out with us. I don't know—I must've given him my number or something." Sammy would pop by Stephen's apartment regularly, bearing stuffed animals and gifts from his brother Marvin's novelty store. "It was kind of cute, I guess," Stephen said. "He was probably working for his brother, and his brother was taking care of him—gave him a busy-work job. It was all these people in their twenties and then Sammy in his mid-fifties, hanging out with us. He was living with Suzie at the time, and that was a strange relationship. I was on the phone with him once. He was talking on and on and I kind of hear her talking in the background and Sammy goes, 'Hey Steve—if I wanna get fucked, I gotta get off the phone!' Sammy would call me a lot for romantic advice, and I'm the last person in the world to give out romantic advice. He'd call me with his women troubles. Mostly Suzie troubles." When Sammy and Suzie broke up, they remained friends and continued to work together.

Sammy got involved with a public-access show with Al Goldstein, the founder of *Screw* magazine. "He was doing a tape for public access that was gonna be his big break—his big comeback. And it was done with strippers," Stephen said. "I guess they took the place of Suzie after they broke up. He didn't have a VCR, so he'd bring this tape over every time and he would work on it. It was a bit with a psychiatrist sketch and it was this stripper

Sammy relaxing with Stephen Kroninger.
Photograph by and courtesy of Mark Newgarden.

from *The Robin Byrd Show* or something. They tried to give her a hundred bucks to do it, and she couldn't deliver her lines—it was terrible.

"Sammy always thought that he was on the verge of stardom. It was sort of nice. That's not a bad way to go through life, right? To think, 'It's just around the corner,' when it really isn't. And everybody knows it—his brother knew it—it *isn't* just around the corner; it's not gonna happen. But he believed it was gonna happen. 'It's just around the corner—as soon as I finish this tape.' When he finished it, it never even got shown on public access. One night we watched *Brooklyn Gorilla* with him and he said every line of dialogue—not just his lines, but every line of dialogue, a beat before they said it on the screen, so that was fun. He was doing lots of colleges with *Brooklyn Gorilla* and I don't think he ever really saw that they thought that it was so bad that it was funny. I just think he thought that the audience had finally appreciated it."

Sometimes Stephen would take Sammy out for dinner in Little Italy. One night, Sammy smeared cream cheese on his face like shaving cream and asked Stephen's friend Alison Mork, who played Chairy on *Pee-wee's Playhouse,* to shave him. Alison refused, so Sammy went to another table. "There was this young woman in her twenties and she shaved him and then they danced. When he came back, he goes, 'I got her number!' It was amazing. Many times these girls would come out of nowhere and just talk to Sammy." Stephen was friends with a few people who worked on *Pee-wee's Playhouse,* and Stephen did what he could to try to sell them on Sammy, possibly playing Pee-wee's father: "Pee-wee's doing his variation on Jerry Lewis and Sammy as his dad would've been funny, but they found him really scary,"

Hanging out with Sammy brought a barrage of stories, and Stephen wondered if many of them were really true or not: "Sammy said that Howard Hughes loved Mitchell and Petrillo. There's one story about Sammy hanging out with Howard Hughes and Lenny Bruce up in Howard Hughes's penthouse in Las Vegas. Lenny Bruce went outside to the terrace and closed the sliding glass door and he ripped up an envelope and was sprinkling the paper on his head going, 'It's snowing! It's snowing!' Sammy also said that he ran into Bela Lugosi one time in Hollywood and Bela Lugosi was so broke that when he would buy salt he'd have the guy fill up a little cup full of salt, 'cause he couldn't buy the whole box. Sammy ran into him at a grocery store buying this salt, and he offered to buy the box for him. Lugosi brought him back to his apartment, and Sammy said that the apartment had a giant wall-painting of Lugosi. He said that was the last time he said he saw him."

Don D'Carlo, Sammy's main Pittsburgh agent, died in 1989, and Sammy moved in with his parents, Anna and Skelly, in Delray Beach, Florida. He produced and directed a new-age show called *Enlightened Encounters* for WAQ, a UHF station in Palm Beach. Featuring astrologers, parapsychologists, crystal experts, and holistic and medical practitioners, Sammy boasted to the local papers that "It is the only kind of show of its kind in the country." Sammy's old pal, the Ed Sullivan impressionist Will Jordan, bumped into Sammy down in Palm Beach. "He wouldn't tell me anything," Will said. "I said, 'Sammy, the whole fucking world wants to know how you are and where you are!' But he just wanted to remain a recluse. I couldn't understand why he didn't want any of us to say hello to him."

Sammy wrote and starred in a kiddie show for WAQ called *Uncle Sammy's* that would run public-domain cartoons in between Sammy's comedy segments. He also ventured into a business with Marvin to ship Canadian prescription drugs down to the States, where they were supposed to sell cheaper than the generic versions. "Sammy was brilliant," Marvin said. "He had a good brain in his head. We said, 'Move

Over, Canada—here comes Only America.' And yet it never took off. I never understood it. The theory behind everything was great. I wish I had a brain in my head like he did."

In the latter half of 1991, Sammy moved back to the suburbs north of New York City, where he picked up some work. Appearing at the Best Western Inn in Nyack, on a night titled *Comedy Done Right,* where the admission charge was $1.98. Sammy was billed as "The Zany and Hilarious Star of *Bela Lugosi Meets a Brooklyn Gorilla*." He moved in with Suzie and her new husband Rocco Fiore in nearby Ardsley, where he became godfather to their two children. "He loved my little boy so much," Suzie said. "He adored him, and I guess his family was always jealous about that."

Sammy brought Suzie and her two young kids with him for a second appearance on *Beyond Vaudeville* and it was a little sadder than the first visit. Sammy didn't have his dentures in and looked noticeably older. Suzie explained that they didn't have a babysitter and Sammy mock-complained about doing TV shows that don't pay any money. "We took time out from living on the subway to do this thing," Sammy joked. "It wasn't clear to me what his relationship with Suzie was," *Beyond Vaudeville*'s host Rich Brown said. "It was an odd arrangement."

The last time that Stephen Kroninger spoke to Sammy was in the early '90s while Sammy was living with Suzie's family. "He called me up needing more advice," Stephen said. "I took the kid out for a walk and the kid ate some snow. 'Can he die from that? 'Cause there's chemicals that came down from the rain and the kid ate the snow. You're sure he can't die from that?' I told him the kid wouldn't die from eating the snow. 'No, I wanna know, 'cause I took the kid for a walk and I'm responsible for the kid.'"

These were confusing times for Sammy. His cousin Martin recalled seeing him go up after a Sam Kinison set at Dangerfield's, Rodney Dangerfield's comedy club on the Upper East Side. "It wasn't long after Rock Hudson died, and it was the beginning of political correctness. He said, 'They buried him face down. That's so his friends would recognize him.' He's expecting the laugh because if it was '62 it would have brought the house down. At Dangerfield's you heard groans and it threw him off. I remember coming back with him in an open-top Jeep, and Sammy was going, 'They just don't understand.'"

APTER 21

THE BOTTOM LINE

In 1992, Sammy spent his fifty-eighth birthday performing at the Bottom Line, the influential 400-seat cabaret-style club in the heart of Greenwich Village. The event was a release party for Shanachie Entertainment, who were reissuing every episode of the Abbott and Costello TV show, spread out over thirteen videotapes. "Uncle" Floyd Vivino, a local-TV legend and the missing link between Soupy Sales and Pee-wee Herman, was recruited to emcee the evening. Floyd's cult kiddie-show-which-was-not-a-kiddie-show was broadcast over UHF stations in various East Coast cities, creating a small yet rabid following. Uncle Floyd's charmingly silly persona was a natural fit for a night of fuzzy nostalgia. Billed as "An Evening of Classic Burlesque," Floyd brought Sammy on board along with Michael Townsend Wright (an *Uncle Floyd Show* regular) and the funnyman Joey Faye. Known at the time for portraying a bunch of grapes in a Fruit of the Loom underwear commercial, Faye's career stretched back to the Catskills hotels and Minsky's burlesque, countless Broadway and movie appearances, and even East and West Coast critically acclaimed runs in Samuel Beckett's *Waiting for Godot*. Joey Faye had claimed credit for writing the iconic "Niagara Falls" (a.k.a. "Slowly, I Turned") sketch, an assertion also made by vaudeville pioneers such as Samuel Goldman and the early Bud Abbott partner Harry Steppe. Faye had been Michael Townsend Wright's onstage partner for a number of years, providing

Floyd with at least one well-oiled act. There would be a look-alike contest not only for Bud and Lou, but for the ancillary characters Stinky, Bacciagalupe, and Mr. Fields. The judges were Lou Costello's daughter, Chris; Bud Abbott, Jr.; and the legendary burlesque stripper Ann Corio, now aged eighty-three. Musical interludes were to be provided by Vince Giordano's Nighthawks, the best vintage jazz orchestra in the business. This was a big night.

The day before the show, *Backstage* ran a promo piece featuring a double head shot of Sammy and Suzie. Suzie, with a flower in her hair, is smiling a toothy grin. Sammy is cross-eyed, his mouth flung open to reveal his top four middle teeth are missing. Starting in the '70s, Sammy wore a bridge but, more often than not, didn't. "He used to walk around without the bridge in," his nephew Stuart said. "We'd say, 'C'mon, Sammy, we gotta meet someone,' and he'd say, 'Okay, Okay, I'll put the bridge in." Then, after that, they were false teeth, tops and bottoms. And eventually he never wanted to wear them, and then he would put them in after not wearing them for so long and complain about how they used to hurt his mouth. He hated it."

On October 24, 1992, Sammy arrived on time at 8 p.m.; however, his teeth didn't. Michael Townsend Wright remembered, "We chatted backstage quite a bit. Here's the funny thing: he got there, and he lived nearby apparently, and he said, 'Oh my God, I forgot my teeth!' and he ran home, got them, and came back."

Sammy might have grabbed his teeth from back home, but he hit the stage that night as toothless as the day he was born. Sammy's attire for the evening was a selection of 1970s-era rumpled and mismatched shirts, jackets, and trousers. Possibly misreading the classic comedy audience, Sammy was working blue right out of the gate.

> SAMMY: If a guy had a sixteen-inch penis growing out of his forehead, how many inches would he see?
> SUZIE: All sixteen.
> SAMMY: Nope. He wouldn't see any.
> SUZIE: Why?
> SAMMY: Because his balls would be in his eyes.

And:

> SAMMY: I look at you and I feel like Napoleon.
> SUZIE: How's that?
> SAMMY: I feel like beatin' my bone apart! [Sammy laughs maniacally

and sticks the entire microphone in his mouth, pretends to shave with it, and then licks it like an ice cream cone.] I love Howard Johnson!

Throughout the evening, treading some dicey ground, Sammy touched on all the bases of lowbrow strip-club humor—sexist, racist, and homophobic gags. He did impersonations, whipping out Porky Pig, Bugs Bunny, Yogi Bear, and Fred Flintstone in quick succession. For an Elvis impression, he lay down on the stage as though he were dead. Requesting a Kleenex from the audience, Sammy stuffed it into his mouth for some Brando *Godfather* schtick. Suzie asked him if he had a son, and Sammy said, "I do have a little son. He's beautiful. He waves bye-bye. He says 'dada.' Thirty-seven. He's a moron." Perhaps mistaking the upscale Bottom Line for the Lincoln Lounge Tornado Room in Staten Island, Sammy remarked on the dust and general uncleanliness of the club. He heckled patrons without any instigation. "Boy, oh boy, look at you," he said to a woman. "What are you celebrating—a menopause?" Sammy told a man with a beard and a mustache that he looked like an armpit. The crowd was friendly, but Sammy had lost them early on.

He appeared in a few other skits, including a hoary burlesque staple, "The Honeymoon Scene," which consisted of a married couple loudly trading insults. Both Sammy and Suzie appeared lost at times, forgetting some lines, rushing and punting others. Joey Faye fared better, hilariously performing the "Niagara Falls" routine with his longtime partner Michael Townsend Wright. As two bums on a park bench, they killed their respective roles with the gravity and playfulness of a Samuel Beckett play. The Uncle Floyd–hosted *Abbott and Costello Show* look-alike contests were the meat of the evening, as the amateurs and non-amateurs evoked the comic spirits of the past. In many ways, the night was a farewell to old-school burlesque and the funnymen and funnywomen that trod its dusty boards. With the exception of Vince Giordano's Nighthawks, hardly any of the other performers that evening would ever work at such an upscale venue again. As of this writing, it was also the last known Joe-Besser-as-Stinky-the-Brat look-alike contest held on the island of Manhattan.

Burlesque would rise again, however, without Sammy. By the end of the decade, fueled by the underground fetishism of the pin-up queen Bettie Page, a new, scrubbed-up version of burlesque was revived. Looking to challenge social and sexual taboos, Dirty Martini, the Pontani Sisters, Dita Von Teese, and other strippers reclaimed burlesque from its sexist, male-gratifying roots. Promoting self-expression and playing to the women in the audience, this new feminist brand of striptease created a cottage industry that exists to the present day. The last emcee that the New York City hipsters wanted or needed was a toothless Jerry Lewis impersonator.

With nightclub work dried up, Sammy started another business with his brother Marvin. Still living in Riverdale, Marvin worked at an offtrack-betting facility down on Canal Street in the city and drove a yellow cab at night. Sammy and Marvin tried to interest the singer Chubby Checker in promoting a bicycle-safety jacket that sported two built-in speakers, but the deal fell through. They shot a pilot for a TV show called *Ask a Lawyer,* with "Grandpa" Al Lewis and Joe Franklin, that was never picked up.

There was also a two-minute commercial Sammy and Marvin filmed down at Grampa's, Lewis's Italian restaurant in the Village. "We had 500 of these knockoff clapper keychains—where you would clap your hands and turn lights on and off," Marvin said. "Our Uncle Benny put out the money for this, but there was a problem with a lady out in California who wasn't processing the orders. We won our lawsuit against her but lost $50,000 in orders." Uncle Benny, also known as Dr. Benito Rish, was a well-known New York plastic surgeon. "He did the Gabor noses," Sammy's nephew Stuart Hersh says, "and Hedy Lamarr's facelift. He was one of the pioneers with the whole transsexual thing. When you see *Dog Day Afternoon*—in real life, he did that operation" (sex reassignment surgery).

Sammy's showbiz ventures at this point consisted almost entirely of autograph shows and fan conventions. Sammy would often accompany his signature with a little cartoon sketch of himself. Kevin Mulligan was a fan who bought a signed *Brooklyn Gorilla* lobby card from Sammy. "He was very happy to pose for pictures, and he did a straight face for the first photo," Kevin says. "Then he said, 'Let's do one where I make a funny face,' and, to be honest, they looked pretty much the same!" One film collector, Gary Balaban, observed Sammy chain-smoking at his table. "He had glossies. He did okay," Gary says. "He did a lot better than Patricia Neal!" The horror and sci-fi movie historian Tom Weaver helped Sammy move his dealer's table: "[Sammy] let out a shout when his hand got caught between his table and the next. That's *my* Sammy Petrillo story!"

Stuart Hersh would be instrumental in getting Sammy booked at these events. Enraptured by old-time radio and TV as a kid, Stuart would initiate contact with retired comics and showbiz types, writing letters and interviewing them long-distance. Turning his passion into a vocation, Stuart ended up managing Bobby "Boris" Pickett, the singer of the original "Monster Mash," and booking his childhood heroes into fan conventions. Aside from handling Professor Irwin Corey, John Astin, and Gavin

MacLeod, among others, Stuart also co-wrote and produced Tiny Tim's "I Saw Mr. Presley Tiptoeing thru the Tulips," as well as a 45 by his own duo act, Hersh and Chipkin—"Disco Toilet" (released on Flush Records).

Stuart set Sammy up at the Ray Court autograph show at the Meadowlands in New Jersey, followed by other signings, including the popular Chiller Theatre Expo at the Parsippany Hilton. "The first time Sammy came out, I was explaining to him how this went," Stuart said. "I found photos for him, some great shots from [Jerry] Ohlinger's [movie material store], repro'd those shots for him, set him all up. Next thing I knew, he was doing shows with Rick Saphire, so I said, 'Oh, okay. There we go.'"

Rick Saphire's uncle was Ernest D. Glucksman, *The Colgate Comedy Hour* human punching bag, who had managed Jerry Lewis's career for an astounding fourteen years. As a kid, Rick was an aspiring comedian and magician, and, through his uncle, had a guest spot during the two weeks that Jerry Lewis hosted *The Tonight Show* in 1962. Jerry, looking out for Rick, secured him a job as social director at Brown's Hotel in the Catskills, where he mingled and did business with the stars that came through. Rick got a taste for celebrity management and liked it. In addition to a career as a professional photographer, Rick opened a magic shop in Cherry Hill, New Jersey, but continued to manage talent. His clients have included Rip Taylor, Mickey Rooney, Hayley Mills, Jerry Mathers, many of the Little Rascals, and Charlie Callas. In the early 2000s, Rick took on a client he had had his eyes on since he was a kid. "After my uncle, Ernest D. Glucksman, and Jerry [Lewis] parted ways in 1964, a great guy named Joe Stabile took over the task of being Jerry's manager," Rick said. "Joe was the brother of Martin and Lewis's longtime orchestra leader, Dick Stabile. I became Jerry's manager—even though Jerry was often unmanageable—some time after Joe's passing." After a few years, Rick realized that there wasn't a lot that he could do with Jerry. "I wasn't going to help promote the speaking engagements that he was doing," Rick said, "because nine out of ten times he just offended the audience so badly. Some people wanted their money back." He continued to sometimes manage Jerry's events as well as managing Jerry's son Gary and the latest version of the Playboys.

Sammy was sitting in front of a large poster of *Bela Lugosi Meets a Brooklyn Gorilla* at an autograph show when he met Rick. They struck up a friendship, and Sammy started getting bookings from Rick instead of Stuart. "Sammy and I became fast friends," Rick said. "I did what I could to secure some personal appearances and such. I did not have a lot of success in securing nightclub performances for him and his lady partner, unfortunately, because nightclubs were pretty much gone. I helped him generate some publicity for himself, but generally we became good friends."

Rick had an idea about getting a message to Jerry from Sammy. He videotaped Sammy at an autograph show, telling him that he would get it to Jerry Lewis. In the three-minute clip, Rick comically goads him on—"So Jerry stole your act, he stole your partner, he stole your looks, and he stole your name ..."

"Oh no! Oh no! Sammy Petrillo!" Sammy says while pointing a finger into the camera. "Hey listen, Jerry, you better stop doing the act, all right? You had an Italian partner. I had an Italian partner. He sang. Mine sang. Yours had a nose job. Mine was born that way. Jerry, I've tolerated you long enough. You're a nice guy, but I think that's enough." This goes on good-naturedly for a couple of minutes until Sammy lowers his voice and says half-jokingly, "Send me a little royalty every once in a while. I don't have enough money. I gotta sit here, scrimping with autographs. Throw a little bread this way, all right?" Visiting Jerry on his boat in San Diego, Rick showed Jerry the video. "Jerry watched in pensive silence," Rick said, "and then asked to see it again. This time, he did not say a word as the three-minute video ended."

In the spring of 2006, *Bela Lugosi Meets a Brooklyn Gorilla* screened on a bill with *Kid Monk Baroni* at the Egyptian Theatre in Hollywood, as part of their American Cinematheque series. The night was a tribute to Realart's founder, Jack Broder, a celebration of his life from Polish immigrant to idiosyncratic producer. Jack had left the business in 1954, two years after *Brooklyn Gorilla,* and bought the swank California Racquet Club, which sported large swimming pools, tennis courts, a dining room, a ballroom, and a cocktail lounge. In 1966, Jack took one last stab at producing with two low-budget thrillers: *Women of the Prehistoric Planet* and *The Navy vs. the Night Monsters*—both filmed with the same sets and crew, in typical Broder style.

Jack passed away in 1979. His grandson, David Kopple, is a successful Hollywood literary manager who shares his grandfather's obsession with monkeys and gorillas. For a grad-school paper, David wrote about apes and movies in Los Angeles, contrasting Aldous Huxley's novel *Ape and Essence* with *Bela Lugosi Meets a Brooklyn Gorilla.* David is proud of his family's gorilla-inspired exploitation past and engineered the Realart Pictures tribute at the Egyptian. The *Kid Baroni* stars Leonard Nimoy and Jack

Sammy with Ernest Glucksman's nephew Rick Saphire. Courtesy of Rick Saphire.

Larson agreed to take part in a discussion between the features. However, one other very-alive star from the Realart stable of talent was missing.

"I tried to get Sammy to come out here, but he wouldn't get on a plane," David said. Undeterred, he set Sammy up with a director in New York to shoot an intro for *Brooklyn Gorilla*. In the video, Sammy comes across as humble and flattered to be asked for his thoughts. He recounts showing up at 5:30 in the morning for makeup, and he perpetuates the rumor that Ramona the Chimp was really Cheeta. In regard to copping Martin and Lewis's act, Sammy ruminates, "I don't know if that was a blessing or a curse. I guess it was a blessing. Who knows if I would've broken into show business any other way?"

The following year, David was in New York and took Sammy out for burgers. "He was making eyes at the waitresses and the waitresses loved him," David said. "He was doing that sort of old-man comedian thing with the waitresses." Sammy signed a photo for David, spelling his name Patrello, with an "a."

"It was very sweet. I had an automatic connection to the guy. I wasn't prepared for it to be that emotional, for this one guy who was in a movie fifty-five years before, but he had very fond memories of my grandfather, although he might have confused him with Maurice Duke. He felt that they had given him his break. It was a fatherly thing, and I think that Sammy probably felt that connection inversely to me."

Shawn Patrello, Sammy's eldest son, realized at an early age that a life in show business was inevitable. Sammy had essentially cut all ties with his four sons in Dallas when he left town for good in 1969. This resulted in conflicted feelings on Shawn's part as he contemplated the idea of entertaining people for a living. "There were many times when I thought that I didn't want to be like Sammy in any way. That's how much anger and hurt I had," Shawn said. "But in the end, like anybody that's in show business, there was nothing that I could do about it. If it's inside of you, you have to do it. You don't have a choice. I had the brains to become anything that I wanted to be—a doctor, a psychiatrist or whatever—but I have show business in my blood, like Sammy had it. Like Skelly had it, and probably everybody before them. It was in my blood and I didn't have any choice, and frankly I make a horrible living doing the things that I do, but I'm in show business."

Shawn's life, in his words, has been "a roller coaster of good and bad times," and his decision at age twelve to accept Christ into his life was, for him, the right decision at the right time. As a young man, working as a character actor in local theaters in Dallas, Shawn joined the national franchise comedy troupe Comedy Sportz and developed a passion for improvisation. He formed his own company, Rubber Chicken, as well as Himprov (later known as Fish Sticks), an improvisational ensemble that taught problem-solving and math to school children. Shawn dabbled in ventriloquism and took the occasional character roles in local plays; however, his most rewarding work was performing as Dr. Scribbles, a therapeutic clown in hospitals across Dallas. "It's the hardest and best thing that I've ever done in my life," Shawn said. "I've been with kids with a broken toe to two kids that were probably going to pass away within a couple of months. Anything I can do to be with them for five minutes at a time to make their lives better and take them away from that sickness, that's what I want to do."

Shawn was in New York in 2006 for a week-long clown workshop at the Flea Theater in Tribeca. Cousin Stewie, Stuart Hersh, stopped by to visit, and suggested that perhaps Shawn should see his father. "I had maybe talked to Sammy three times in my life on the telephone," Shawn said. "Sammy would say, 'How's it going?' and, 'I miss you,' and make a promise that he would never keep like, 'I'm gonna send you pictures of this,' or, 'I'm gonna send you some money,' and that was just the way that it went every time. He really did have a negative effect on my brothers and myself, and any absence of any father does that. I thought that, when I saw him, I would let him know *this* happened and *this* happened and you missed *this* and you could've been there for *this*. I thought that when I saw him I would go into that and I would finally get to have my say."

Stuart arranged for Shawn to meet Sammy on a street corner in SoHo, not far from where he was staying. "After about five minutes, this little old lady, a real small, shriveled, gray-haired old lady, started walking towards me, and I thought, 'Well, this New York stuff just happens,' and she put her arms out and she said, 'Shawn! Shawn!' and then I realized—that was Sammy! It wasn't a little old lady. It was this little person with gray hair and no teeth, and it was him, and I thought, 'Oh my gosh.' I literally froze. He came with his arms towards me. He said, 'Shawn!' He reached out to hug me. I hugged him back and, at that point in time, everything that I thought that I would say I didn't say. I tried to think, after that, why that was, and the only thing that I could think was to draw an analogy. If you were a wolf, and you were chasing prey, and you could hear it rustling in the bushes and it was evading you, and you just thought to yourself, as a wolf, 'Man, when I get this prey I'm going to devour it,' and this prey comes out of the bushes, and it's a tiny, tiny mouse—if you're any kind of a decent wolf, you let the mouse go, because it's too pathetic. It's not worth devouring him. That's what I felt like."

Sammy took Shawn uptown to 47th Street for a Joe Franklin Comedy Show in the basement of a TGI Friday's. The comedian Bob Greenberg, who had come in second at the Bottom Line in the Lou Costello look-alike contest, spotted Sammy from the stage and introduced him. "I asked him to stand up and the audience gave him a big hand," Greenberg said. "He looked so happy when he stood and bowed. Later he found me and told me how much he liked my Jackie Gleason and Lou Costello impersonations."

In an awkward moment, Sammy proudly introduced the crowd to his son. "I'm sitting there and of course nobody cares who the hell I am," Shawn said. "At that point, Sammy leaned over to me and he said, 'Shawn, I haven't eaten all day. I'm gonna run upstairs. I'm gonna go outside and get a hot dog and bring it in. Do you want anything?' and I said, 'No, thank you,' but I remember feeling that if you knew your son was coming after thirty-something years of not seeing him, you might take him to dinner. You might do something. At least he did offer me a hot dog. I thought, 'This is Sammy, and Sammy's always going to be Sammy, he always was, and always will be, and this is who he is."

Shawn's clowning workshop ended with a reprise of acts that had been worked on during the week. "I did this clowning stuff while Sammy was sitting out there. When it was over, he was, of course, very complimentary and very nice, but then the other typical Sammy thing was that he said, 'Oh, I wish your mother would've sent you to me years ago. I could've made you into something.' I said, 'Just stop it right there,' because he always blamed my mom for him being gone. He's the one that chose to leave. He always blamed her, and he was doing it again, and I said, 'You know what, Sam? You could've come and gotten me any time. Nothing stopped you from coming to see us or coming to us. Let's not talk about this anymore. Let's not talk about it.' After that I think I saw him just one more time, to get a falafel with Stewie, and that's the last time I saw him."

CHAPTER 22

FRONT ROW SEATS

Along about your thirteenth minute of fame, you start thinking that maybe fifteen minutes isn't gonna be enough.

—Sammy Petrillo (told to Gil Reavill, a customer at the used-car lot)

Sammy was dying.

"It was colon cancer," Shawn says. "He had this fear of getting a colonoscopy because someone's gonna put a finger up your ass. Stewie and Martin would try to convince him all the time. Sammy would just put it off and put it off, and eventually he was already stage four, and there was nothing he could do."

November 22, 2008. Knowing that his time was short, Sammy took Rick Saphire up on his invitation to see *The King of Comedy: Jerry Lewis in Conversation with Peter Bogdanovich* at the Times Center in the *New York Times* building. It had been fifty-eight years since Sammy and Jerry were, for a moment, partners in comedy, astonishing and convulsing half the nation in their shared performance. Fifty-eight years of Sammy skittering around the edges of fame, while Jerry's bright star shone fairly steady in comparison. Fifty-eight years and seventeen blocks straight up Eighth Avenue from the *New York Times* building, Sammy and Jerry, together, put one over on millions, from the stage of the International Theatre in Columbus Circle. It was a mutual history that could not be denied.

There's a publicity photo of Sammy, Dean, and Jerry snapped backstage at the International Theatre during rehearsals for *The Colgate Comedy Hour*. In the photo, Jerry and Sammy are standing side by side, their arms folded identically. Their mouths are wide open and their eyes are bugged out. Dean stands to their left, clutching his head with both hands, with a look of astonishment mixed with terror. Sammy possessed a copy of this photo and was planning to ask Jerry to autograph it, as if proof of their past. Whether the autograph might lead to a conversation with Jerry, a possible acknowledgment, closure, or maybe even an apology from the man who sabotaged his career—this was all to be determined.

The tickets were $50 each and general admission. Sammy arrived early with his cousin Martin, Martin's wife Nancy, Joe Franklin, Rick Saphire, and Rick's newest client, Jerry Lewis's illegitimate daughter Suzan Lewis.

Raised by the fashion model Lynn Dixon and an alleged mobster, Hy Uchitel, Suzan wasn't aware of who her true father was until she was in her mid-twenties. Dying of cancer, Suzan's mother disclosed her three-year affair with Jerry as well as her time spent with Milton Berle, who "gave comfort" when her husband was in the army. Discovering as an adult that Jerry Lewis is your biological father would be disorienting for anyone, and it was especially so for Suzan. "[When] my mother admitted to me that she was unfaithful to her husband . . . I was numb, and all I could do was look into the bedroom mirror, which actually had been telling me the truth from the time I was a child. I finally knew who I was, because the face in the mirror was the face of Jerry Lewis."

Suzan looks more like Jerry than Sammy does. From the dark and thoughtful eyes, down to the identical dimple in the chin, it's a resemblance that only familial ties could provide. Going beyond a rubbery, Sammy Petrillo parody of an expression, Suzan's resting face is proof of genetic lineage. Not long after the Jerry Lewis event, Suzan aced a DNA test that Gary Lewis provided a swab for. Suzan Lewis is not an imposter, she is the sequel—*Daughter of the Nutty Professor*. Unfortunately for Suzan, she was the sequel that Jerry didn't ask for.

In the early 1980s, Suzan met her father in a hotel where he was staying in France. "We spent a warm and very special day together in his suite," Suzan said. "It was his idea to place an overseas call to Mom. After he talked to her, he seemed more relaxed and accepting of me." The fatherly love was short-lived. Jerry avoided Suzan from that day forward. There would be rough times for Suzan. After a divorce, and leaving her two kids in France with the ex, she was in a head-on car accident that caused brain damage, affecting her short-term memory. Broke and living on the streets or out of a car at various times in Boca Raton and northeast Philadelphia, Suzan looked up Rick Saphire, then personal manager for Gary Lewis and the Playboys and unofficial manager for Jerry Lewis. Rick signed her up to his talent roster with the intent of bringing her to the immediate attention of his most famous client. *The King of Comedy: Jerry Lewis in Conversation with Peter Bogdanovich* looked to be the perfect time to bring all of Rick Saphire's worlds together—three cherries in a row, or rather, three *Jerrys* in a row.

Trouble started as soon as the doors opened. "When somebody noticed that the lady that I was with was using a cane," Rick says, "they said, 'Oh, why don't you come with us?' They took us right up front, to the right of center stage. We kinda looked at each other and snickered a little bit, because this was not expected, but it was just kinda fun that we were up front there. Nothing was pre-planned. We didn't tell anybody that Sammy Petrillo was there, we didn't tell anybody that Rick Saphire was there (like anyone would care), and we certainly wouldn't tell anybody that Jerry Lewis's daughter was there. That was not our intention. I figured that we would sit anywhere. We would just quietly see the show, and we thought, maybe, if Jerry did autographs afterwards or something, Suzan would just quietly say hi to Jerry, and that would be satisfying, because she was his biological daughter."

Rochelle Slovin, founding director of Astoria's Museum of the Moving Image, who had arranged the evening, came down the aisle and asked Rick, Sammy, and Suzan to move to different seats. "She said, 'Mr. Saphire, you know the three of you are going to have to move your seats to the back of the theater.' I said, 'Why?' and she said, 'I can't really tell you why, but you're gonna have to change your seats,' and I said, 'I can't tell you why, but we're not gonna change our seats.'"

Rochelle walked away and came back ten minutes later, with two "sizable men" and a slightly more compelling message. "Either you move your seats, or we'll have to ask you to leave."

Sammy called his lawyer. According to Rick, upon hanging up, Sammy said to her, "Listen—we paid $50 a seat. In the state of New York, that constitutes a license, and that license is irrevocable, and it doesn't expire until the end of the show. That's how a ticket is handled in New York. We've done nothing wrong, and we're not leaving. If you want us to leave, you'll have to call a policeman and let him figure it out." At this point, they noticed the comedian and Jerry Lewis insider Richard Belzer leaning against a nearby wall, in shades. His arms were folded like a detective as he stared down the interlopers.

"I knew what was on Jerry's mind," Rick says. "I knew better than he did. He was afraid that if he did a Q&A, Suzan would pop up and say, 'I'm your daughter, Suzan,' which we would never do, or Sammy would pop up and say, 'Do you remember me, Jerry? You had me blackballed.' The stupidity is that he knew me better than that. He knew me my entire life, and at that time I was fifty-six."

Rochelle came back a third time with tears in her eyes. She told them that they didn't have to go anywhere. Forty minutes past showtime, stagehands turned the two onstage chairs forty-five degrees away from Saphire and company, stage left. Most of the audience saw a profile of Jerry that evening.

The conversation, oncc started, was contentious. Sucking angrily on a lozenge, the eighty-two-year-old comedy legend was in a foul mood. The previous year he had taken flak for an anti-gay slur during the Muscular Dystrophy Telethon and was forced to apologize. Only one month earlier, when asked his opinion of cricket at a news conference in Sydney, Australia, Jerry again made a homophobic remark, as he mimed effeminately swinging a cricket bat. No apologies were offered. And now, having to appear onstage twenty-five feet away from one or more of these look-alike parasites from the past had him fuming.

The director, actor, and historian Peter Bogdanovich had cut his teeth interviewing the most difficult of the old-school Hollywood types—the directors Howard Hawks and Henry Hathaway, among other formidable and taciturn men. Jerry Lewis, that night, would provide Bogdanovich with a late-career opportunity to be publicly humiliated.

"Stick the fucking notes in your pocket," Jerry barked at a surprised Bogdanovich. "Whatever I'm going to tell you now, it is all bullshit." When asked how he and Dean met, Jerry replied that anyone who would ask such a question is "a moron—present company *included*." Jerry steered the conversation away from his movie-making process, which is what the evening was presumed to be about, and towards his philanthropy and Nobel Peace Prize nomination. "Look what this Jew from Newark pulled off," Jerry crowed.

"Jerry never once looked in our direction," Rick says, "which meant that one-third of the audience never got Jerry to look at them, which was so stupid and so silly. That was the last time I was together with Sammy. Sammy was really, in his heart, hoping that he'd be able to close the deal with Jerry and say hello. Sammy knew how sick he was. In his mind, he was gonna say goodbye."

Bob Greenberg reintroduced himself to Sammy in the men's room. "He knew my name and everything," Greenberg says, "and he gave me a little red sucking candy wrapped in plastic. I still have it and never opened it." After the show, camera in hand, Greenberg, hoping for a little backstage time with Jerry, was disappointed. Exiting quickly in a wheelchair, Jerry rolled past Greenberg, and did his "Oh, hello! How are you!" high-pitched schtick as they wheeled him off into the night.

Standing on Eighth Avenue and 41st Street after the event, Rick and Suzan approached Peter Bogdanovich. "He had a solemn expression as he looked intently at Suzan," Rick writes in his memoir, *The Real Jerry Lewis Story*. "Offering her hand to Bogdanovich, Suzan introduced herself. 'Hi,' she said. 'My name is Suzan. I'm Jerry Lewis's daughter.' Peter Bogdanovich peered into her face, scrutinizing it, but remained expressionless. Suddenly, he understood. 'Oh?' he remarked. '*That's* what it was all about.'"

Walking out in the lobby, Sammy was recognized. "There were about a dozen people surrounding Sammy asking for his autograph," Martin remembered. "Sammy just loved it."

In August 2009, Stuart sent Shawn a message that read, "If you ever want to talk to your father again, you're probably gonna have to talk to him now." Shawn called Sammy at the hospital. "He was in a pretty bad place, so he was like, 'Oh, Shawn, my boy, my boy, I love you.' I said, 'I love you' back. I said goodbye, and that was it."

Sammy died on August 15, 2009, of colon cancer. He did not go easily. By Suzie's account, other factors contributed to Sammy's demise, including septic poisoning, a concussion, and a bladder infection. Unable to pay for a funeral, Ray Book enlisted the help of Joe Franklin, who in turn procured burial money from the Actors Fund. Sammy is interred in Kensico Cemetery in Valhalla, New York, twenty-seven miles north of Hanson's Drugstore in Times Square. His tombstone simply reads, "Sammy Petrillo 1934–2009."

Two years after Sammy's death, in his comfortable upstate home overlooking the Hudson River, Cousin Martin recalled the later, fun years with Sammy. Marvin and Sammy would sporadically work together in some sort of business—be it selling fake perfume door to door or Martin hiring Sammy to hack for his limo company. The Patrello men all gravitated towards livery jobs. Sammy's brother Marvin drove a cab when he wasn't working at off-track betting, and their father Skelly owned his own taxi in Miami Beach. Martin opened a used-car business and was happy having

Sammy man the phones and ring up air fresheners. A lobby card from *Bela Lugosi Meets a Brooklyn Gorilla* hung conspicuously on the wall of the office, which would invariably lead to conversations with inquisitive customers. Tales of Sammy's life filled the room, and the punchlines and back-and-forths flew fast and furious.

"We would be talking," Stuart says, "and then out of nowhere, 'Do I love you? 'Deed I do!' Sometimes Sammy would follow it up with a *baby baby baby*.' He was always 'on.' And it wasn't a phony 'on.' It wasn't an 'on' like some entertainers feel like they always have to be 'on.' It was just Sammy being Sammy."

"A few years ago, I was throwing around an idea with Sammy, " Martin says. "He was sitting in my office, and I said to him, 'You gotta do a show called *The Last Gorilla Standing,* like a one-man show,' and he says, 'Yeah, we'll do a one-man show,' and he says, 'These are the people we'll get for the show,' and I said, 'It's a *one-man show,* Sammy!'"

Todd Rutt wrote the first modern-day article assessing the careers of Duke Mitchell and Sammy Petrillo for *Psychotronic Video* in 1991, titled "Those Two Fireballs of Fun." Todd tracked down a copy of the 1950 babysitter skit on *The Colgate Comedy Hour,* a performance which Sammy had never actually seen. Unfortunately, Todd wasn't able to show a copy to Sammy, so he described it for him.

"Sammy's memory of it was different from what actually happened," Todd says. "In his memory, he had been in the entire sketch. And then I had to tell him, 'No, you're in it at the very end. He was surprised to learn that. I'm sure that it was a big, overwhelming moment for him to do that show with those people at that time. I don't think that he was lying when he thought that it was him the whole time."

A few years later, the episode of *The Colgate Comedy Hour* containing the babysitter sketch was released as a budget-priced videotape. Martin bought a copy and called Sammy up, telling him to come by so he could play it for him. "Usually I would watch anything with him, and ten seconds would go by and he would have a comment, he would crack a joke. I played that for him, and he sat there silent. I never saw him that still. And he sat there and watched it, and he didn't say a word, and then he said, 'Can you play that again?' So I rewound it, and as we were watching it again, he turned to me—I'll never forget—and he said, 'That Jerry Lewis is great.'"

OH NO, ’M SAMMY PETRILLO!

I hold the record for being the world’s youngest has-been.

—Sammy Petrillo, WFMU-FM, 1992

I’ve been working on this book for fifty years.

As a kid growing up in New Rochelle, New York, a suburb “forty-five minutes from Broadway,” I gravitated toward old black-and-white movies. An obsessive Marx Brothers fan since the age of ten, I would set my alarm for 2:45 a.m. so I could sneak down to the basement to watch *The Big Store*. Often I would record the audio on cassette, mic positioned carefully in front of the TV, make a cover for the cassette, and then actually listen to it. My other great loves were the Universal horror movies, particularly *Frankenstein* and *Dracula*. I was drawn to Bela Lugosi. Acting-wise, I saw what he was doing, and I liked it. Lugosi’s over-the-top style appealed to me at a base level and made me realize that mysterious and creepy wasn’t a terrible way to go through life. Fortunately, the local TV stations ran Lugosi’s lesser-known Universal movies along with dozens of his Poverty Row quickies. I don’t remember much else about my childhood aside from watching these crummy old movies.

I didn’t feel like the other kids. Shy and poorly coordinated, while others were playing sports, I sat in my bedroom, cutting myself off from the groovy ’70s with the blinds drawn, watching 8mm versions of *Nosferatu* and Buster Keaton two-reelers. As a budding geek, I realized, even in my single digits, that one required a schtick, a gimmick, to cut through all the noise. I was a poor student in school, and even with the Coke-bottle glasses that made me look like an Einstein, I knew that I needed an edge if I was to ever meet a girl, or even make a friend, in my lifetime. I borrowed books from the library on ventriloquism and bought *Sneaky Tricks* in paperback, which would show you how to roll coins across your knuckles and how to crack an egg with one hand. My bible was the advertisements in the back of comic books, promising X-ray vision and joy buzzers that would make you the life of the party. I was always looking to better myself. Always looking to be someone else.

There were essential reads in my collection of books that fed and heightened my love for the movies filmed decades before I was born. Leslie Halliwell's massive *Filmgoer's Companion* got a workout, as well as *The Marx Brothers at the Movies* by Paul D. Zimmerman and Burt Goldblatt and Leonard Maltin's *Movie Comedy Teams,* which I reviewed for my school newspaper. On a random bookstore visit when I was twelve years old, I espied a new hardcover in the movie section. *The Count: The Life and Films of Bela "Dracula" Lugosi* by Arthur Lennig would become the first book that I would read in one sitting, from start to finish. I was knocked out by the comprehensive filmography and the stories behind the making of my favorite Lugosi movies. Little-known facts about Lugosi were revealed—his political activism and his passion for stamp collecting—that fleshed out and humanized this strange character. Near the end of the book, a paragraph jumped out at me, about a Lugosi movie that I had never heard of—*Bela Lugosi Meets a Brooklyn Gorilla*:

> Thin and haggard, [Lugosi] played a scientist on a lonely tropical island who tries to contend with (God preserve us!) a British imitation of Dean Martin and Jerry Lewis. Bela put in a good performance, but the film was poor.

Obviously, Lennig had not seen the movie; however, he sure as hell must have seen *Mother Riley Meets the Vampire,* judging by how many pages he spent on that. This is a timely reminder that, before the Wild West of the internet, books could be just as inaccurate as the web.

The concept of a movie called *Bela Lugosi Meets a Brooklyn Gorilla* starring Martin and Lewis impersonators ate away at me. I needed to see this movie. Growing up a train ride away from the city, I had my pick of revival houses—the Thalia, the Elgin, Cinema Village, the Regency, the Bleecker Street Cinema, the Carnegie Hall Cinema, and Theater 80 all switched up their double bills every day—and *Brooklyn Gorilla* never made an appearance. I fastidiously checked the *TV Guide* for airings of *Brooklyn Gorilla* without realizing that I missed multiple showings of the retitled version, known as *The Boys From Brooklyn.*

The thought of this bizarrely named Lugosi movie continued to haunt me for years—not just because of a fake British Dean and Jerry—there was also the gorilla to contend with. I developed my fascination with monkeys and gorillas at a young age, no thanks to the New Rochelle public school system bringing the performing chimp Mr. Jiggs to my second-grade classroom. Mr. Jiggs roller-skated, mixed drinks for the faculty, and snapped Polaroid photos, not to mention looking at his wristwatch for sixty seconds before peeling off the toxic layer of emulsion from the front of the photo. My introduction to an anthropomorphic chimp raised more questions than it answered and led me down the questionable road that I tread daily. The concept of the great Bela Lugosi meeting a gorilla from Brooklyn made the movie even more fantastic and unattainable. I realize now that my studies and sleep were affected by even the knowledge of the existence of such a movie.

In 1987 I was twenty-five years old and living in Brooklyn, working a schlub pollster job in Rockefeller Center, where I spent most of my time writing, pasting up, and xeroxing my zines, *Ahunka Elvis* and *Rock + Roll Equations*. I hosted a weekly music radio show on WFMU-FM out in East Orange, New Jersey, which was a dream volunteer gig. I also sang lead/shouted into a microphone and co-wrote songs in a novelty punk band, the Sea Monkeys, with one of my few pals as a kid, Andy Maltz. An ex-member of the Sea Monkeys (we had a lot of those at the time), Paul Rubin, taped *Brooklyn Gorilla* off a cable channel and gifted me with the tape. I wasn't disappointed. Sammy's performance as Jerry Lewis was a revelation. I had never seen anyone so committed to anything as Sammy's off-the-charts Jerry Lewis act. I knew nothing else about this guy. His life, for me, began and ended within the length of the film.

The Sea Monkeys always tackled the tough issues—Archie Andrews, bad haircuts, Iowa Tests, etc.—so a Sammy Petrillo song was a given. I came up with terrible verses and Andy wrote the music and the chorus and hook for the song:

I look in the mirror . . .
Oh no! Oh no!
I look in the mirror . . .
Oh no, I'm Sammy Petrillo!

Our bassist, Tom Cassar, ran a record label out of the East Village, Vital Music Records, and pressed up 500 copies of "Oh No, I'm Sammy Petrillo!" backed with an ode to another icon, "Nipseyland." In the '90s, the comedian Nipsey Russell's address and phone number were listed in the White Pages, along with those of Henny Youngman and Joe Franklin, so Nipsey was easy to contact. We called him once, or maybe twice, asking for one of his signature limericks, which he happily delivered. Not wanting to bug him with more phone calls, we recorded a song about a utopian paradise where you could slam-dance to a "Nipsey band" and play Nipsey Whac-a-Mole all day. We sent Nipsey a copy of the record and he said that he enjoyed it, so mission accomplished.

"Oh No, I'm Sammy Petrillo!" was grimmer, with obnoxious lyrics about being an "ugly jerk." This song was written without any intention of ever meeting this obscure comic from a two-dollar movie. That would be like crossing paths with Franklin Pangborn or Zasu Pitts. In the days before the internet, this kind of thinking was not far-fetched, at least not in my crowd.

Our first indication that Sammy Petrillo walked among us was when the Sea Monkeys appeared on Uncle Floyd's TV show in early 1992. This

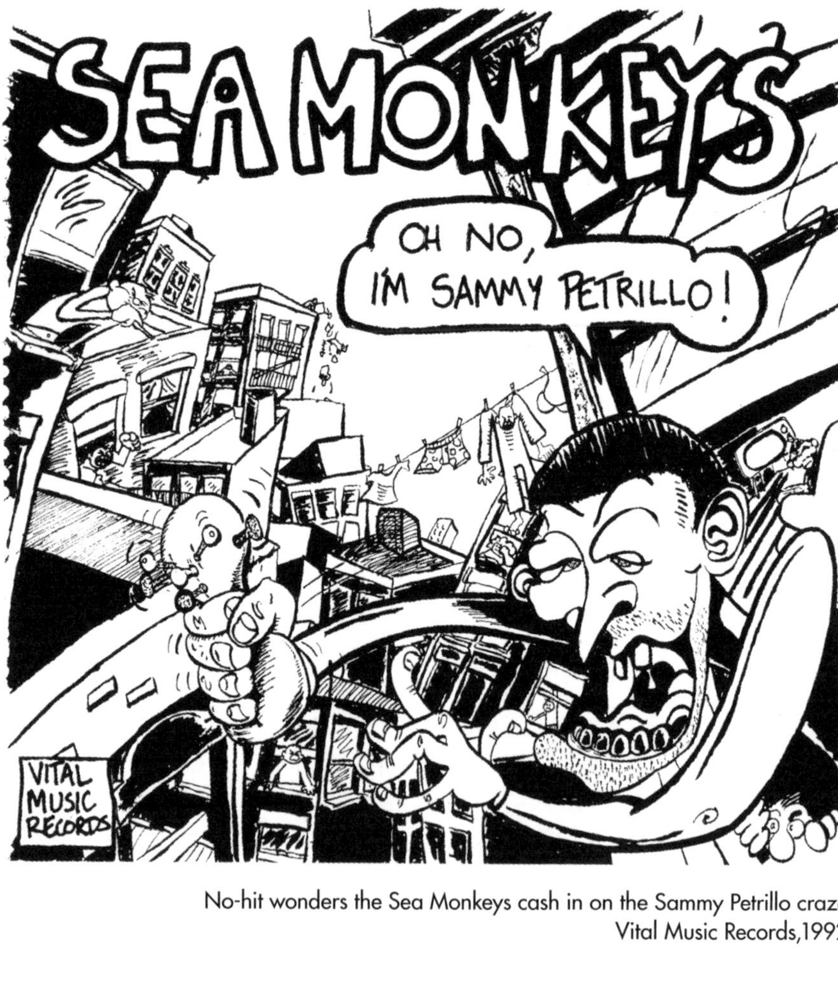

No-hit wonders the Sea Monkeys cash in on the Sammy Petrillo craze. Vital Music Records,1992.

Smithereens drummer Dennis Diken flanked by Sammy and Suzie. The Bottom Line, New York City, October, 1992. Courtesy of Dennis Diken.

was not the "classic" version of Uncle Floyd, with his cast of zany sidekicks, but the later period when he hosted local bands, mostly of the hair metal variety. Floyd appreciated that we were, first and foremost, committed to the stupid when it came to punk rock, and he loved our version of the "Food Emporium Theme," complete with manager specials. We sat with Floyd for a goofy interview and lip-synched a handful of songs, including our new single about Sammy Petrillo.

"I know him!" Floyd shouted, to our mutual shock. When asked after the taping how we might get in contact with Sammy, Floyd said that he had lost track of him.

In October of that year, I saw the ad in the back of the *Village Voice* promoting the Abbott and Costello look-alike contest at the Bottom Line, and Sammy's name was listed. The Sea Monkeys had a show that night at some dive bar in the East Village, maybe Downtown Beirut II or the Spiral, and I was crushed that I wouldn't be able to attend. The next-best thing seemed to be to leave a vinyl calling card. Early Saturday evening, on the way to the Sea Monkeys show, I dropped off a copy of the record at the box office with instructions to pass it along, with my phone number, to Sammy Petrillo. Years later, Dennis Diken, the Smithereens' drummer and a Bud Abbott aficionado, told me that his wife Donna was working the box office that night and remembered this odd interaction. Donna got the record and phone number to Sammy. A few days later, I came home from work to an answering machine message:

> Oh no! Oh no! I'm Sammy Petrillo! Wow . . . anyway, Dave Abramson—this is Sammy Petrillo. Everything looks sensational, and uh, I got your note, of course. I got your record. I want to find out how to buy some, and I'd like ta talk to ya. If you give me a call anytime after 11 a.m., up until 9 p.m.

He stumbled over the phone number when repeating it and said, "Sometimes I forget because . . . I'm Sammy Petrillo. So, gimme a call. Thanks. Bye."

I called him back at what appeared to be a number in Westchester with a 914 area code. We chatted for a bit and I apologized for the idiotic lyrics, which he seemed to be okay with. At one point, he jokingly said, "How would you like it if I went around saying, 'Oh no, I'm Dave Abramson?'" I set up a date to interview Sammy live on the air during my radio show. WFMU is a rare breed among radio stations—free-form to the point of encouraging disc jockeys to play whatever they want, including and even encouraging detours into on-air interviews with obscure comedians from Bela Lugosi movies. The forty-five-minute interview went well, largely thanks to Todd Rutt's Duke and Sammy piece in *Psychotronic Video,* which helped me prep the questions. The name of my show was, and still is, *Music to Spazz By*. When informed of this on-air, Sammy said, "Next thing you know, they'll have 'Interviews to Vomit By.' " Towards the end of the interview, Sammy turned philosophical:

> A lot of people are doing jobs that they're not really happy doing. But it's nice to dream. It's nice to do what you can do, when you can do it, for some kind of fulfillment. Just living and being able to pay your bills and being able to eat—that's a form of success in itself. People who strive to do showbiz but still do regular-type jobs and they have to do show business on the side—there still is a fulfillment in that. There's an old saying and I believe in it: "Each show that you do is a success within itself." Whether you perform for a hundred thousand people or for two people—to make them happy and to be able to lift them into another world momentarily—that's a form of success.

I recorded a cassette of the broadcast and transcribed it into an article, "Sammy Petrillo Speaks Out!" for WFMU's station magazine *Lowest*

Common Denominator (*LCD*). When the piece went online in 1998, it became the quoted-verbatim reference for any subsequent writings about Sammy, including his *New York Times* obituary.

About a week after the interview, Sammy called me again. He said that he wanted to buy a quantity of Sea Monkeys 45s, so he could sell them at autograph shows. Oddly enough, we had actually sold out of records at that point—all 500—which, at our bottom-feeder level, was known as a "gold record." I told him that we could repress them, but the minimum order from our pressing plant in Nashville was another 500 copies, costing about a dollar apiece (plus record cover and postage). Sammy said that he would buy 500 of them. We had pressed the first run on orange vinyl, and I asked Sammy what color records he would like. "Plaid!" Sammy exclaimed. We went with purple. When the records came in a few weeks later, I called Sammy's number but it wasn't in service. Sammy and I never spoke again.

My feeling at the time was probably correct. Sammy couldn't afford to buy the records—even a small quantity of them. He had haphazardly arranged a large purchase without thinking the plan fully through. It always comes down to scratch. (Naturally, there are 500 copies still sitting in our bass player Tom's basement, waiting for the rush on anything Sammy Petrillo–related after the wild success of this book.) A few years later, in 1995, I was amused to see Sammy name-drop us in the hallowed pages of *Filmfax* magazine. "You know there's a rock group called the Sea Monkeys," Sammy said. "They recorded an underground hit record titled, 'Oh No, I'm Sammy Petrillo' [laughs], so the film certainly influenced them."

In 2007, the film historian Leonard Maltin listed *Brooklyn Gorilla* as the first on his list of the "Best of Hollywood's Worst" for a piece in the *New York Post*. "This one is always at the top of my list. It's a film you watch in utter amazement," he championed. A few years earlier on the syndicated news magazine show *Entertainment Tonight,* Maltin had dubbed *Brooklyn Gorilla* the worst movie of all time on his first "Turkey" show. Sammy was mystified by the attention. "I have no idea why Leonard Maltin keeps trying to dig this movie out of mothballs to bash it!" Sammy complained. Martin Jackowe showed Sammy a videotape of the *Entertainment Tonight* episode in question, and Sammy said, "Play that again! I'm gonna sue him!" Clearly, Sammy appreciated laughs on his own terms and was unfamiliar with this particular kind of respect. His nephew Stuart went to a showing of *Brooklyn Gorilla* at a revival house, the Thalia, in the '80s and recorded the audience's reaction on a tape recorder. "They get to the last scene where

Lugosi shoots Sammy and the audience cheers!" Stuart says. "And I played this for Sammy, and he said, 'Why did they cheer?' and he was really hurt. He was really perturbed by that. I had to soften it for him." Sammy did admit that it was funny when Soupy Sales was quoted as saying, "[*Brooklyn Gorilla*] is shown in eight states as capital punishment."

In the '80s, the cult mystique of *Bela Lugosi Meets a Brooklyn Gorilla* and, in particular, the idea of a Jerry Lewis impersonator began to slowly permeate the outer reaches of the mainstream. The cartoonist Matt Groening, before creating *The Simpsons,* had taken inspiration from *Brooklyn Gorilla* to illustrate a novelty "Flicker Snickers" postcard featuring Sammy's image. The indie-rock icon Marshall Crenshaw's 1996 album *Miracle of Science* opens with a short clip from the Jungle Hut sequence in *Brooklyn Gorilla.* For decades, syndicated TV columns in local newspapers depended upon the random question in their "mailbag" about whether Jerry Lewis was ever in that "Two Guys from Brooklyn" movie or if Jerry's name was really Sammy Petrillo. In 2008, the Hernandez Brothers, in their critically acclaimed *Love and Rockets* graphic-novel series, included a story about a pair of Dean Martin and Jerry Lewis impersonators named Duke and Sammy who are flung into another dimension where they attain godlike powers.

Praise for *Bela Lugosi Meets a Brooklyn Gorilla* has been trickling in over the years. In Fredde Duke's documentary *Fuck 'Em,* about her father, Maurice Duke, she recounts the time that he received a special plaque for *Brooklyn Gorilla.* "My dad knew that all of his movies were shitty. He said, 'I made 103 pieces of shit, and the shittiest one won an award.'" According to Fredde, while spending time with the Second City comedy people in Canada, she realized that "They all love the movie because they know about it from Christopher Guest. Christopher Guest is a big fan."

Gilbert Gottfried, who until his death in 2022 co-hosted the *Amazing Colossal Podcast* with Frank Santopadre, was quoted as saying that Sammy Petrillo was a "true original." Sammy was a recurring topic on the podcast, along with Gilbert's other unsung oddball comedy heroes, making his interment in the same cemetery in Valhalla as Sammy, along with Danny Kaye and Guy Kibbee, all the more appropriate.

To Sammy's credit, even the principals in the Petrillo story, though often at odds with each other, all agree: Sammy Petrillo was funny. Even Duke Mitchell's son, Jeff, who doesn't have a lot of positive things to say about Sammy as a person, concedes that "He was funnier than Jerry Lewis! And better, I thought. I mean that movie's fucking hysterical. Sammy's great!"

Sammy and Elaine's separation was contentious for all involved, but, according to Shawn, his mother didn't suffer any bad-mouthing of Sammy: "She would tell us that Sammy was one of the funniest people she's ever known. She said it was sad that he didn't get further in show business, but she always gave him accolades, as far as that was concerned."

Considering Sammy's obvious failings as a father, which had a chilling effect on his sons, Shawn reassesses his upbringing: "I probably empathize a lot more with Sammy in my life now than when I was growing up. As a kid, I knew that I missed my dad. It's that simple. As an adult, you realize—well, my brother just said it the other day: 'Who knows what he went through mentally? Who knows? And he had a life that was up and down, and sometimes good and sometimes bad, and we don't know what he dealt with . . .'"

Jerry Lewis enjoyed a fairly thorny final act. After numerous extramarital affairs—he boasted of flings with Marilyn Monroe, Marlene Dietrich, and his *Nutty Professor* co-star Stella Stevens—Patti Lewis finally filed for divorce in 1980. Three years later, Jerry married SanDee Pitnick, a dancer and stewardess who was twenty-five years his junior. They adopted a daughter, Danielle, three years later. Fulfilling a long-sought-after dream, Jerry made his Broadway debut as the devil, Mr. Applegate, in *Damn Yankees* in 1995. He toured with it nationally and stole the show in the London production. Jerry executive-produced the critically successful, and lucrative, Eddie Murphy *Nutty Professor* remake in 1996 and its sequel in 2000. In 2009, Jerry regretted his role in producing the movies, saying, "I have such respect for Eddie, but I should not have done it. What I did was perfect the first time around and all you're going to do is diminish that perfection by letting someone else do it."

In 2011, the organization that Jerry was most closely aligned with throughout his career, the Muscular Dystrophy Association, had reached its Jerry Lewis saturation point, severing all ties and firing him as the host of the telethon. No explanation was given besides that Jerry had "completed his run" as the MDA's national chairman.

At the Cannes Film Festival in 2013, Jerry made headlines by disparaging female comics, saying that he did not enjoy seeing women do broad comedy. "I can't see women doing that," he said. "It bothers me." When asked who his favorite female comedians were, he said, "Cary Grant . . . Burt Reynolds . . . I don't have any." Leaving his hand and footprints at Grauman's Chinese Theatre the following year, Jerry doubled down on his comments: "Seeing a woman project the kind of aggression that you have to project as a comic just rubs me wrong."

In his essential 1996 biography, *King of Comedy: The Life and Art of Jerry Lewis,* Shawn Levy writes, "He once claimed to be one of the most recognized people on the planet—and at moments in his life that was true." Jerry Lewis passed away at age ninety-one on August 20, 2017, and, for one last time, the worldwide community was reminded of him. The memory of Jerry as the maudlin, yet not-quite-zany-enough telethon host was a lasting image that the general population remembered, along with the vague idea that he used to be half of a team with a singer called Dean Martin. Jerry disinherited all of his sons from his marriage with Patti, leaving his fortune to second wife SanDee and daughter Danielle.

In Greek mythology, Prometheus steals fire from the Olympian gods and passes it down to humanity, so that technology, knowledge, and human ingenuity could one day invent the dribble glass. Jerry was the modern day God of Fire—obsessively learning his trade inside-out, the nuts and bolts and the screws and those little things with the wingnuts—whaddaya call those things because I think I just ate one . . . ? He then foisted all of this chaotic knowledge and experience upon an unsuspecting world, and spit-takes were never the same. The original Prometheus story has a downer ending. A pissed-off Zeus ties Prometheus to a rock and instructs an eagle to painfully peck away at his liver—a liver that would miraculously grow back overnight, only to get pecked at by that eagle all over again the next day. Jerry never paid for his sins like that, but perhaps in the agony of his mid-life Percodan addiction and withdrawal, he might have had a painful glimpse into what that eagle-pecking-at-your-liver brand of hell felt like. (Insert chopped liver joke here.)

After Dean died on Christmas Day in 1995, Jerry sought to reclaim and reshape the story of their collaboration and friendship. Partnering with the notable novelist and journalist James Kaplan, Jerry co-authored *Dean & Me (A Love Story)* in 2005. In a series of unpublished interviews with Jerry in 1999, Kaplan asked Jerry about Sammy Petrillo. Through the generosity of James Kaplan, who went on to write definitive volumes about Frank Sinatra (*Frank: The Voice* in 2010 and *Sinatra: The Chairman* in 2015), this interview is presented here for the first time. Jerry's revisionist take of the "meeting Sammy" story is accompanied by his misremembering of the famous sketch; however, his tone and attitude are genuine. In a weaving of truths and untruths, Jerry still gets to the essence of what it's like to have a doppelgänger.

JK: Whatever happened to Sammy Petrillo?

LEWIS: Jesus, I don't know. I heard he died.

JK: Really?

LEWIS: Yeah. I heard he died. He overdosed or something. Crazy kid.

JK: I never cast eyes on him. Did he really resemble you?

LEWIS: God, you couldn't tell the difference in the same room. I found him walking in the street in New York, and we were doing a sketch where I wanted very much to do something in television that's never been done and get the audience fooled. So I'm on stage left, and I hired the kid, and he's on stage right, and he's looking at the audience and I'm looking at the audience, and I look at him and he looks at me, and he leaves and I leave—and it was a wonderful joke. But what a monster I built. We couldn't get rid of him. [laughs] He meets a guy named Duke Mitchell—they team up to do everything that Dean and I did in a picture called *Brooklyn Gorilla* or something . . .

JK: Something like that. Godzilla. Something.

LEWIS: They were harmless. They didn't do anything to hurt anybody. And interesting that Duke Mitchell sang pretty good. He was a pretty good singer, that kid.

JK: But no looks, right?

LEWIS: No, he didn't look like a helluva lot. But anyhow, that was it. Jesus Christ, where did you read . . . Did you read about Sammy Petrillo somewhere? We stunned the *Colgate Comedy Hour* audience with that. Nobody could understand it. They know it's not recorded, they know it's live. How did they get him over while he was over here? [laughs] It was great. And the wonderful thing was that I made sure that the shot was a knee figure, no more, *a knee figure* and a two-tit figure on Jerry.

JK: You lost me there. Two-tit figure . . .

LEWIS: Yeah, this is two tits.

JK: And knee figure is from the knee up?

LEWIS: From the knee up. So I had Jerry—"Well, you can't miss; it's Jerry," and then when you pop to the shot down to the knees, it's Jerry—*bang, bang,* it's there. Then when he turned, we walked away on this close shot of the back of his head. And it was an incredible . . . I've had more people ask me about that.

JK: I thought the kid who came up to you at the Actors Studio looked a little bit like you as a kid. Do you remember him? He was being a pain in the ass. He wanted something. Don't you remember? He wanted to know who your casting director was for your next . . .

LEWIS: Oh, you mean backstage?

JK: Yeah, after . . . backstage.

LEWIS: Yeah, I remember. Anytime you see a kid with large lips they will tell you, "I've been told I look like you." Okay, God bless you. The world ain't ready for another one. [laughs]

I had my own run-in with Jerry Lewis, thanks to the brilliant cartoonist and illustrator Drew Friedman. Interviewing Jerry Lewis would be a real "get," so Drew took on the formidable task of asking Jerry to speak to me about Sammy. Jerry loved Drew's work, and Drew was risking his friendship with Jerry, asking him to address one of the two subjects that you were never meant to bring up with him. Unless you were an official biographer, inquiring about Sammy Petrillo or *The Day the Clown Cried* were verboten. The first time Jerry returned my phone call from his Las Vegas office, it didn't go well. I thanked him for calling me back, and told him that it was an honor to speak to him, and that I would take up very little of his time. That's when he cut me off.

"Wait, wait, wait. I don't do phone interviews. I'm all jammed up and very busy. If you would like to speak with me, then you'll have to figure out some other way of doing this that doesn't involve the telephone. Let me know what you want to do."

"I'll do that. Thank you, Mr. Lewis."

"Goodbye."

Thankfully, Jerry called back a few weeks later, abruptly awakening me from a nap. The terror that I felt on the receiving end of Jerry Lewis is a feeling that I'm certain that many in Jerry's orbit throughout the years had endured at one time or another.

"I just want you to know that I wouldn't be doing this for anyone else in the world besides Drew Friedman," Jerry explained.

I agreed that Drew was the greatest, which he is. I complimented Jerry on his pioneering use of Video Assist technology, which is the secret handshake into his world. Jerry lobbed the first question and he sounded pissed off.

"WHY are you . . . writing . . . a book . . . about . . . *Sammy Petrillo*?"

I explained that of course, nobody could touch Jerry's genius and that the Sammy Petrillo story was epic in scope and Shakespearean in tone, as mistaken and unmistakable identities played out in the world of pie-in-the-face comedy. Jerry seemed satisfied with that and girded himself for questions. It was brief.

"I don't know anything about him. I saw the kid in the street and put him on the show that week. That's it."

"Did you sign him to a contract?"

"No. Your information is wrong.

"I only used him once more—it was a stage-left walk-on—it was a big joke visually . . . I had no other dealings with him."

I didn't want to push him. Getting off the phone, I ordered up a dried fruit and nut basket from the legendary Manhattan appetizing store Russ & Daughters and had it shipped to his Las Vegas office. Jerry shared his side of the story with me, and for that I was grateful.

Piecing together the minutiae of a private man's journey into a linear, coherent form can be a challenge. Sammy's disconnect with his family and the world at large was part of how he moved through life. Some of his hermit-like behavior is endemic to the business that he was in. While zooming down a Los Angeles highway, on his way to a gig, Sammy's pal Chuck McCann expounded on his cell phone about the setbacks of fame:

> In this business, you move away, you're on the road, you don't see each other—we're not like human beings, you know what I mean? Comedians and actors, we're constantly on the move, and there's no one taking care of us but us. You're kinda guiding your career around—it's like sailing a boat or gliding a plane—you're on your own. You try to get some help, somebody to talk you into the airport, or a manager, or something, but your whole life is like that. You're by yourself. We're traveling all the time, so we're constantly making movies, on the road, doing TV, burdened down with lines and scripts, so it's kind of hard to have friendships from the past. When you get two guys that are in the business together, like Sammy and I were, you have to do a lot of reaching out and stuff, and he didn't do too much reaching out.

After Sammy's 1995 interview in *Filmfax* magazine, I didn't hear anything about him at all for the next ten years. WFMU's station magazine *LCD* took a hiatus from its print format in the early aughts and was replaced by the blogging website *Beware of the Blog*. I signed up for two postings a month, where I wrote about whatever came to mind. I whipped up *Dragnet* haikus and explored the early rock 'n' roll records of Ronnie James Dio and the later prog recordings of Louis Prima. On March 7, 2005, I received an email from Rick Saphire. After finding my online article about Sammy, he was looking for contact info for his management company. I told him that I didn't have a clue, but I would put out the word. That evening, I drafted a piece for the FMU blog, wondering aloud what might have ever happened to Sammy Petrillo. Three years later, this simple act evoked a maelstrom of Sammy activity, involving Sammy, his brother Marvin, his son Shawn, and the former exotica producer Kirby Allan. Sammy, who lived and worked through the technical innovation that was live television, was now tackling another technology—the nascent world of the internet.

Two years after my original post, Shawn left a comment, stating that he was Sammy's oldest son and that, in the quest for success, Sammy had tossed aside his family: "He forgot to be our dad. Just completely forgot us."

That comment sat there for a year, until 2008, when one of Sammy's old pals, Kirby Allan, stumbled across the blog. Kirby's hit exotica records in the '50s had made it possible for him to comfortably retire to Mesa, Arizona, where he unsuccessfully ran for mayor nine times from 1982 to 2000. Tragically, Kirby perished in 2011 after saving his longtime female companion from a house fire. Kirby was always one of Sammy's cheerleaders, and he would look fondly back on their days in L.A., where they hatched plans over plates of cheeseburgers at Coffee Dan's. Regarding Sammy as a major, yet troubled, talent, Kirby's salacious anecdotes, whether true or fabricated, make for some over-the-top blog reading. Recalling the night that Sammy dumped a salad bowl over the head of a drunk woman in front of her mobster pals, Kirby puts himself right in the action: "The three mobsters ran after [Sammy] causing an uproar all through the club. I told him to meet me in my car and ran out and started it up. He ran toward the open car door and we sped off just in the nick of time. I asked him why he would do such a dumb thing—you could have been killed? He told me that he was overwrought over what happened on his wedding night last night when he kept waiting all night for his new bride and she never came. He then said, 'I couldn't take it when I found out my partner had fucked her on MY wedding night.'"

Kirby also recounts on the blog about the time he accompanied Sammy to a psychiatrist appointment. "The psychiatrist asked Sammy to draw his partner's face on the pillow," Kirby writes, "and then get on the bed and punch it, calling him everything [his] partner called Sammy. The psychiatrist threw me out of the room when I busted out laughing at Sammy punching and saying, 'Cocksucker, motherfucker, asshole, etc.'"

The eighty-year-old Kirby cluelessly cites a handful of racist and homophobic jokes that Sammy made over the years, before publicly consoling Shawn on his absent father. "Your dad was caught up in show business, like many have in the past," Kirby explains. "Sammy, as I knew him, seemed not to want to think about the past, and seemed to cloud it out of his mind, like so many have done before."

Sammy himself chimes in, first addressing Kirby: "I remember you as a nice, creative person. However, the stories you tell about me are not exactly accurate. I never had a wedding night in my entire life, and I was married only once in my life. I do not ever recall even thinking my wife cheated on me, particularly with my partner." Then Sammy tells Shawn that he sent money to the family regularly but lost track of everyone after Elaine remarried and changed her name. In a bitter exchange, Shawn accuses Sammy of physically abusing Elaine and refers to him as "Daddy Dearest." Accusing his father of being self-pitying, Shawn says, "Martyrs suffer or die for a noble cause. What is your noble cause, Sammy? What was worth the loss of your children?" Sammy asserts that he asked Shawn and his "talented children" to be in a remake of *Brooklyn Gorilla* he was planning, but no one got back to him. The comments turn nastier as the accusations and recriminations play out under the harsh lights of the internet. After decades of estrangement, Sammy and Shawn are at this point only able to speak to each other in a public chat forum for all to witness. Sammy tells Shawn he has a chip on his shoulder that cannot be undone by "years of brainwashing." Shawn responds that Sammy's "truths border on insanity." Taking a swing at Shawn's Christian faith, Sammy counters with, "Flowery words and talk of God don't do it. Jim Jones was spiritual, too. Take the beam out of your own eye, learn the truth and it will make you free." Legal action is threatened by both of them. Father and son publicly say goodbye to each other forever, closing the door on ever repairing their relationship.

After a few weeks of silence, Sammy and Shawn returned to continue to air their dirty laundry in public. This time the comments use handles like "Big Sammy Fan," "Hollywood Harry," and other aliases (including anonymous postings) with telltale I.P. addresses that lead back to the fighting Patrellos. The hurtful stabs at each other return as well. Marvin checks in, boasting that, "Sammy is the best brother in the world," and Kirby adds loopy updates about LP and CD reissues of his Chaino records. In the midst of the reanimated insults between father and son, Kirby blithely posts an observation:

> Sammy, glad to see that you are OK. Your subtleness is hysterical. I don't know if you entertain now, but having much success in choosing talented winners, I strongly believe you should. Your time is now.

ACKNOWLEDGMENTS

I am indebted to the expertise and patience of my interview subjects, without whom this book would be about three pages long. Being able to speak to both Sammy Petrillo and Jerry Lewis was, in a word, priceless. Sammy's family were equally invaluable: Sammy's brother Marvin Patrello, Sammy's son Shawn Patrello, his cousin Martin Jackowe, and his nephew Stuart Hersh all contributed greatly to thc narrative.

Sammy's longtime manager King Broder's reminiscences were inestimable, as well as recollections from his partners and pals Kirby Allan, Ray Book, "Lady Mary" Cochran, Will Jordan, Rocky Kalish, Steve Kaplan, Stephen Kroninger, Chuck McCann, Jeffrey Mitchell, Henry C. Parke, Suzie Perkovic, Rick Saphire, and Michael Townsend Wright.

Fredde Duke, Madelynn Kopple, and David Kopple unsparingly gave me crucial details regarding Jack Broder and Realart Studios. David shared the shooting script for *Brooklyn Gorilla* with me, an act for which I'm eternally grateful. Poring over pages of dialogue that never made it to the screen, such as Muriel Landers and Charlita lazing in adjoining beds discussing their double wedding plans, is revelatory—for me, akin to stumbling across the nineteen minutes that Kubrick cut from *2001: A Space Odyssey*. Fredde Duke and Michael Barrie were excellent sources for all things Maurice Duke. Track down Fredde's documentary, *Fuck 'Em!*, about her father Maurice Duke. It's a hoot! Thanks to Marco Joachim for his recollections of his parents Barbara Loden and Larry Joachim. Marco also shared Sammy's script for *The Army Needs You, Marvin*.

The writers Michael Barrie, Leonard Maltin, Gary D. Rhodes, Nick Tosches, Frank Dello Stritto, and Tom Weaver generously contributed their knowledge and opinions. Special thanks to James Kaplan for the unpublished Jerry Lewis transcript. Also thanks to Rich Brown, Mark Buniak, Bob Greenberg, Bob Madison, and "Uncle Floyd" Vivino, who all shared their anecdotes and expertise with me over the many years of research. Their help was invaluable.

Kudos to Jeff Abraham, Peggy Ahwesh, Pedro Alvarez, Tony Arena, Jake Austen, Jon "Bowzer" Bauman, Keith Bearden, Jack Blanchard, Joe Bob Briggs, Brian Chidester, Dennis Diken, Donna Diken, Rex Doane, Sherwin Dunner, Scott Engel, Charlotte Ercoli, Amber Ann Faulds, Gaylord Fields, Michael Flores, Otis Fodder, Bob Fumanek, Vince Gaudio, Sim Gershon, "Little Anthony" Gourdine, Bob Gramegna, Lisa Hirschfield, Jason Isaac, David Johansen, Glen Jones, Joe "the Phantom" Kane, Paul Karasik, Larry Karaszewski, Owen Kline, Nate Knaebel, Craig Scott Lamb, Cosmo Lee (Park Slope Desk), Laura Lindgren, Miriam Linna, Bob Madison, Monroe Mann, Deanna Martin, Andy McCarthy, John McElwee, Clare McKeen, Giovanna Melchiorre, Billy Miller, Josh Mills, Glen Morris, Kevin Nealon, Kliph Nesteroff, Mark Newgarden, Andy Paley, Kris Parrish, Kurt Patrello, Samina Pitrello, Victoria Price, Howie Pyro, Joyce Randolph, Gil Reavill, Cathy Rich, Fabio Roberti, Jack Roth, Jeff Roth, Paul Salos, Frank Santopadre, Scott Schinder, Michael Shelley, Stan Stolpiec, Ward Sutton, Chante Tenoso, Brent Walker, Wayno, Peggy Webber, Michael Weldon, and Brynn White. Irwin Chusid was especially helpful with scanning and legal stuff.

Shout-out to my bosses and buddies at WNYC and WQXR—Steve Shultis, Jim Stagnitto, and Steve Uckerman, along with all the other patient hosts and engineers who would tactfully walk backwards out of Master Control as I espoused details of Sammy's life to them. And no, the irony isn't lost on me that WQXR is at the same spot on the NYC radio dial, 105.9 FM, as Sammy's radio shows on WHBI in the '70s. Or that my boss at Multicultural Radio (five AM stations based on Broadway just off Canal Street) was the hilarious Mark Buniak, who also worked with Sammy at WHBI. To quote the WFMU air personality Rex Doane, "Radio people are good people."

Speaking of radio people, WFMU's station manager, Ken Freedman, has kept me out of trouble for the past how many years. Ken's impact on my life has been substantial—from letting me on the air in 1987 to taking my submissions for the station magazine, *LCD* (*Lowest Common Denominator*), to letting me edit a few issues in the '90s. He even named his dog Sammy in tribute to my many years' worth of Sammy Petrillo research, for cryin' out loud! And, of course, WFMU is the greatest, but we all knew that.

Intrinsic to my life as a spazz and as a Sammy Petrillo devotee are the members of the Sea Monkeys, who let me show up at rehearsals and join them onstage for the past forty years: Tom Cassar, Kevin Clark, Sam Elwitt, and Andy Maltz.

I can personally vouch that the fiery trash bin known as Facebook is good for one thing and one thing only—the Sammy Petrillo Appreciation Society, where fans, friends, and family unite for one singular purpose: In Search of Historic Sammy. John Wendler, in particular, in that group, was gracious with his time and assistance in answering the tough questions and digging up vital Sammy ephemera.

My unofficial copy editors were incisive, brutal at times, and almost always correct. Scott Alexander, Bruce Bennett, Jesse Jarnow, Ira Kaplan, and my wife/muse Nancy L. Weber crucially took my mess of a manuscript and helped me sculpt it into something.

In 2008, when Sammy and his estranged son Shawn were slinging insults at each other in the comments section of my blog, it was Nancy that said, “You should write a book about this!” This is all her fault. Equally to blame are Scott Alexander and Drew Friedman. Their unlimited inspiration and faith in this project, along with the scores of phone numbers they both supplied, kicked my ass across the finish line. They are the true heroes of the Sammy Petrillo story.

And thanks again to Sammy Petrillo. Look what you started by getting that haircut!

Dave Abramson
Brooklyn
September, 2026

BIBLIOGRAPHY

BOOKS

Ahwesh, Peggy, *The Films of Doris Wishman*. Inpatient Press, 2019.

Bojarski, Richard, *The Complete Films of Bela Lugosi*. Citadel Press, 1980.

Bonanos, Christopher, *Flash: The Making of Weegee the Famous*. Henry Holt and Company, 2018.

Bruck, Connie, *When Hollywood Had a King*. Random House, 2003.

Chapman, Aaron, *Liquor, Lust, and the Law*. Arsenal Pulp Press, 2012.

Cheeta, as told to James Lever, *Me Cheeta: The Legendary Autobiography of Hollywood's Greatest Animal Star*. (Ecco, 2010)

Corman, Roger, and Jim Jerome, *How I Made a Hundred Movies in Hollywood and Never Lost a Dime*. Delta, 1990.

Dello Stritto, Frank J., and Andi Brooks, *Vampire over London: Bela Lugosi in Britain*. Cult Movies Press, 2015.

Felix, Arthur (Weegee), *Weegee by Weegee*. Ziff-Davis Publishing Company, 1961.

Gabler, Neal, *An Empire of Their Own: How the Jews Invented Hollywood*. Vintage Books, 1988.

Greene, Richard S., *Marketing Mayhem! Selling Dean Martin and Jerry Lewis to Post-War America*. Bear Manor Media, 2022.

Grey, Rudolph, *Nightmare of Ecstasy*. Feral House, 1992.

Hayde, Michael J., *Side by Side: Dean Martin and Jerry Lewis on TV and Radio*. Bear Manor Media, 2018.

Hayes, David, and Brent Walker, *The Films of the Bowery Boys: A Pictorial History of the Dead End Kids*. Citadel Press, 1982.

Kazan, Elia, *A Life*. Da Capo, 1997.

Kearns, Burt, *Lawrence Tierney: Hollywood's Real-Life Tough Guy*. University Press of Kentucky, 2022.

Lear, Norman, *Even This I Get to Experience*. Penguin Press, 2014.

Léger, Nathalie, *Suite for Barbara Loden*. Dorothyproject.com, 2012.

Lennig, Arthur, *The Immortal Count: The Life and Films of Bela Lugosi*. University Press of Kentucky, 2003.

Levy, Shawn, *King of Comedy: The Life and Art of Jerry Lewis*. St. Martin's Press, 1996.

Lewis, Jerry, and Herb Gluck, *Jerry Lewis in Person*. Atheneum, 1982.

Lewis, Jerry, and James Kaplan, *Dean and Me (A Love Story)*. Broadway Books, 2005.

Lewis, Patti, and Sarah Anne Coleman, *I Laffed till I Cried: Thirty-Six Years of Marriage to Jerry Lewis*. WRS Publishing, 1993.

Maltin, Leonard, *Movie Comedy Teams*. Signet Film Series, 1970.

Marx, Arthur, *Everybody Loves Somebody Sometime (Especially Himself)*. Hawthorn Books, 1974.

Millard, Andre, *America on Record: A History of Recorded Sound*. Cambridge University Press, 1995.

Nesteroff, Kliph, *The Comedians: Drunks, Thieves, Scoundrels, and the History of American Comedy*. Grove Press, 2015.

O'Dowd, John, *Kiss Tomorrow Goodbye: The Barbara Payton Story*. Bear Manor Press, 2006.

Rhodes, Gary D., and Bill Kaffenberger, *No Traveler Returns: The Lost Years of Bela Lugosi*. Bear Manor Media, 2012.

Rhodes, Gary D., and Richard Sheffield, *Bela Lugosi: Dreams and Nightmares.* Collectables Press, 2007.

Saphire, Rick, *The Real Jerry Lewis Story: A Memoir*. York Publications, 2024.

Saul, Scott, *Becoming Richard Pryor*. HarperCollins Publishers, 2014.

Schoell, William, *Martini Man: The Life of Dean Martin*. Cooper Square Press, 2003.

Skal, David J., *The Monster Show: A Cultural History of Horror*. Penguin Books, 1993.

Sloan, Will, *Ed Wood: Made in Hollywood USA*. OR Books, 2025.

Svehla, Gary J. and Susan (eds.), *Bela Lugosi*. Midnight Marquee Press, 1995.

Tosches, Nick, *Dino: Living High in the Dirty Business of Dreams*. Doubleday, 1992.

Van Meter, Jonathan, *The Last Good Time: Skinny D'Amato, the Notorious 500 Club, the Rat Pack, and the Rise and Fall of Atlantic City*. Bloomsbury, 2003.

Von Schilling, James, *The Magic Window: American Television, 1939-1953*. Haworth Press, 2003.

Weaver, Tom, *A Sci-Fi Swarm and Horror Horde: Interviews with 62 Filmmakers*. McFarland and Company, 2010.

Weldon, Michael, *The Psychotronic Encyclopedia of Film*. Ballantine Books, 1983.

Weldon, Michael J., *The Psychotronic Video Guide*. St. Martin's Griffin, 1996.

Zemeckis, Leslie, *Behind the Burly Q: The Story of Burlesque in America*. Skyhorse Publishing, 2013.

ARTICLES

Abraham, Jefry N., "All Comedy Aside, 'The Gorilla' was No Joke to Either the Ritz Brothers or Darryl Zanuck." *Filmfax,* no. 13, 1988.

Barnes, Mike, "Jerry Lewis Double Sammy Petrillo Dies." *Hollywood Reporter,* August 17, 2009.

Berman, Gary, "You Wouldn't Say That If My Writers Were Here!" *Nostalgia Digest*, Summer 2023.

Bowen, Michael, "Doris Wishman." *Psychotronic Video*, no. 26, 1997.

Crust, Kevin, "Looking Past the Moguls." *Los Angeles Times*, March 9, 2006.

Dello Stritto, Frank J., "At Long Last Lugosi: Film History's Evolving View of Bela Lugosi." *Cult Movies,* no. 13, 1995.

Dello Stritto, Frank J., "The Lugosi Curse: Evolution of the Vampire Myth, 1927 to 1956." *Cult Movies,* no. 27, 1998.

Dello Stritto, Frank J., "The Vampire Strikes Back." *Cult Movies,* no. 24, 1997.

Dello Stritto, Frank J., and Andi Brooks, "Dracula's Last Hurrah: Interviews with the Cast and Company of Bela Lugosi's Last, Lost 'Dracula.'" *Cult Movies*, no. 33, 2000.

Galbraith, Stuart, "The 'How to' of Making a Monster Movie! An Interview with AIP Producer Herman Cohen." *Filmfax,* no. 37, 1993.

Handy, Bruce, "Never Again: A Jerry Lewis Story." *Spy*, May 1992.

Headrick, Robert J., "France's Le Roi de Crazy! The Cinematic Comedy of Jerry Lewis." *Filmfax,* no. 36, 1993.

Hevesi, Dennis, "Sammy Petrillo, 74, an Actor and Nightclub Comedian." *New York Times*, August 24, 2009.

Martin, Dean, and Jerry Lewis, "Why We'll Never Split Up." *TV and Movie Screen,* vol. 2, no. 4, 1955.

Mitchell, Lisa, "Midnite Deli." *Videosonic Arts,* vol. 1, 1990.

Newson, Ted, "Confessions of a Hollywood Gorilla." *Filmfax,* no. 16, 1989.

Okuda, Ted, and Scott MacGillivray, "Confessions of a Brooklyn Gorilla: An Interview with Sammy Petrillo." *Filmfax,* no. 53, 1995

Okuda, Ted, and Scott MacGillivray, "Play It Again, Jack! Remembering Realart, the Re-releasing Company." *Filmfax,* no. 39, 1993.

Parke, Henry C., "My Boss, Sammy Petrillo." *Stalling Tactics* blog, January 11, 2010, http://stallingtactics.blogspot.com/2010/01/my-boss-sammy-petrillo.html.

Rutt, Todd, "Duke Mitchell and Sammy Petrillo: Those Two Fireballs of Fun." *Psychotronic Video,* no. 22, 1991.

Server, Lee, "An Interview with Huntz Hall." *Filmfax,* no. 23, 1990.

Szulkin, David, "Duke Mitchell." *Scream,* no. 30, 2015.

Voger, Mark, "'Call Me Sam' (Arkoff, That Is!)." *Filmfax,* no. 26, 1991.

Williams, Sharon, and Rudolph Grey, "Inside the Mind of Director Joseph Green: The Man That Gave Life to 'The Brain That Wouldn't Die.'" *Filmfax,* no. 18, 1990.

PODCASTS

Maron, Marc, "Episode 779, Martin Landau," WTF with Marc Maron Podcast, January 22, 2017.

Santopadre, Frank, "Lights! Camera! Inaction! Abandoned, Unfinished and Unproduced Movies w/ Drew Friedman, Owen Kline and Barrett Leddy," Fun for All Ages! Podcast, November 11, 2025.

DVDS

Abbott and Costello Rarities. Colgate Comedy Hour, featuring Bud Abbott with Martin and Lewis. Thunderbean, 2017

Bela Lugosi Meets a Brooklyn Gorilla. Video interview with Sammy Petrillo. Image Entertainment, 2001.

Kid Monk Baroni. Video interview with Madelynn Kopple. Image Entertainment, 2006.

Lugosi: Hollywood's Dracula. Alpha Video, 2013.

Massacre Mafia Style. Interview with Jeffrey Mitchell, *An Impressionistic Tribute to Jimmy Durante* TV special. Grindhouse Releasing, 2014.

Wanda. I Am Wanda, an hour-long documentary by Katie Raganelli filmed in 1980; audio recording of Loden speaking to students at the American Film Institute in 1971; segment from a 1971 episode of *The Dick Cavett Show*; essay by Amy Taubin. Criterion Collection, 2019.

RECORDS

All about Cleopatra, featuring Will Jordan, Sammy Petrillo, Dave Starr, and the First Family of Egypt. Topical Records, 1963.

My Son, the Phone Caller, featuring Sammy Petrillo, Surprise Records, 1963.

INDEX